A HOOPOE ON THE NISPERO TREE

OUR ANDALUSIAN ADVENTURE CONTINUES

SABINA OSTROWSKA

Amazon ASIN: B09TB3VQFB

Paperback ISBN: 978-84-09-33873-3

Cover art and Chapter 8 painting by Sally Campbell

Formatting by www.antpress.org

To receive updates about new books and to read additional chapters of my books, subscribe to my website or follow me on social media:

www.sabinaostrowska.com

Facebook @sabinawriter

Instagram @cortijob

Published by: textworkshop.org

WHAT READERS AND AUTHORS SAY
ABOUT SABINA'S BOOKS

"Sabina Ostrowska's wonderful romp through Andalucia had me laughing at the antics of her rustic neighbours, agape at the foibles of demanding B&B guests and impressed at her expat ability to navigate through multiple frustrating situations. A truly wonderful read." Simon Michael Prior, author of *The Coconut Wireless: A Travel Adventure in Search of the Queen of Tonga*

"This is a delightful book, filled with humour and the realities of navigating tortuous Spanish bureaucracy, learning the hospitality trade, and adapting to the rural culture of Andalusia. The author has packed the story with shrewd observations, outstandingly witty diatribes, and sketches that had me laughing out loud. If you're looking for an intelligent, fun read in a beautifully drawn setting, I heartily recommend a few days in Sabina's company." Jacqueline Lambert, author of *Fur Babies in France: From Wage Slaves to Living the Dream*

"I've been drawn into the world of Sabina and Robert, transported to Andalusia through the pages of this book. The authors description of the little stone cottage in a mountain valley made me want to pack my bags and start a new life in Spain. [...] The authors sense of humor, descriptions and keen observations of those around her make this a great read, highly recommended." Sharon Hayhurst, author of *Travels with Geoffrey: If It CAN Go Wrong, It Will*

"Sabina Ostrowska has a sharp eye for the eccentricities of British ex-pats (including those of her English husband) and an even keener eye for the customs and foibles of her new rural neighbours in rural Andalucia. [...] the author reveals all the missteps they make with humour and self-deprecation." Ronald Mackay, author of *The Kilt Behind the Curtain: A Scotsman in Ceausescu's Romania*

"Searching for a more fulfilling lifestyle, Sabina and her husband Robert give up their well-paid jobs and luxury lifestyle in the UAE and move to a remote, charming but dilapidated house in Andalucia. [...] I loved the quirky way this book was written, the humour, the wonderful descriptions and I also loved the beautiful pictures at the start of each chapter. It's a super read." Rebecca H. reader

"It is in fact almost a literary work. Joseph Conrad too was Polish; Sabina can be proud to follow in his footsteps as she wields her pen, or rather flutters her fingers across her keyboard." Bibliofilia Vine Voice

"What a great read! I found it hard to put down once I'd started." Martin, reader

"I laughed out loud and giggled at some of the descriptions and analogies. this was a very entertaining story of moving to Spain." M. Murphy, reader

As always, to my husband, Robert Ryan,
who has always been my biggest supporter.
XXX

One need not be a chamber to be haunted,
One need not be a house;
The brain has corridors surpassing
Material place.

Far safer, of a midnight meeting
External ghost,
Than an interior confronting
That whiter host.

Far safer through an Abbey gallop,
The stones achase,
Than, moonless, one's own self encounter
In lonesome place.

by Emily Dickinson

CONTENTS

PROLOGUE
DOING YOUR HOMEWORK

'I can't understand why people come here if they haven't done their homework,' I heard an Englishman say at an expat book-swap meeting in Alcalá. 'They have no idea about the weather, their water supply situation, no jobs, little money, and they can't even speak the language.'

I sat quietly. He knew that I had written a book about our move to Andalusia. His wife, who was sitting next to me, even remembered the often-confused title correctly.

'*The Crinkle Crankle Wall*, isn't it?' she had asked me just ten minutes earlier.

It was obvious that no one at the table had read my book because they were, in fact, describing Robert and me far too accurately — two fools who rushed in without a plan. While I was hoping that they'd drop the topic of 'uninformed expats moving to rural Spain', Robert seemed oblivious to the fact that the man had just described us to a tee and felt that he needed to express his own feelings of indignation about these clueless foreigners who think they can waltz into another country and start a new life.

'The problem is that they're not committed to this place. They keep on going back and forth to the UK.'

This was greeted with nods, and others around the table shared stories of expats who struggled to settle in Spain.

'They live here for ten years and don't speak any Spanish.'

'They don't have any Spanish friends.'

'Their cars are right-hand drive.'

'They don't eat Spanish food.'

The accusations were raining down. Everyone felt self-righteous and better than 'those other expats' who don't seem to be able to assimilate. While the others kept on exchanging anecdotes, I wondered what it meant to 'do your homework' before you move to another country. I knew for a fact that Robert and I did not do our homework at all. We had resigned from our teaching jobs in the United Arab Emirates, left our friends and colleagues behind, and moved to a country that we knew very little about with no foresight or planning. All our hopes and dreams about the new life in Andalusia were based on a romanticised idea of a pastoral life.

Apart from buying a flight ticket and occasionally booking accommodation for the first night or two in a new destination, Robert and I have never been great fans of planning ahead. This, of course, has led to many marital disputes and heated exchanges of opinions, like the time we spent hours wandering along the beach in Koh Samui, with our suitcases getting heavier and heavier by the minute, looking for a place to sleep. Or the time when we went hiking in the Tatra Mountains without checking the weather forecast and ended up in a snow blizzard at the top of the mountain, even though it was the last day of July. Or another holiday was when we decided to spend a month with a family of nomads in Mongolia but did not realise that there was no food available that we were used to eating. Getting lost, having nowhere to sleep, being surprised by the weather, and starving ourselves of food have been part and parcel of most of our travel experiences.

If I didn't know other people, I would have assumed that this was the way most people planned their holidays and, by extension, their lives. Growing up with divorced parents in the 1980s meant that very little of my life was properly organised. I never knew who would show up outside the kindergarten to collect me. If it was my mother, we'd go home, and I would have to do hours of tracing letters in my little notebook before I could go outside to play. If it was my father, I'd spend the rest of the day as a passenger in his rickety communist-era van in a cloud of cigarette smoke while my father finished his deliveries. One day it was my mum, another my dad, but most of the time, it was a lottery; anyone would show up at the school door — my grandmother, my uncle, one of my aunts, or even a friendly neighbour whose child was in the same group.

If it was my grandmother, we'd go on a very long tram journey across the city of Gdańsk. Martial law was still in place, and so it was not uncommon to see tanks blockading the main roads or special brigades patrolling the streets. If there were riots on the street, I would stay with her for a day or two and 'help' her cook copious amounts of food and preserves. At the time, there was very little in the grocery shops that could be described as comestible.

Should my uncle come to fetch me from school, I'd end up as a spectator at a moto-racing track watching him drink beer after beer throughout the afternoon and lose all the money he had earned the previous week by working at a mechanic's workshop. It was a shame because he was my grandmother's only son who lived past infancy in penicillin-deprived post-war Poland. If one of my father's sisters came to get me from school, we'd take the tram to the predominantly *volksdeutsche* part of the city, where I would spend many quiet hours colouring in and watching my aunts sew dresses and shirts to make a little extra money. From the moment I started to form memories, almost every day of my childhood was different.

It came as a shock to me in my early teens to find out that not every family lived their lives with such a lack of routine. I must have been twelve or thirteen when my best friend invited me to go on a short holiday with her parents. I don't remember where we went or what we did. But one thing that stayed with me was the folder that the father carried around everywhere we went. Inside the folder, he had filed away an itinerary, passes to the attractions, tram and train tickets, and lots of little papers that made the whole experience run smoothly. Perhaps that is why the holiday was quite forgettable.

I think that the way we travel often reflects the way we live our lives. Many, if not most of us, hate the unforeseen. We want to know what to expect and anticipate what may happen. We don't want nasty surprises or random incidents. If you are the type of person who 'does the homework', who travels through life with a little folder with an itinerary, you may find my story infuriating. You might find it shocking and unacceptable how little Robert and I had prepared to move to another country, not to mention how little we researched opening and running a guesthouse. If you hate the intentionally unexpected, you might throw this book away into a corner after the first few chapters, or if you're reading an eBook, you may decide to stop reading after the first two chapters and write an angry review telling the whole world how foolish or mad our adventures were. This is a risk that I'm willing to take.

If you want to read about 'living the dream', there are plenty of fantasies out there. They weave a flawless tapestry of the good life: a glass of sangria in one hand, a plate of delicious tapas on the table, accompanied by a flamenco band with dancers tapping their shoes and clicking castanets to the rhythm. I can't take you on such a journey. It wouldn't be honest, and it wouldn't be fair. Our story is not about chasing a dream; it's about escaping the mundane.

I was in the middle of my teaching career when I got sick and tired of going to work. I didn't mind the work itself. It was literally the fact of having to get up early in the morning, get dressed, do my hair and make-up, and drive to work. It was that part that I could not face anymore. After a while, coming home from work, too, started to destroy my spirit day by day. Finishing every day, spat out and uninspired, started to weigh heavily on my soul. Since Robert had never had a strong attachment to his academic career in the sense that it identifies who he is, we decided it was time to see if there was something else out there for us to do.

It was in 2012 when we first came to Spain in search of a rural property. Neither of us had ever visited Spain before, and neither could we speak any Spanish. What attracted us to Andalusia were the endless olive groves, patios shaded by grapevines, ancient bay leaf trees, cascades of red geraniums hanging from the windows, and enchanting white villages, each boasting its own Moorish castle — or so it seemed at first. We loved everything about this part of Europe and decided to buy a stone cottage with a little bit of land to grow vegetables and fruit trees attached to it.

Two years later, we moved all of our earthly possessions plus two Arabian Maus rescued from the streets of Al Ain in the Emirates to our tiny cottage, a few minutes outside the village of Montefrio in Andalusia. It was the first time that we tried living without steady jobs. The first eighteen months of our move to Spain were consumed by endless house renovations, learning about the new place, meeting our neighbours, and preparing to open a guest house. Every day of that period was new and different. It bore new challenges, most of which we could not have predicted.

Book One of our adventures of starting a new life in Andalusia ended on the night of New Year's Eve in 2016, when we received our first paying guests. Even though the rental apartments were far from ready, we had to start taking in guests to help with our dwindling finances.

ONE
THE FEBRUARY FROM HELL

The almond blossoms saved us that winter. On those sunny winter days, our guests would drive up the small hill to our *casa rural* and be enchanted by the views of the olive hills. In the distance, they'd catch a glimpse of the snow-covered Parapanda and Sierra Nevada Mountains. They would park outside the crinkle crankle wall and get out of their car to be welcomed by a symphony of pink and white almond blossoms against the deep blue skies. There are eight almond trees at the top of our driveway. Since it had been an unusually warm winter, the trees' natural cycle was confused, and they had bloomed a month or so prematurely.

Fortunately, these trees served as a misdirection. Despite parts of the property looking like a construction site, we managed to get excellent reviews that winter. The guests would often stand on the terrace and admire the views of the olive hills and the mountains. They'd take selfies with this backdrop and tell me how *desconectado* or relaxed they felt. It made me feel happy to see them satisfied, even though in the back of my mind, I knew much more had to be done before the summer season arrived when people would stay for longer and perhaps be more discerning. Notwithstanding this, it was a foretaste of what I hoped our place would be one day.

Welcoming guests when the weather is sunny is a pleasure and leaves you with good feelings about the whole business of renting apartments to tourists. Since winter is not the most popular time for foreign tourists to visit Spain, we did not have many bookings. The few bookings that we did get for January were a great success and gave us good practice in providing hospitality — a trade that was new to both of us. But in February, things took a turn for the worse.

Since we did not have any guests in the first two weeks of February, we used that time to build more furniture for the apartments. I was hoping to start writing a new textbook for Cambridge, which I had been contracted to do in December. But the project was getting terribly delayed, and so I began to really worry about our financial situation. As a textbook writer, you usually receive an initial payment from the publisher when you deliver fifty percent of the book. So, with the two-month delay and the starting date set for the end of February, I would be lucky to see my first payments in June. We managed to survive on Robert's translation and editing work, but we also needed money to build kitchens for the apartments to rent them to self-catering visitors. There were also a million projects around the house that needed money to finish. We needed to install gutters, build a room around the outdoor gas hot-water heaters to protect them from the weather, pave our driveway, and find a solution to our continuous water worries. We needed every penny we could get, so we stayed open for bookings.

The next visitors were booked for the Valentine's Day weekend. I prepared their apartment with a lot of care — and left a box of chocolates and a bottle of pink sparkling wine on the table. Since it was a cloudy day, I lit their fireplace so the apartment would be nice and cosy on their arrival. As I sat on the patio with a book, I could not help but notice that the sky above was getting darker and darker. By the time their car appeared on our driveway, a slight drizzle was falling.

I showed them to their apartment and explained what was what, but they did not seem very impressed with the décor; nothing in the apartment seemed to evoke a spontaneous *¡que chulo!* or *¡que precioso!* They walked past the upcycled French farm furniture, the Indian coffee table with hand-engraved rural scenes, and up the hand-crafted staircase made of upcycled wood and colourful tiles without a word. The traditional white and blue caliphate-style tiles in the bathroom, marble washbasin, wardrobe made of upcycled pallets, or hardwood chest of drawers from India — nothing seemed to prompt a comment or compliment. They handed me the forty euros for the night and ushered me out.

'How are the guests?' Robert asked when I returned to our quarters.

'A bit strange.'

'Did they say anything?'

'Not much,' I felt disappointed with the guests' underwhelmed reaction, but I kept these feelings to myself. Little did I know that things were going to go downhill from there.

By the time we went to bed, it had been raining steadily for several hours. The first proper rain in many months that year. I was woken up around two a.m. by the sound of something smashing. I could not identify the sound, so I got up and went to the window to see if it was coming from outside. It was pitch black. I could hear torrential rain and a storm raging outside. Every few seconds, through the storm and howling wind, I could hear a sound 'bang!' and again 'bang!'. I woke Robert up.

'What's that sound?' I asked.

'Rain?'

'No, no. Wait.' I lifted my finger to indicate silence, and there it was again 'bang! bang!'.

'It's the window shutters. They didn't close them, and they are banging against the window and wall.'

This explanation made sense. In my desire for a picture-perfect cottage, I had requested the carpenter in Granada to put our shutters on the outside instead of the inside of the windows, which was the local tradition. When we first installed the windows, the effect was very picturesque, and I could not understand why more people didn't put their shutters on the outside. However, it soon became apparent that this setup was utterly impractical. To open or close the shutters, you had to open the windows and lean out quite far to fasten them to the window frame.

Another problem had also just become apparent. In heavy wind, the shutters would smash against the window frame and the wall outside. I did not know what to do. The tempest that was rolling over the olive groves outside was loud enough on its own. Add the regular banging of the shutters, and there was no way these guests could sleep.

Why don't they close the shutters? How can they sleep with that noise? I could not understand.

I wasn't willing to go to their apartment at two a.m. to close the shutters in their bedroom and living room. And so, I spent a heavy-hearted, sleepless night listening to the hurricane outside. As soon as the sun rose, I looked out of the window of our bedroom. The downpour and the wind had not slowed down overnight. The trees were half-bent under the strain of the heavy wind, and the rain was now horizontal. By ten a.m., the rainstorm had transformed itself into a hailstorm that covered the fields with ice. Since it seemed as if we were in the middle of the ten plagues of Egypt, I wasn't able to go outside to check on the guests. I was sure they'd be hiding inside like everyone else.

Thank God, I don't have to serve them breakfast, I thought.

I could not imagine how I would have been able to bring the trays of food to their living room in this wind and rain. As we sat in our tiny living room waiting for them to check out, I had a sinking feeling. I knew that they did not have a comfortable stay, and I worried about the bad review that was forthcoming. Around eleven, as the rain subsided for a few minutes, I heard them knocking on our door. They were ready to leave. Avoiding the puddles, we escorted them to their car and waved them off. I could not help but notice that our driveway had turned into a clayey mud bath in the heavy rain.

Because the soil in our area contains a lot of clay, the driveway is fine when it is sunny and dry. When dry, it is hard as stone and thus easy to drive on. However, even a little bit of rain turns it into an impossibly sticky quagmire, where the clay sticks to your shoes forever. If I walked down the driveway to the gate after heavy rain, I would gain ten centimetres in height due to the mud that would stick to the soles of my boots. I could only imagine the mess this made inside the guests' car once they had walked across the driveway and entered their pristine city car.

But perhaps that was karma for smoking dozens of cigarettes inside the apartment, where I had posted a clearly visible 'non-smoking' sign. I only noticed the cigarette butts after they had left. On the stone patio outside the window of their living room, I spotted a sprawling collection of butts, clearly thrown out of the window onto the stone paving as if they were at a London pub during the World Cup. Robert joined me to inspect the damage. He was livid when he saw how the patio had been turned into an impromptu ashtray.

Inside the apartment, I was rudely confronted by the smell of cheap perfume. Since I used to be a smoker myself, I knew exactly what had happened. They had whiled away the evening smoking their lungs out in front of the fireplace and then had attempted to cover the smell by dousing the apartment with madam's perfume. Soon my anger at them melted away when I spotted a giant puddle of water that had formed at the back of the room. It was clear to me that water had somehow penetrated the back wall of the house.

Another puddle had formed at the entrance to the apartment, where the horizontal rain must have gone under the door. It all looked somewhat dreadful and could not be described as 'luxurious' by any means or standards. I was feeling very dejected. All the work we'd put into this place to make it comfortable for guests seemed to be for nothing. I went upstairs to check the bedroom and bathroom.

The bedroom smelled like burnt chorizo. The odour had penetrated deep into the room. I didn't know what it was, but I could also smell the guests' cigarettes and cheap perfume beyond the unknown toxic smell. I opened the windows to close the noisy shutters. One of them would not close properly because the hinge had been bent out of shape during the windy night. It took several days and a lot of frankincense to get rid of the smell. I had to wash all the bedding, including the pillows and duvets, because they were saturated with cheap perfume and cigarettes. As expected, we did not get a sterling review for that short stay.

'Seven-point-five out of ten,' I told Robert as soon as it was posted. 'It's not *so* bad considering their apartment got slightly flooded, and the shutters banged all night.'

A few regional expletives from the Scouse dialect were used as Robert was still fuming over the smoking and throwing the butts out of the window. There was nothing to add.

The disastrous Valentine's Day booking had revealed several problems with our guest accommodation. The shutters that were fixed to the wrong side of the windows, the leaky walls, muddy driveways, and smelly chimneys all had to be sorted out. As it rained day after day, each day colder and wetter than the next, I closed our availability on the booking website until the inclement weather passed. The first thing that we attacked were the shutters. We spent several hours moving from window to window, removing the shutters and re-fitting them on the inside. Now the guests would be able to open and close them even during a storm without getting wet. It also prevented any future middle-of-the-night banging.

The smelly chimney flue was a more serious problem. I didn't realise that the burnt chorizo smell was coming from the chimney itself until we were visited by friends from the nearby village, Venta Valero. Keith and Delia moved to rural Andalusia in 2014, the same year we relocated from Abu Dhabi. Robert had met them the year before on a Spanish-for-beginners course that I forced him to take soon after we had arrived in Spain. Many students in his class were the stereotypical simultaneously-pale-faced-and-sunburnt bargain Brits in the sun who insist on having lunch at noon, tea at five, and celebrate English bank holidays as if they hadn't left their homeland. But Delia and Keith were a bit different, so Robert invited them for drinks and a BBQ one day.

'Don't be put off, but she's a raw vegan,' he informed me a few hours before their arrival.

'What does it mean?'

'She doesn't eat cooked food.'

So why did you invite her for a barbecue? I thought to myself.

This was going to be fun. From personal experience, it is difficult enough having vegetarians around for a meal since they have a tendency to constantly interrogate the host whether any of the vegetables have touched the meat during the cooking process. And, God forbid, should the same serving utensils touch a chop and then serve roasted vegetables to a vegetarian. All hell has been known to break loose.

'What's she going to eat?' I enquired of my dear husband, who dropped this bombshell on me as soon as the food was ready.

'Can't she have a salad?'

'I don't think so. I've sprinkled grated Parmesan all over it.'

'Oh,' it must have dawned on Robert that cheese was not vegan. 'What about the pomegranate salad?'

'It's with couscous,' I couldn't believe that he could not understand what 'raw vegan' meant.

'Do we have *anything* to feed her?' I could see he was worried.

I looked in the fridge and spotted some lettuce and tomatoes.

'She can have some lettuce leaves and tomatoes.'

Delia, an aspiring yogini in her late fifties, had a lot of youthful energy only accentuated by two buns on top of her head and a collection of turquoise tattoos on her arms and legs. She was a good sport and accepted the leaves and tomato wedges as her main course with grace. As that was clearly not enough food, she ate some non-raw and non-vegan salads and didn't fuss about the Parmesan cheese. Our bumbling lack of respect for her dietary choices did not put her off, and since then, we'd often meet up and chat about our projects.

They, too, had plans to open a B&B and yoga retreat, and, like us, they were constantly renovating and making improvements to their cottage. Because we had so much in common at the time, we became instant friends. We'd spend hours discussing bricklaying, flooring, tiling, and problems with builders and material supplies. We'd also share our ideas about who our future customers would be and how we could entice people to come to rural Andalusia for their holidays. Even though Delia didn't drink and was a raw vegan, we managed to have fun together.

We invited Delia and Keith over for wine and tapas about a week after the disastrous Valentine's Day booking. Because our own living room was not presentable to guests, or even friends, we set up some food and drinks in one of the guest apartments. It was a treat for us to sit in a clean and spacious room. Before they arrived, I lit the fireplace and went downstairs to our quarters to finish preparing some tapas — mainly olives, local cheeses, and sundried figs. For someone who didn't drink, Delia consumed a good number of our boozy figs. I felt happy to see her eat something with gusto and restrained myself from pointing out that the syrupy liquid in which the figs were naturally coated was most likely fermented sugar.

Once they arrived, we went upstairs to the rental. As soon as I opened the sliding glass doors, I smelt the toxic odour again. It permeated the whole living room.

'I think you have condensation in your chimney flue,' Keith informed us. 'Is your flue insulated?'

Keith was a lanky man in his mid-sixties. In his previous life, he was an HR manager, but now he filled his days reading about and planning his house renovations. It transpired that he had had the same problem the year before. He had a new firebox installed in his kitchen, but once it was lit, it filled the house with a terrible smell, a mixture of soot and fat. The reason for the poisonous stench, as explained by one of his neighbours, was that his flue was exposed and was not insulated. In cold weather, condensation formed inside the vent whenever the fire was lit.

'Why didn't Dani tell us that we had the wrong flue? It's not like it was the first time he was renovating a house.'

Dani was one of the builders who helped us with the reform the year before. I was miffed. We would have bought the expensive insulated flue pipes if we had known that this would happen. There were five men on our building site when we installed the fireplaces. They all had experience renovating houses, and not one said anything to us about the flue being the wrong one. Now, we would not be able to fix the problem.

To start with, the purchase of new insulated flues for both guest apartments would significantly exceed our meagre budget. The other problem was removing the flue which was attached to the chimney and cemented into the chimney stack on the roof. It looked like a big job for which we had neither the time nor the money.

Since our next guests were due to arrive on the twenty-eighth of February on *el Día de Andalucía*, I was hoping for sunny weather, thereby reducing the amount of condensation that might form in the chimney. I placed a chemical chimney sweep log in the burning fireplaces a few times to reduce the foul odour. While we could not do anything with the exposed flues in the living rooms, Robert built a brick encasement around the exposed flue in one of the bedrooms, which also helped reduce the toxic aroma. A few days before our next guests' arrival, another couple booked a weekend stay with us. We would be fully booked for the first time, but the weather forecast remained ominous.

TWO
BROKEN GLASS

'When are the Dutch coming?' Robert asked on the morning of our regional holiday, *el Día de Andalucía*.

'They said between two and three,' I told him for the tenth time.

'And the Canadians?'

'The wife said that they'd be here in the evening, but she didn't say at what time exactly.'

These were our first guests after the Valentine's Day fiasco. Their review had brought our score on the booking sites down, and I was determined to bring it back up before tourists started to look for their summer holidays. I was hoping for nice weather to break the bad spell, but the grey skies told me otherwise. The Dutch arrived shortly after two p.m. The wife, Eva, drove the rental car. She got out, and we greeted each other. It was all very pleasant despite the bleak weather. But as soon as she opened the passenger door for her husband, my heart sank.

Eva struggled for a few seconds to get him out. Once he was on his feet, she passed him his crutches, and we exchanged greetings. Jaap was a giant of a man. As he stood in front of me, he was over two metres tall. He was pretty obese, too. We started walking across the patio to their apartment. While I asked them about their holidays and places that they had visited, in my head, I was trying to solve a problem that would soon stare us all in the face.

The previous December, while we were frantically finishing the apartments before the arrival of our first guests, we realised that we did not have beds for the guests, but we didn't have money to buy them either. In the one apartment, we built a bed frame from pallets and used a spare mattress that we had brought from the UAE. But since we were under a lot of time pressure, we had to figure something out for the second apartment. By a stroke of good fortune, I spotted two single beds for sale in Montefrio for a hundred euros. I instantly contacted the Englishman selling them and asked him to reserve these for us. We drove to the address in Montefrio to inspect them. The beds were almost new and with excellent mattresses. The problem was that, even as singles, they were on the short side, and they were only seventy centimetres, or twenty-seven inches, across.

As we examined them, I could not make up my mind.

'If we connect them, they should be OK. We could advertise it as a twin bed.' I suggested.

Robert seemed to agree, and since I did not think we could find anything better in the short time that we had before the guests' arrival, the Englishman loaded them onto his pick-up and followed us to our house. As it turned out, when connected together, the two singles made an acceptable double bed. Not a king-size bed, but a smallish queen. The guests who had used them in January and February were Spaniards of petite postures. But now, as the Dutch Gulliver was approaching his Lilliputian billet, my eyebrow started to twitch from stress.

In her prior communication with me, Eva had requested that the 'twin bed' be separated. I didn't question it. Many married couples like to sleep in separate beds for one reason or the other. The problem was that once I separated our twin bed into two singles, they looked rather toylike, more like a doll's house display than a bedroom for full-grown adults. I tried to make the beds look larger by puffing up the feather duvets, but even the pillows sagged across each side of the miniature beds. I sighed in despair and went away, hoping that we would host anorexic hobbits. As it turned out, both my guests had the physique of retired NBA players — one taller than the other — and neither seemed to have skipped a meal in the last decade or so. I had to think on my feet.

As I showed Eva and Jaap their accommodation, I first highlighted the positives of the place: the spacious living room, the cosy fireplace, and the large bathroom. They were especially pleased with the walk-in shower because the wife reported that Jaap had struggled to get in and out of the minuscule Spanish bathtubs they had been confronted with thus far during their holiday.

Wait until you see the tiny toy beds I have prepared for you, I thought to myself, bracing myself for the inevitable.

I led them inside the bedroom and could see their puzzled looks.

'You wanted to have two single beds instead of one, is that right?' I asked, knowing the answer very well.

'Yes, but these are too small,' the Dutch are famously straightforward and don't hesitate to point out a flaw.

'OK,' I said. 'I can put another bed here for you if you like.'

I had a plan ready.

'That would be great.'

I left them to unpack and make themselves at home. Back in our headquarters, I explained to Robert the mismatch between the size of our guests and the size of our beds and told him that we had to make another bed for Jaap.

Even though I'm not a very tidy or well-organised person, I have an excellent memory of where I misplace or store things that are not used anymore. Behind our kitchen annexe, there was a bedroom that had not been used since we moved in. Inside, we stored the remaining unpacked boxes, about twenty or so, and anything left from the previous owners that we didn't feel like throwing away yet. In that dark and dingy room, leaning nonchalantly against the wall, was the mattress of our old *cama de matrimonio* on which we had spent many agonising months during the reform.

'Oh, it seems you require my services again,' it said in a French accent while finishing a cigarette.

'Yes, please. Can you help us again? Please! We need you!' I would have pleaded if the bed could talk.

'OK, but don't imprison me in here again.'

'Of course not,' I lied.

We pulled the old mattress out and checked it for stains or mould, but miraculously it was clean and acceptable. While a Spanish-sized *cama de matrimonio* should not be slept on by two people who love each other but don't wish to get divorced by dawn, it can be considered a somewhat luxurious single bed. I was confident that Jaap would fit nicely on it, albeit diagonally. Luckily, we had also kept the steel bed frame that accompanied the mattress. In twenty minutes, we had installed it in their bedroom. Once the bed was all made up, we went downstairs to check if they were happy with what we had done.

'You work so well together,' Eva was delighted with the new sleeping arrangements.

Indeed, we had enough sense not to argue in front of the guests and, for once, we collaborated without questioning each other's methods. We left them in their living room, and I took a moment to sit down on the patio. Even though it was the last day of February, the skies had cleared up to a deep blue, and the olive hills were glistening in the sun. I hadn't sat down for more than five minutes when I heard a terrible crash coming from the guest apartment. I could not identify the sound. Soon enough, Eva appeared round the corner. She was red-faced and out of breath.

'The shelf fell down with all the wine,' she informed me.

This explanation did not make any sense to me.

'What do you mean?' I asked quickly. In the years to come, I would become a much more experienced hotelier. In such situations, I would force a smile and go directly to investigate the problem and solve it. But since I was still learning, I engaged in a lengthy exchange during which a frustrated Eva tried to explain to me in broken English what had happened. After several minutes, she beckoned me to follow her to their apartment. There, in front of the fridge, I was welcomed by what may only be described as a scene from a Greek wedding. Smashed pieces of glass, white and green, were all over the floor. The floor was covered in what I assumed to be a mix of white and red wine. I looked at the dignified woman in her early 60s who stood before me, and I wanted to ask: 'What's happened here? I was gone for five minutes!' But I didn't have to as Eva started to explain again.

'I don't know what happened! I put the wine bottles on the shelf. I always do it like that at home. I never have a problem. But it all goes down. I think this fridge is broken.'

I picked up the plastic fridge door shelf and looked at it. It seemed fine. Obviously, it hadn't been placed correctly inside the fridge door for some reason — I tested it, and it fitted snugly in its grooves on the inside of the door. The previous guests must have taken it out and not replaced it correctly.

'I'm very sorry about this. I'll clean it for you right away,' I said.

I first went to our pantry and got a big bottle of cheap *crianza*.

'What's this for?' Robert asked.

'They smashed five bottles of wine on the floor.'

'What?' he seemed confused.

'I'll tell you later. Bring me the bucket and the mop, please.'

I went back to the guests' living room and handed Eva a bottle to apologise for the incident.

'That's so nice of you,' she said. 'Can we buy some more from you?'

'You don't need to buy it. It's on the house. I'm very sorry once again.'

She opened the bottle of wine, filled two glasses and went out to sit on the patio with Jaap while I grabbed the bucket that Robert had brought.

This must bring us good luck, I thought to myself as I mopped the wine and collected large shards of broken glass by hand.

It's an old superstition that still lives on in Jewish and Polish culture that broken glass brings good luck to the household. Many other cultures in Europe have it too, I'm sure. Of course, you can't just smash up your glassware in the kitchen by yourself, hoping to bring good fortune; it has to be done by accident. I was confident that with this amount of broken glass, we would get rid of the bad luck that was brought by our Valentine's Day visitors. I spent a good half an hour cleaning and vacuuming. As I left the apartment, I passed Eva and Jaap drinking wine on the patio and enjoying the winter sun.

'Is it always sunny in February?' Eva asked.

A sarcastic remark went over in my head, but I didn't think disdain would get me far in the hospitality business. I searched for words. I was in a foul mood after all the work I had done since their arrival; I just wanted to sit down and prepare myself for the arrival of the next couple. I was standing on the patio with a vacuum cleaner in one hand and a bucket in the other, and it did not seem like I would be dismissed from my duties any time soon.

'It can be cold and rainy in the winter. The weather changes,' I informed my new masters of the most basic fact of nature.

Eva seemed convinced that Spain had been stuck in some kind of meteorological Groundhog Day. In my new role as a hotelier-cum-chambermaid, I learned that a common expectation made by travellers is that the atmospheric conditions at their holiday destination should be as depicted in the photographs in the travel agent's catalogue. Later that year, another Dutch woman scored our accommodation down in her review because it rained during her stay. 'It can rain in April,' she shared these portentous words of warning to fellow travellers.

Returning to Jaap and Eva, I explained that it would get cold at night and that it was best if they kept the fire going because then the apartment would stay nice and cosy all day. They told me they knew how to use a fireplace because they had a country house in the Netherlands and proceeded to tell me all about it.

'That bear is very loud,' Japp said enthusiastically, apropos of nothing, while Eva talked about their son.

22

'What bear?' I thought I misheard.

'There's a bear in the forest. Listen, you can hear it every few minutes. Like this.' He uttered a long angry growl to illustrate.

There is a forest at the top of the olive hill in front of the house, but it's home to rabbits, pigeons, foxes, and wild boar or *jabalí*, as they are called in Spanish. I was pretty sure that there were no bears near our house. If bears were roaming these hills, Rafa or José, our Spanish neighbours who grew up in this area, would have informed me about it.

'There it is,' Jaap put his finger in the air in the direction of the hill behind the house.

'It's an olive shaker.' I was loath to curb his enthusiasm for engaging in a close encounter with the local wildlife, *Ursus* or otherwise. I explained that we were still in the middle of the olive picking season. For Robert and me, the sound of the olive tree shakers had become white noise. Until Jaap pointed it out, I would have sworn that the season had come to an end. My explanation generated more questions than I wished to answer. I was still holding the vacuum cleaner and the bucket and was hoping that this would give them a hint to release me, but it didn't.

I put the cleaning utensils down and explained everything that I knew about olive picking and told them that for breakfast, they would have the opportunity to try our own olive oil from the previous December. They seemed satisfied, and since their wine glasses were now empty, Eva went inside to replenish them. I seized the moment and left the patio.

'You need to talk to them,' I informed Robert as I entered our living room.

'About what?'

'Anything,' I said. 'They're hungry for company.'

'Can I have a glass of wine too?'

'Yes, get a glass of wine and entertain them, please. I'll wait for the Canadians.'

As Robert went out, I could hear them on the patio. He told Eva and Jaap that I was busy getting the other apartment ready for the other guests. Jaap had renewed energy in his voice — I assumed they'd refreshed their glasses while I went away — and I could hear them talk about the process of house renovations in the Netherlands. I didn't have anything else pressing to do. I just wanted to lie on the sofa and close my eyes for a few minutes.

It was a real blessing that Robert liked to talk to complete strangers about nothing for hours on end. He was always eager to share his life story with a busy sales assistant or strike up a conversation with perfect strangers on a plane. I used to just roll my eyes and pretend I didn't know him, but now, his social skills became a real asset.

I didn't blame Jaap and Eva for seeking out the company of others during their travels. During our own travels, long and short, Robert and I have made many 'good friends' — not infrequently as the product of his nosiness. I would leave him alone in a bar while I went to the beach to read my book, only to find him a few hours later chatting away and laughing with complete strangers as if they were his long-lost friends. We'd often spend a significant part of our holiday with these people and then completely forget their existence once we returned home. I was reminiscing about the hordes of 'friends' we had made during past holidays while waiting for the Canadians.

It was six p.m., and the sun was starting to set. I went out to check on Robert. He and the guests were no longer on the patio. It was getting cold, so they must have gone inside. I knocked on their door in search of my husband. While his talkative nature might be considered a blessing for our little hospitality business, he also doesn't know when to stop talking. I wanted to check if he was not overstaying his welcome. Inside the cottage, everyone seemed happy, sitting by the roaring fire with glasses of wine in hand. Nevertheless, Robert got the hint that it was time to let guests be by themselves, and he politely excused himself. I went to the other apartment and put the outdoor light on, and lit the fire for a warm welcome.

Where are they? I was getting frustrated. *It'll soon be pitch-black outside.*

The hill in front of the house blocks any possible light pollution from Montefrio, which is about six kilometres away as the crow flies. The only light in the valley visible from our house is a small electric bulb outside José's property on the top of the hill, but it only dimly illuminates his outbuildings. The olive hills and the oak groves around us are thus left in complete darkness. I was sure that driving to our cottage through unlit, narrow, and curvy mountain roads would put our foreign guests in a bad mood from the start. But there was nothing I could do about it.

'It's very far,' Kevin, the Canadian husband, informed me as soon as he exited his rental car and greeted me.

'Far?' I didn't understand what he meant.

'It's a long way to Madrid Airport.'

I blinked in disbelief a few times, not knowing how to respond. I had to admit that he had his facts in order.

'Yes, we're about five hours from Madrid Airport.'

I took them to their apartment, which they both liked very much. They enjoyed the lit fireplace and immediately took off the puffy winter jackets that they had obviously brought from Canada. They were truly a catalogue couple — despite the car journey, their jeans looked freshly ironed, and they wore matching white cotton shirts. While exploring the room and asking questions, Carol told me everything that I needed to know (and more) about her family and her kids and suggested that I subscribe to the travel newsletter that she was writing during their sojourn in Europe. After twenty minutes, I felt I'd been sufficiently courteous and had heard enough about their private lives and travels. I explained that I'd be bringing them their breakfast on a tray in the morning. And I wished them good night.

I was woken in the middle of the night by the howling wind and a storm outside.

Here we go again, I thought to myself.

Luckily, this time the window shutters were fastened to the inside of the windows and did not bang and keep everyone awake. Because both sets of guests had ordered breakfast, I got up early to prepare their morning meals. By seven a.m., the wind had died down, and it was once again quiet outside. So, there was a glimmer of hope for good reviews. At first light, I ventured out to see if there was any damage outside caused by the wind, but — to my surprise — I was welcomed by a scenery devoid of colour.

What was, the day before, a lush green landscape with pink

almond blossoms and blue skies was now a dull monochrome abstract painting. The olive trees, the patio, the driveway, and the hills were all covered in a thick blanket of snow. The guests' vehicles looked like two odd bulges on the landscape. Without knowing that cars were parked in those spots the night before, one would think they were just two small woodpiles. I couldn't believe my eyes. I closed the door and went back into the kitchen to prepare the breakfasts.

Try not to slip on the icy steps with these breakfast trays; I made a mental note.

A few minutes later, Robert bounced down to the kitchen with the exciting news that it had been snowing all night. Neither he nor I had seen snow in over a decade since 2005, when we had swapped the frozen Swedish pine forests for the sunny sand dunes of Abu Dhabi. While it was somewhat exciting to see snow again, I was also immediately reminded why I resented snowy weather so much.

'The guests will be stuck inside all day. We need to do something special for them,' I suggested.

In the months leading up to hosting our first guests, I had spent a lot of time reading reviews left by customers of other guest houses and B&Bs in our area. I wanted to get an idea of their expectations, their likes and dislikes. During the course of my investigation, I learned that while cleanliness and tranquillity are paramount, good hosting and unique experiences could make up for any misgivings people might have of an amateurish enterprise like ours.

'We can take them for a walk up the hill,' Robert decided.

'Jaap's on crutches,' I reminded Robert.

'Ahh...shall we offer to make a barbecue for them?'

'In the snow?'

'It will melt by noon,' Robert was somewhat optimistic.

'If it melts, we can invite everyone for a barbecue in the afternoon. I'll ask Carol and Kevin if they'd like to go for a hike.'

As Robert predicted, most of the snow was gone by noon. Only the north-facing side of the valley had patches left here and there, but the roads themselves were clear. The Canadian guests were more than excited about the prospect of a hike with 'the locals', as they referred to us. We took them up a curvy path to the top of the steep hill opposite our house to inspect an abandoned ruin. There are several abandoned ruins just a short hike away from our *cortijo*, and each one makes for an excellent destination for a walk with friends or family.

Our guests loved the little escapade and took numerous photos on the way up. The winter skies had again turned blue, and the air was so clear that you could easily see the village of Montefrio in the distance. The ragged rocks with the sandstone church and Moorish ruins at the top of the village looked quite spectacular.

Kevin and Carol told us more about their family life, friends, and finances during the hike. I wasn't listening particularly closely to their life stories, however. Instead, I was musing on the human tendency that we have where we travel thousands of kilometres across continents and oceans, only to use every opportunity to tell complete strangers about the life that we'd temporarily left behind.

Robert and I are guilty as charged. I vividly remember us, years earlier, during a summer holiday in Mongolia, sitting outside a yurt in Ulaanbaatar with German backpackers and telling them about our life back home in Al Ain. Our impromptu audience would patiently wait their turn to share with us personal details about their lives in Berlin. Why do we do that? At home, we are somebody; our identities are delineated by the suburbs in which we live, the jobs we have, and the friends and family who are close to us. But once we venture abroad, these identities are erased, and we become nobody, just another face in the crowd.

As we were climbing up the hill, I was learning a crucial aspect of hosting travellers — you have to listen to their life stories to help them re-establish their sense of being. Later that day, we prepared a tasty barbecue for everybody, and I was relieved to see that our guests seized the opportunity to tell each other about their lives. All I had to do was keep on topping up their wine glasses, so Robert and I could relax from our duties.

Our guests stayed for two more days. However, the Dutch couple seemed exceptionally hapless since they also managed to break the glass door on the fireplace and had a few other disasters.

Some people, I thought, *are just followed by misfortune.*

Or was it a function of the inherent clumsiness that some people seem to possess? We bent over backwards to please them to make up for any misgivings they might have had about our budding establishment. Robert took them up the hill tracks in the 4X4. He showed them the thousand-year-old olive tree outside Castillo de Locubín and took them to see the ruined castle in Montefrío. It all seemed to work because, despite the tiny beds, broken wine bottles, a glassless fireplace, leaky walls, and smelly chimneys, they left us excellent reviews online.

'Excellent hosts and a cosy fire with olive wood. The views of the olive groves and the oak forest. Stylish decorations. Beautiful place in nature. Ten out of ten.' I read Carol's review to Robert.

'And the Dutch?' he asked.

'Nine point five out of ten.'

'That's not bad, considering all the disasters.'

'No, but we can't spend so much time with all the guests. We need to fix these beds, sort out the leaks, and build kitchens so that I don't have to serve breakfast.'

'If we install gutters, it will reduce the amount of water that ends up at the bottom of the walls,' Robert sagely suggested.

'Yes, but that's like a thousand euros. We don't have that kind of money. What about the tiny beds? Can we buy a new mattress and make the bed frame ourselves?'

We had an action plan laid out for the spring. I took out a piece of paper and wrote down what we needed to buy and do to make our lives as hosts bearable and not worry about complaints. Once done, I totalled everything up.

'If we build the bedframe ourselves and make the kitchen cupboards from the pallets, we still need about six thousand to get the apartments ready for the summer.'

There was dead silence. We did not have six thousand euros lying around. Every penny that we made from translating, writing, and editing went straight into the house, and we never seemed to get ahead with our finances. Money was a constant worry. I would spend sleepless nights going over the state of our account in my head over and over, hoping against all hope that I had forgotten about a secret payment that we were due to receive.

While Robert's editing and translating work paid for our groceries, petrol, and other monthly expenses, there was nothing left to save. I was about to start writing a new coursebook, but I would only get paid for the first half of the book on its delivery in June. To move this project forward, there was only one solution.

'We need to take out a small loan,' Robert broke the silence.

Despite the feeling of defeat, I agreed. We had fought for a long time against the idea of borrowing money from a bank; we both have strong opinions about living on credit. The principle we try to live up to is that if you can't afford something, you do without it. We were now going to break this rule that had spared us from becoming debtors and the fear that the bank would threaten us with repossession. There did not seem to be another way forward, however. I convinced myself that since I was getting paid in June, we would pay the loan off very soon.

'We can go to the bank tomorrow morning,' I announced and went upstairs to look for the purple folder that contained all our documents. I was not looking forward to doing the paperwork.

THREE
RED TAPE

T he brightest minds in the world can't beat the complex network of circular logic and Catch-22 scenarios that is otherwise known as the Spanish bureaucracy. Like the Spanish Armada, this machinery of mindless paperwork is formidable and resilient to change. It's also quite resistant to reason or common sense. Should a humble member of the general public try to point out a flaw in its perfection or suggest an improvement, they might never be heard of again. More pragmatic members of society might argue that there is no point in fighting the setup and recommend that you try to work with it. But in reality, trying to work with a system of bureaucracy that has been developed by generations of imperious clerks is as easy as trying to tame a rabid dog.

The sole aim of the apparatus is to provide cushy jobs for armies of civil servants, generate tons of paper, mounds of used staples, and a series of inter-related files that could fill an infinite number of office filing cabinets. Where these filing cabinets are stored — I don't know, perhaps on giant container ships in the middle of the Atlantic. In short, the bureaucratic organism was designed by a cruel psychopath in order to break people down, one by one, and spit them out onto the street with a folder filled with copies of an almost incredible number of documents.

Our first encounter with this cruel organisation was in the summer of 2014 when we came to Spain from Abu Dhabi intending to be self-employed. One of the first things that we had to do was register our residency so as to avoid paying import tax on our personal belongings that were arriving at Malaga harbour in a matter of weeks. Robert seemed quite well-informed about the ins and outs of the process.

'First, we need to get a *padrón*,' Robert informed me.

'What's that?' Between packing boxes, selling things that we didn't want to ship, arranging feline transport across the continents, and closing down nine years of our life in Abu Dhabi, I had not researched how we would obtain Spanish residency. I assumed that holding European Union passports would facilitate the process. Robert had spent hours reading blogs and forums by other expats, and he seemed convinced that the first step was to get a *padrón*.

'It's a list of residents who live in a municipality,' I was informed.

Since I'm not much of a planner and hate reading about something before actually doing it, I was pleased that at least one of us had an idea where to start. Once in Spain, on a fine August morning, I gathered all the documents we had accumulated since we had bought the house. Because my Spanish was somewhat rudimentary and limited to greetings and salutations, I had no idea what most of these documents meant or what their purpose was. I kept a purple folder with separate partitions where I 'filed' one paper after another, suspecting that they were all somehow important. Inside the folder, I included bank receipts, our *catastral*, or the title deed, tax numbers, the architect's contract, the electricity contract, and lots of other papers from different establishments, including, most importantly, our NIE documents.

The NIE is your personal Spanish identity number or the *Número de identidad de extranjero*. Without this number, the Spanish government cannot recognise your legal existence. More specifically, you don't exist in the eyes of the Spanish tax office, which seems to be the most essential branch of the government. To buy the house, we had to acquire NIEs. This necessitated a trip to Jaén and a wait of several hours at an empty police station, followed by lots of subservient bowing and scraping before a power-hungry office clerk. After hours of doing nothing in the empty waiting room, we now had to run to the nearest bank to pay the fees before all the offices closed for the day. After the payment of nine euros and ninety-seven cents exactly, we ran back to the police station before it, too, closed. Finally, once we were done with more curtsying and thank-yous to the omnipotent dead-faced clerk (who must have been furious that we had made it back to the office just as she wanted to leave for the day), we received two pieces of paper with our NIEs. We managed to complete these steps in only half a day with the help of our estate agent, who came with us and anticipated each obstacle placed in our way.

The estate agent must have known that no average foreigner could accomplish the task of obtaining the NIE if left to their own devices. If she had told us that we had to drive alone to the province's capital, find parking near the main police station, fill in numerous forms, and spend several unhappy hours being humiliated and looked down on, I might have withdrawn our offer on the house. She must have anticipated that should any prospective buyer be left to deal with this madness on their own, the estate agent would never make a sale. I knew that I would have given up after the first two hours of waiting at the police station if we were there alone. I would have encouraged Robert to abandon the whole plan of buying a house and convinced him that we should go to the beach in Malaga instead. Such was the arrogance we were confronted with at the police station in Jaén.

Two years later, when we finally moved to Andalusia, we decided to face the Spanish bureaucracy on our own and obtain our residency by following the steps outlined online. To be listed on the *padrón*, we had to go to the town hall. The *ayuntamiento* of Montefrío is beautifully located in what once was a very affluent part of the village (parts of it remain so, of course). We passed the round church, the roof of which is home to thousands of swallows that nest in its trusses. I looked up to see flights of swallows in the sky and the ruins of the Moorish castle ahead. As we climbed the steep stone street, we passed renaissance buildings with beautiful wooden shutters and large windows. The town hall itself was a former palace. It was built in the seventeenth century and used to be the home of a wealthy family. The residence was purchased from them in the twentieth century to become the village's headquarters. As we walked through the giant hardwood door decorated with beautiful arabesque carvings, the palatial past of the dwelling was evident in its high ceilings, marble floors, and balustrades. In the middle of the palace, we spotted a shaded stone patio lined with palm trees and a shimmering fountain. Built from thick sandstone, the interior was nice and cool despite the forty-degree heat outside, or hundred- and four-degrees Fahrenheit.

As soon as we turned left inside the building, we were back in the modern world. The oversized brown wooden counter of the reception area formed a formidable barrier between the public and the officials who populate the office's inner sanctum. As we approached the counter, I could see piles of papers of different sizes and colours and an array of printers hailing from different epochs and old computer monitors no longer in use. I explained in broken Spanish that we wanted to register on the *padrón* and were directed to the first floor, second door on the left.

In stark contrast to the enormous wooden windows and marbled ground floor, the first floor was divided up into a series of small pokey offices. I could see desks and chairs arranged neatly in each office through open plywood doors. Precarious stacks of papers were perched on each desk. I could hear printers humming in the background, and a friendly, welcoming atmosphere pervaded this part of the building. A secretary ushered us down a narrow corridor and inside one of the cosy offices. From this office, we entered yet another office.

Despite the no-smoking signs posted on every door and window, it was clear that everyone who worked in these offices smoked, at least passively. The wide-open windows did not manage to clear the air fast enough. I didn't mind. It reminded me of my student times when, during oral exams, we'd be seated in the office of a chain-smoking literature professor. His ashtray was overfilled after hours of listening to students regurgitate 'their' take on postmodern poetry. Thus, encountering a middle-aged man in a crinkly grey suit and a yellowish shirt with an ashtray hidden, presumably, in his desk drawer was a familiar tableau.

Once we were seated, I put my purple folder on my lap and started to take out any documents that contained our address and personal details. The clerk was surprisingly helpful. He took my paperwork from me and copied whatever information was needed into his database. Then, he printed our *padrón* papers and wished us good luck in Monetfrio. That was it!

This was very different from our previous experience at the police station in Jaén, so I decided to take my chances and asked the kind man how we should proceed to obtain Spanish residency papers. Of course, even though I could form the question, I could barely grasp the answer that came in rapid Spanish and made a large number of assumptions about my knowledge of the country's administration. I understood *oficina de extranjeros* and asked the clerk to write down the exact name of the office for me so that I could google the address.

As we walked back to the car, I felt optimistic. In those days, we had not yet located the municipal car park, and so we used to park at the bottom of the hill to avoid getting stuck in one of the narrow one-way streets that radiate off from the centre of Montefrio. We walked past manicured orange trees and balconies generously decorated with pots of geraniums. Teens motored up and down the narrow streets on noisy two-stroke scooters. Old ladies carried their grocery bags home with baguettes sticking upright out of their shopping bags. They'd stop every few minutes and chat to their neighbours who they met on the street.

We were one of them now — I thought to myself — *a resident of Montefrio*.

I liked what I saw. I liked the people who surrounded us. I felt that perhaps the impenetrable fortress of the Spanish bureaucracy was just a myth and nothing to worry about.

Oblivious of what lay ahead, the following day, we set off for the Immigration Office in Granada. After driving around the district where the office is located for over half an hour looking for a place to park, we were waved down by a Moroccan man who kindly indicated that there was an open parking spot in a side street. We followed his directions, parked and then gave him a small tip for his services. Armed with my purple folder, we marched into the Immigration Office. After a security check by a uniformed policeman who was smoking at the front door, the receptionist asked us what we wanted. Since we were both from the EU, we were given a stack of papers to fill in and told to get a ticket and wait for the clerk in the glass office on the right to call us. I looked to the left and then to the right again and breathed a sigh of relief.

On the left of the reception desk were the counters for non-EU citizens. There was a babel of voices coming from the numerous queues on this side of the reception area — families from Venezuela, Brazil, Ecuador, Ethiopia, Ghana, Algeria, and many other South-American and African countries were respectfully queuing with papers neatly arranged in hand, awaiting their chance to speak to an Immigration Office clerk. It was not only the fact that they had to wait in a long queue while the EU citizens' side of the office was almost empty that made me gasp. The apparent vast discrepancy in power and social standing that was played out before our eyes made me wince in embarrassment.

At that moment, there was no time to dwell upon the social injustice of it all and the role that the 'luck of one's birthplace' so often plays in our lives because we had to fill out reams of papers with different codes and numbers. We filled out these forms together as a team: I'd decipher what piece of information was needed and then translate it to Robert. I left blank whatever I did not understand and hoped that the clerk would fill it in on our behalf.

We were barely finished with the paperwork when our queue number was called. The short-haired brunette did not even look at us from behind her computer screen. There was no enthusiastic *¡Hola!* or

¡Buena! that I was used to hearing in the shops, bars, and other public places in our little village. By contrast, we were welcomed by a direct, big-city inquiry: *¿Que quieres? — What do you want?*. The female clerk already seemed bored with speaking to us, so I cut to the chase.

'We would like to be residents of Spain?' I explained in slow and probably mispronounced Spanish, but she got the gist — we were, after all, in the Immigration Office, so what else would we need, a loaf of bread or perhaps a haircut?

It's often an unmistakable mark of the bureaucratic mind that, no matter how obvious the purpose of your visit is, a true civil servant will make you explain it.

'Where are you from?' she asked, still looking at her screen.

'I'm Polish, and my husband is English,' I explained in Spanish.

'You need to fill out the forms N-025, Y-536, and X-78,' she recited.

'These ones?' I showed her the bunch of papers that we had half filled out in the reception area.

She finally looked up and took the papers from me.

'Passport copy,' even though the syntax and intonation were wrong, I assumed it was a question.

The clerk was surrounded by printers, scanners, and several photocopiers.

'I have the passports here,' I put both our passports in front of her.

'I need a copy.'

'Can you make a copy?' I enquired.

'No,' she snapped. 'There's a café outside. They make photocopies.'

She browsed through the papers, spoke as fast as was humanly possible, and ticked different places in the documents to indicate their importance.

'Complete these, make five copies of those, and bring your passport photos,' was all I understood. The rest of her imperious instructions were plain gibberish.

It was clear from her tone that we were not to ask any further questions at that point of our interaction. I hastily gathered our paperwork and exited the building.

'What did she say?' Robert asked.

'We must make five copies of these in the café outside.'

Robert was confused and angry and started to argue with me about the absurdity of the situation.

'Why can't she fill out the missing information and make copies?' he demanded to know.

I tried to stay calm and looked at the 'huddled masses' on the other side of the Immigration Office. The friendly receptionist noticed our marital dispute and decided to help. He looked at the paperwork and the sections that the sociopath inside the office had ticked off. He then explained in slow Spanish what information was needed. Then, he stepped outside the main entrance of the building and directed us to the café that made photocopies.

To the casual passer-by, the place we were told to go looked like a regular café. Most of the tables were occupied by people drinking coffee and finishing their *tostadas con tomate*, a typical Andalusian breakfast. I was thus a bit wary of going inside and demanding photocopying services, but I had faith in our newly-acquired friend — the receptionist. Inside, we found a bar and an Arabic grocery shop. There were different Egyptian-style beans and canned meals, varieties of hummus and halva, and bags of rice from North Africa on the shelves.

There was also a price list for photocopying services. We were in the right place. A very competent Algerian bartender-cum-shopkeeper understood immediately what we needed — the fistful of documents in my hand was a clear giveaway. He took the papers from me and browsed through them.

'OK, you'll need five copies of these. Do you have passport photos?' he spoke in excellent English. Obviously, it was not his first time helping applicants from the Immigration Office.

'Yes, I do have the photos. Thank you.'

He went to the back, and I could hear the gentle humming of the photocopy machine. He came back after a few minutes with our documents neatly arranged and stapled, all ready to present to the sour brunette in the glass office.

'Good luck!' he shouted as we left the café.

Back in Satan's lair, we were instructed to sit down and wait for madame to finish whatever she was reading on her computer. We then patiently watched her chat to her colleagues, ostensibly laugh at a joke some other trainee despot was telling her, engage in an obviously private matter on the phone, go out and make herself a cup of coffee, come back and print out some pointless documents, and then meticulously attach some stamps on some other documents. Once our status as deplorable lowlifes who did not deserve her precious attention was well-established, the real power games commenced. She took our paperwork from across the desk but didn't even bother to check it.

'Papers from the hacienda,' I assumed she was asking about something.

'Hacienda?' I was confused. 'No, we don't have a hacienda. We have a small *cortijo*. It's outside Montefrio.'

'No, hacienda, hacienda,' she repeated twice as if that would make me understand. 'We need your tax information from the hacienda.'

'I have no idea what she's on about,' I turned to Robert.

'I think *hacienda* is the Spanish tax office,' he suggested.

'No, it's a big estate,' I argued.

'It's also a tax office. *Impuesto* means tax.' Robert explained to me. For someone who could barely explain where he was from and what his job was, he sometimes surprised me with such nuggets of random information. I accepted this and turned back to the goblin behind the desk.

'We have NIE numbers, and we've paid tax on the house.'

'No, you need a letter from hacienda with your tax returns,' the word *impuesto* — the most beloved word of any Spanish bureaucrat — was uttered several times until I understood what she wanted.

'But we just moved here two weeks ago. We don't have any tax returns.'

'What about your tax in Abu Dhabi?'

'There are no taxes in Abu Dhabi,' I told her. She must have thought that I was a real cuckoo because we exchanged the same question and reply a couple of times before she gave up on this thread. She changed the angle of her interrogation.

'Do you have a job?'

'No.'

'Do you have social insurance?'

'No.'

We went rapid-fire through the things that we definitely did not have. Once done with us, she opened a drawer and gave me a photocopy. It was an A4, or American letter size, paper filled with bullet points. I could see this paper was a copy of a copy as it contained some old notes made by someone else and had been copied askew.

'You need these documents to apply for the EU residency.'

'What about these documents?' I asked, pointing at the pile of photocopies that I handed her at the start of the interrogation.

'These are just application forms.' Was that a glimmer of a smile? 'You need these too.' She ticked each of the items off the list that was on the desk. Each point seemed to increase her sense of power over the situation since each subsequent tick was accompanied by a flourish of her pen that became more extravagant as she moved down the list. In fact, the list was awe-inspiring and did well to represent the labyrinth of bureaucratic madness that is 'the Spanish system'.

I looked at the monstrous document and at her cold eyes. I was feeling faint. Based on the list, we'd have to go to at least three different government buildings in Granada. I knew we would be forced to repeat the same song and dance we had just been subject to at each institution. I didn't know where these places were and which department we were to look for in each location. I collected our photocopies, put them inside my purple folder, gave the clerk a cold stare and left. Robert followed.

'What now?'

I gave him the list.

'We need to go to all these offices and get a piece of paper from each one of them.' I explained.

'Is this a joke?'

There was nothing else to say. It was already one o'clock, and it was apparent we wouldn't be able to get anything else done that day in Granada because government offices close at two p.m. sharp for lunch. We were both hot and exhausted. I felt defeated, and we decided to go home and clear our heads with some cold beer by the pool.

We discussed our predicament all the way from Granada to Montefrio but couldn't figure out how to overcome the obstacle that the Spanish bureaucracy posed for us. A few days later, when meeting an English friend for some drinks, we were presented with a solution. We were sitting at El Parque café in the centre of Alcalá la Real. It's always a nice place to meet up with other people because of the beautifully maintained flower gardens that border the park and the stunning view of the castle above. We explained to Tony our adventures at the Immigration Office.

'You need a *gestor*,' he said, pronouncing the initial *g*, as it sounds in *George*.

'A gestor? Who's that?' Robert asked.

'It's a fixer. They deal with the red tape — they do your taxes, any paperwork with the social security office, anything you need doing in a government office,' Tony explained.

'Do you know one?' I asked.

'Yes. Go to Diego. His office is over there.'

Tony pointed to some shops and offices behind the fountain. The word *gestoría* was printed in bold capital letters on one of the windows.

'Does he speak any English?' I asked.

'He speaks perfect English. He studied in Tennessee.'

An Andalusian accountant who studied in the South — I liked him already. Once we finished our drinks and tapas, Robert and I went to Diego's office. Once inside, we were greeted by a tall, lanky man who immediately identified us as foreigners and welcomed us in American English. Without further ado, he invited us from the waiting room lined with accounting tables into his spacious office. On the wall behind his well-padded black leather chair was a large framed poster from the University of Granada that included photographs of all the graduates of administration studies in his graduating year. There were other diplomas and certificates from different institutions of learning dotted around the walls of the office — it's an Andalusian tradition for small businesses to display their owners' credentials on the wall. But I didn't have time to study them all as we had to explain what we needed. We went over our exasperating trip to the

Immigration Office, but Diego interrupted him and cut to the chase before Robert finished talking.

'OK. I know,' he said in a mixture of thick Southern American accent mixed with Andalusian Spanish. 'First, you need to register as an *autónomo*. It's like a freelancer. Can you do that?'

I looked at Robert. This was perfect. We planned to work as freelancers anyway — Robert was an editor and translator, and I wrote textbooks.

We are going to kill two birds with one stone. I thought to myself.

We hired Diego on the spot, and from then on, he minimised our future interaction with the Spanish bureaucracy. That is, until almost two years later, when we decided to take a dreaded bank loan to finish our guest apartments. To secure this loan, we had to venture into the world of banking bureaucracy.

FOUR
MOVING FORWARD

The first step in securing a loan was very straightforward. I sent a text message to our banker to ask him if we could get one. The benefit of being a bank customer in a small town of about twenty thousand people is that you can text your banker directly. In a town like Alcalá la Real, everyone is somehow linked to each other. The banker knows your plumber, the plumber is the husband of your dentist, the dentist is the mother of the nurse who helped bring you to this world, the nurse is the cousin of your hairdresser and a sister-in-law of the waitress in your favourite café, who, in turn, is the wife of the manager of the funeral home whom everyone is doomed to meet sooner or later. Because of these close links, there is a certain level of trust which means you can send a text message to your banker at eight o'clock in the morning — an hour and a half before the bank opens and ask:

'Hola Enrique! Hope you're well? How is baby Hugo? We need to borrow some money from your bank to finish two kitchens in our guest apartments. Is it possible?'

We'd been Enrique's clients since we purchased the house, and he knew all about our plans to open a holiday home, so there was no need to explain the message any further. After ten minutes, I received his text.

'Yes, of course. Can you come to the bank this morning or tomorrow?'

I sent him a thumbs-up icon and told Robert that we had to go to the bank that morning to apply for our loan. I grabbed my purple folder. As we entered the bank, Enrique led us to the director's office, where we were seated on plush black leather chairs. Enrique stayed with us to translate. We went over our situation one more time and decided on the amount that we were going to borrow to finish our project. Then Enrique left us to attend to his other customers, and we sat there while the director filled in a seemingly endless series of forms on his computer screen. Occasionally, he would ask us some simple questions needed to complete the application form, but he generously did all the paperwork for us. This was greatly appreciated as I could see that I would have given up after page one if I were left alone with all these forms.

Once all our personal details were inputted into the bank's software several times over, the bank director started to print out the paperwork. Printing papers and filing them is one of the essential marks of a solid bureaucratic organisation.

'It will take a few minutes,' the director warned us. 'Maybe you'd like to go out for a cup of coffee and come back.'

It was a cold March morning, and a gentle spring rain was falling. I did not feel like leaving the cosy office, so we declined and said we were fine waiting here. This was, of course, a mistake. Watching paint dry might have been more fun than watching the slowest printer in Andalusia spit out our application page by page. Not only was the printer ancient, but the document itself appeared to be the longest book in the world. *Remembrance of Things Past* would have seemed to be a short novella if it were placed next to the tome that was growing in front of our eyes.

The director himself did not feel like he had to suffer through the protracted birth of the document and thus left his office for fifteen minutes or so, just enough time, I reflected, to have a cup of coffee. On his eventual return, our magnum opus seemed to be nearly ready. He started to collect the papers from the printer tray and arrange them into small piles, which were then stapled together. He placed tick marks at the different places where we had to sign.

I was handed the first lot of papers and added my signature where indicated. Once I was done, I passed them on to Robert. I don't think I have ever signed my name so many times in one day. I was starting to get a cramp in my hand when the director announced that our application form was complete.

'Did you bring your tax return form for the last year with you?' he asked in Spanish.

I pulled out my purple folder and searched for the pocket that contained our tax documents for our house. To be honest, I never read any of the letters we received from the tax office. If anything looked important, I would take a photo and email it to Diego to sort it out. He would always write back:

'OK. Thanks. Don't worry about it.'

And with these magic words, he made any concerns I may have had about these tax letters disappear from my life. Of course, I kept the hard copies that were sent to our home address and so now presented a thick stack of the hacienda's communications to the bank director. He seemed perplexed but browsed through it.

'It's not here.' He declared after searching through the pile of tax office letters.

'Do you pay taxes?' he seemed to start to regret spending so much time on our application form.

'Yes,' I assured him. 'Diego does our taxes.'

On hearing Diego's name, he instantly cheered up.

'Perfect. I'll call him and ask for your tax papers. Is that ok?'

'Yes, of course.'

He called Diego without searching for his number, which made me think that he worked with our gestor a lot. After a short chat, he hung up his phone, and I received a phone call on my mobile. It was Diego. He wanted to know if it was OK to give the bank director our tax information.

'OK. I'll bring it in thirty minutes,' Diego said.

It seems that in a bureaucratic regime, nothing can be done electronically. By now, it was raining heavily, and we once again declined the offer to go out for coffee. However, we exited the room and waited in the bank's general waiting area until Diego showed up. We then went back into the director's office, where Diego handed over our tax information. He then translated for us some finer details of the loan contract.

'Now, you need to go to the notary to sign this agreement,' Diego explained.

'A notary?' I echoed.

We had visited the notary four years earlier when we purchased the house, but I would not have been able to find that office again. Sensing my slight despair, Diego offered to escort us to her office. This was very generous.

'That would be fantastic,' I said.

Outside, we opened our umbrellas and walked quickly through the narrow streets. At the notary's office, Diego explained to the secretary what we wanted. He must have sensed that we were not going to get through the bureaucracy of the notary's office on our own and decided to stay with us. We had been waiting for some time on a row of hard wooden chairs when Ms Notary waltzed in through the main entrance, presumably refreshed after her morning coffee and toast.

In her fake Chanel suit, white leather high heels, and expensive haircut —— she barely gave us, two scruffy country bumpkins, a look. She must have thought we were a couple of homeless people sheltering from the rain in her pristine waiting room. She ignored Diego, too, even though she must have dealt with him in the past. He was a well-known gestor in Alcalá.

She turned 'ignoring us' into an art form. First, she made a spectacle of putting away her umbrella, then chatted to her secretary about nothing. Next, she walked in and out of the different offices that could be accessed from the waiting room offices several times for no apparent reason. She appeared to be very busy, but it was not clear to anyone watching her what exactly she was doing. It was a dance, a painful exercise of power, but Diego wasn't having any of it.

He followed her into one of the offices. After a few minutes of lively conversation, he came out and asked if we had our NIE papers with us. I opened my purple folder and fished out our NIE documents. He took them and the loan contract and returned to the office where Her Highness, Ms Notary, resided. A heated discussion could be heard through the open door. I could tell that things were not going our way. After a few minutes, Diego came out and, in an exasperated voice, asked me if I had the originals of our NIE documents.

'Are these not the originals?' I asked.

'No, the originals have a green stamp. This one is grey, so it's not an original.'

I realised that I must have mixed up the originals with the copies over the last few years. I searched the folder but could not find them.

'But the identification number is the same. It doesn't change — it's recorded by the tax office and the social security office,' Robert tried to bring logic to the table.

'I know,' Diego replied. 'But she wants to see the originals.'

'But it does not matter. The original is only valid for three months anyway. It expired in 2012.'

This was true. The original NIE document that we got from the dead-faced policewoman in Jaén included a line of minuscule small print that stated that the document was only valid for three months. In fact, at the time, all NIE documents were good for only three months. Diego went back to the office to present these arguments to Ms Notary. But he wasn't there long when he jumped out of the office like a jack-in-a-box.

'Let's go,' he told Robert and me. 'I'll never do any business here ever again.'

We followed him dutifully, trusting his judgement. Once we were outside, he explained that the notary was making it impossible to sign the bank contract; the monster demanded more paperwork.

'We're going to see my notary,' he announced. 'She's in Castillo de Locubín.'

Castillo de Locubín is a small village fifteen minutes outside Alcalá. Diego offered to take us there. On the way to his car, he was constantly on the phone.

Ms Notary must have really angered him, I thought.

We got into his car and drove off. Before we left Alcalá, he stopped on the main street outside his office, where his secretary was waiting for us with a manila envelope in hand. Robert opened the passenger window, and she gave him the envelope with the originals of our NIE documents.

That's where we left them. I suddenly remembered that we had handed over the original NIEs to Diego two years earlier.

With these precious documents in hand, we drove at speed to Castillo. Whether it was the adrenaline built up after his exchange at the first notary or just traditional machismo, Diego whisked us off to Castillo like a professional racing driver, cutting corners, overtaking other cars, and almost taking off on the speed bumps. Once in Castillo, 'Fernando Alonso' parked just a few metres outside Castillo's notary office.

Our business was completed in minutes. We met the notary, signed the loan contract, and raced back with Diego to Alcalá in time to present the papers to the bank manager before the bank closed for the day. Two days later, the much-needed funds were deposited into our account. We could now continue the project and finish the holiday rentals before the summer.

FIVE
BEARDED IRISES

For fellow admirers of Van Gogh's flowers and landscapes, springtime in Andalusia is a real treat. Wherever you look, it feels like you've just stepped inside one of his paintings from Provence. Because Van Gogh drew his inspiration from southern France, I never expected to see it come to life in rural Andalusia. But it seems that the light in both places has the same magical quality, which gives the flowers and trees the vibrant expression which is so well depicted in Vincent's thick brush and knife strokes. From the blossoming cherry orchards to the olive trees that glisten in the moonlight, the landscapes of Provence and Andalusia are wonderfully similar.

Springtime around Montefrio starts with the sprouting of the first almond blossoms. The almond tree is an early flowering tree, and so the flowers appear before the leaves. The pinkish and white blossoms contrast against the deep blue skies throughout February. In late March, the bearded irises start to bloom. They are one of the most common springtime flowers in our area. Planted on uneven terrain, hillsides, escarpments, and ridges, they require little attention or care. They are never watered or deadheaded. The purple flowers grow in abundance in spring and frame the whitewashed cottages. Like the almond branches, the stems of bearded irises are gnarly in shape. Not unlike the fingers of an old farmer, weathered by extreme cold and heat. This may be why these two plants were favoured by the famous artist.

That March and April, I made both apartments unavailable for bookings so that we could build kitchens for prospective summer guests. After constructing a giant wardrobe and bedside tables out of recycled pallets, Robert was confident that we could make kitchen units from the same material. He noticed that our neighbour had a stack of old pallets next to his house, or *casa de campo*, as he referred to it since he only visited it on the weekends to enjoy nature and to cool off in his swimming pool in the summer. The next time we saw Juan, we went over to ask whether we could have the pallets. He looked at us suspiciously.

'You want to take these old pallets?' he must have thought that we used a wrong word.

'Yes. These old pallets. Can we take them?' I reiterated.

'These pallets?' he wasn't getting it. He couldn't understand why someone would want a pile of junk. His wife Carmen approached.

'They want to take these pallets,' he explained to her.

'That's excellent,' Carmen seemed quicker on the uptake than her husband. She had the expression of a woman delighted to have found two idiots willing to take away her husband's rubbish for free. As Juan still did not understand why anyone would want a pile of old pallets, I explained that we were going to make kitchen furniture from it.

'Furniture?' he was even more confused, but his wife gave him a friendly jab to stop him from asking further questions.

We brought our trailer around and loaded it with the pallets. Carmen and Juan watched us, pleased. She told us that they would plant some watermelons in the spot where the pallets had been stacked. Once finished, we all congratulated each other on a job well done — us pleased with the free materials and them happy with a clean spot of land. We drove the few hundred metres back to our land, where we offloaded the pallets.

We spent the spring tearing down the pallets and building the kitchens. When I wasn't helping Robert prepare the wood to make the kitchens, I was writing a new textbook, and he, too, was juggling translation work with kitchen-building. It was an easy-going spring, and in contrast to the heavy workload of the previous years, which involved cement mixing, tiling, and living in a cloud of dust, building things from wood was rewarding and creative. Another advantage of working with wood is that it is much easier to adjust to your needs than tiles or bricks. Since both Robert and I are terrible at measuring things precisely, I was happy to see that, for once, our miscalculations didn't lead to disastrous consequences.

One afternoon, I was walking in front of the house and carrying tools from the garage-cum-carpentry-workshop to one of the apartments when I saw a young boy in a fluorescent green jacket furtively climb over my neighbour's two-metre fence. My neighbour, Mercedes, has a small house, or a *nave*, on the other side of the track that runs along our valley. From our position on the hill, we can see the entrance to her cottage quite well. Since her husband, Juan Carlos, had passed away the year before, she hardly ever visited the place. She was over seventy years of age and lived in an apartment in Montefrio. Because Mercedes did not have a driver's licence, Old Gabi had to chauffeur her around whenever she wanted to leave the village and visit her *campo* house.

Mercedes and her brother had been born in our house, and it was Old Gabi's son, Young Gabi, who sold it to us. The younger generation did not care for country life *per se*, and the older generation did not seem to miss living in their ancestral home either. In

Montefrío, Mercedes could walk anywhere she wanted without needing a lift. Unlike in her *casa de campo*, she had running water and central heating in her apartment and lots of activities that she could engage in with other pensioners in the village.

Old Gabi, too, seemed to enjoy his widower's lifestyle in the town of Huétor-Tájar, where he had retired. From his frequent descriptions of the fiestas and dances organised by the town hall for the *mayores*, or senior citizens, I gathered that he was quite the attraction for the ladies. Neither of the siblings was particularly interested in living in the *campo* permanently. It was unmistakable that they appreciated the creature comforts that living in a village could offer.

Since we were good neighbours, I was concerned about the youth in the fluorescent green jacket who had just climbed over Mercedes's fence. I went inside the garage where Robert was constructing the frames for the new kitchens and told him what I had just witnessed. After a brief discussion, we decided that we had never seen a young lad of this description in the area.

'Could it be one of their nephews?' I asked. They were at least a dozen nephews between Merce and Old Gabi, who we often heard of, but we had only ever seen two of them face-to-face.

'No. Why would he jump over the fence?' Robert answered. 'I'm going to check it out.'

I watched from our patio, but the front of Merce's house was hidden by fig and quince trees. A few minutes later, I saw Robert running up our driveway.

'Bring me the car keys,' he hollered.

I went in and grabbed the keys. Robert jumped into the car and drove away without any explanation. This wasn't unusual. I find that when confronted with situations that require immediate action, men find it difficult to vocalize what has just happened and what needs to be done.

Hoping that he wasn't getting himself into trouble, I went back inside and continued assembling the pieces of wood that Robert had prepared to serve as a frame for the kitchen cupboards. He was following a design we had drawn up together that would fit the existing kitchen appliances. Consequently, many of the pieces were of unique lengths to make space for the fridge, the washing machine, and the sink.

The problem was that while Robert had measured each piece several times and cut them all meticulously, he forgot to number the pieces, and we now had a pile of perfectly cut pieces but no idea which part was supposed to go where. It all reminded me of a wooden box puzzle that we once bought in Thailand. Enthusiastically, we took it out of the box where it was neatly assembled, disconnected the pieces without paying any attention to their rightful place and were never able to put the puzzle together again.

To this day, the disjointed pieces adorn our library shelf as a decorative pile of wooden blocks and homage to certain character traits that we aren't proud of. Unfortunately, this time we could not abandon all the kitchen parts on the floor and walk away, so I gathered my patience and concentration and worked on one section at a time. Half an hour later, Robert was back.

'What happened?' I asked.

'I went down to the road and saw the boy cycling away from Mercedes's house on a pink bicycle.'

'How old was he?'

'Twelve or so. I saw him carry the bike from behind the house onto the road. Then he jumped on it when he saw me coming and rolled down the hill on it.'

'So, you ran back to follow him in your four by four? Wasn't it a bit overkill?'

I simply stated the facts to emphasise the particular power imbalance between a twelve-year-old boy on a tiny girl's bike and a two-metre-tall man in a Nissan Patrol. David and Goliath came to mind, but I kept these thoughts to myself.

'No, it wasn't,' Robert defended his actions. 'He was flying on that bike down the hill. He was past the postboxes and halfway up the first hill by the time I caught up with him.'

Our postboxes are about six hundred metres from the house. Because our postman refuses to explore the country roads of Andalusia, he told our neighbours and us to install the postboxes just before the turnoff from the asphalt road to our dirt track. While the road from our house to the postboxes is downhill, you have to climb several steep hills to get anywhere from there. I felt sorry for the little chap on the pink bike.

'Whose bike is it anyway?' I asked.

'It must be Young Gabi's niece's bike. She was here last Christmas.'

I remembered a small six-year-old girl.

'How did he manage to ride that bike? Wasn't it too small?'

'He rolled downhill on it with his legs up in the air. When I caught up with him, he was pulling the bike up the hill. He couldn't ride it. It's too small for him.'

'Why did he not throw it in the ditch?' I couldn't understand why the boy was hanging on to the tiny bike.

'Obviously, to roll down the next set of hills on the way to Montefrio.'

To Robert, who as a ten-year-old boy in Liverpool in the late 1970s had his share of misdemeanours, this was a perfectly logical thing to do.

'He was going to Montefrio on that bike?' I was shocked.

While Montefrio is only six kilometres away as the crow flies, to get there on foot or by bike, especially one too small for your body, would require a lot of endurance and stamina. I could not understand what a twelve-year-old was doing near our house and why he stole a bike to get to Montefrio.

According to Robert's version of the events that followed, on seeing Robert get out of the car, the boy surrendered the stolen bike without arguing. He explained that he had taken the bike to get to Montefrio to his mum's place because he didn't want to spend any more time with his dad in the countryside. Feeling a little bit sorry for the teen vagabond, Robert followed him down the rest of the hill until he saw a neighbour behind a fence.

'He's the son of the *delincuentes*,' the neighbour informed Robert, while they watched the lad run off towards Montefrio.

Even though it was a new word for Robert, it sounded just like the English *delinquent*, so there was no misunderstanding here.

'Where do these *delincuentes* live?' Robert asked. We were

completely unaware that a family of delinquents lived near us until now. He was intrigued.

'Do you know Encarna?'

'Encarnación? The one with a black BMW?' Robert might not always have been able to recall where the knives and forks were in his own kitchen, but he had an excellent memory of who drives what type of car, make, model, year, and colour.

'Yes, that one. The *delincuentes* live past her house.'

As Robert reported these events to me, we realised that we knew which house the man had referred to. It was a small *cortijo* off the dirt track with a pack of mad dogs roaming around it. We had gone past it once, three or four years earlier, while exploring the area and had to fend off some rabid-looking dogs with sticks and by throwing small stones from the road at them. We had not gone for a walk in that direction since those events.

'And why are they *delincuentes*?' I asked.

'He said that they sell drugs,' Robert repeated what the neighbour had told him. 'Apparently, the father has just come out of prison.'

'Is this why we haven't seen him?' I speculated.

I wasn't too excited about this new information, but we could do nothing about it. Besides, their house was approximately three kilometres away from ours, so I doubted we'd be too bothered by whatever went on there. However, unconsciously, I started to watch the road.

SIX
ASPARAGUS SEASON

Outside the olive season, very few cars pass on the road outside our house. One neighbour, Isabella, would drive her Seat Ibiza to the postboxes where the school bus collected and dropped off her little girl from school. Encarna would go shopping twice a week in her black BMW. Sometimes, José would go past in his old Land Rover Defender, or Pablo would drive to his *cortijo* in an ancient Mercedes van with a big mastiff drooling out of the back window. There are not more than six cars that regularly drive past our house. That's why it was so strange when, one morning, I heard a huge bang outside, similar to a car crash. I went out of the kitchen and saw Robert standing on the stone wall by the end of the patio and looking at the road.

'What's happened?' I asked.

'Javier has just crashed into Pablo's van.' Javier was Encarna's fast and furious son. 'I knew this was going to happen.' Robert had always complained to me about the speed with which Javier races up and down the road.

On the road, which is about a hundred metres, or three-hundred-and-thirty feet, from the house, I could see Pablo's old van stopped right in the middle of the road and Javier's Ford Fiesta stuck sideways across the track, one wheel in the ditch, facing José's wheat field. For two cars to pass each other in our lane, one has to stop either in a passing bay or drive into an olive grove to let the other pass. It was apparent from the cars' positions and the skid marks on the road's surface that Javier had hit the brakes really hard and spun to the side to avoid a head-on collision.

It was not a horrible accident. Admittedly, the front of Javier's car was destroyed, but the van seemed unscathed. The old man, Pablo, got out of his van and immediately started discussing the young punk's driving skills, or lack thereof, in a somewhat raised tone of voice.

'I'm going down in case Pablo needs a witness,' Robert told me.

I stayed and watched the events from the patio wall. It was the most action that we'd ever had outside our house. I wasn't sure about the procedure.

Will they call Guardia Civil or Tráficos? I wondered.

The Spanish police system is complicated and consists of many branches. In Montefrio alone, a village of six thousand people, there is a Guardia Civil station in an old, disused, yet still ominous-looking, Franco-era barracks. There is also a Local Police station next to the town hall. For regular law-abiding foreigners, it is somewhat difficult to distinguish between the different responsibilities that these two law enforcement agencies have. In addition, there is also the Traffic Police, which can often be seen monitoring motorists' speed on the highways, and the National Police, which we only see in big cities and on television. I was curious to see what would happen if we were ever involved in an accident.

As it turned out, there was no lesson for us here. Once Pablo had finished explaining to the young man what was on his mind at that particular moment in time and what he thought about his kind in general and in more specific terms, he returned to his vehicle and drove off. After all, his thirty-year-old van had barely been scratched, and the mastiff in the back looked perfectly satisfied to continue with the journey.

It was Javier who had to turn around and drive home to explain to his mum, Encarna, how he had managed to completely demolish the front end of his Ford Fiesta. I didn't envy young Javier, but I was also quite relieved that he would be off the road for some time.

A few days later, we were planting tomatoes and peppers in our vegetable garden when Encarna's vehicle stopped by our gate. I opened the gate and invited her in. From the back of her car, she collected a small basket and a plastic bag.

'A gift for you,' she said in Spanish. 'The eggs are fresh from our chickens.'

She handed me the eggs and the biggest bunch of asparagus that I had ever seen in my life.

'Wow! That's a lot of asparagus. Thank you so much.'

The asparagus that is cultivated in Granada, Jaén, and Cordoba provinces is thick and bright green. It is harvested in spring, soon after the olive harvest is finished. Throughout the year, the asparagus fields turn from green in the summer to a vibrant orange and yellow in autumn. I didn't know before we moved to Andalusia that harvesting this delicacy requires backbreaking work, which starts when it's still dark outside.

Because picking asparagus is so labour-intensive, most farmers go out into the fields around four a.m. to finish a day's work before it gets unbearably hot. The pickers wear wide-brimmed hats and carry a sack around their waist to collect the shoots. They use short, sharp knives to cut the stalks at ground level. There doesn't seem to exist a special technique that one could use to collect tons of asparagus without developing severe back pain. The work itself is monotonous — it involves hours of bending down, cutting, putting the vegetable in the sack, walking to the next plant, and repeating the same action thousands of times.

The resemblance of this work to slave labour may explain the price of asparagus in most European supermarkets. Despite the arduous labour involved in harvesting it, many of our neighbours grow small patches of asparagus. As soon as the olive picking season is over, they collect the asparagus and sell it to Montefrio's asparagus cooperative.

'We have a lot of asparagus this year,' Encarna explained as we started walking up the driveway to our house.

She wanted to tell me more, but the steep hill was making her lose her breath. I could see she regretted leaving her car by the gate, but she insisted on walking. I knew she walked a lot because in her never-ending fight to lose weight since I would see her several times a week walking with great spirit and determination past our house to the postboxes and back to her house, which is a six-kilometre round trip in total. Even now, she was wearing knee-length leggings, a Decathlon T-shirt, and expensive sneakers. Once we reached the house, I got her a drink, and we all sat down on the patio shaded by the bay leaf tree.

'That's better,' she said in Spanish after taking a sip of the cold drink and putting it down. 'So, to eat the asparagus, you boil it very quickly, then fry it with jamón serrano and eggs. It's very delicious.'

She smacked her lips. '¡muy rico!' or *very delicious*, she repeated two more times in the typical Andalusian fashion of reiterating the same thing several times to make sure its importance sinks in with whoever is listening. Once she cooled off, we showed her the progress that we had made on our rental apartments.

'¡Que precioso! How beautiful! she assessed our work with several exclamations.

Not having much more to talk about, Robert informed her about his adventures with the *delincuentes*' son. Encarna was all ears. Like us, she was a keen gossiper and spiced Robert's tale with regular *ah!*, *hah!* and *uf!* Robert's Spanish was still pretty basic and composed mainly of nouns that the listener had to piece together into a cohesive story.

'One morning, young boy, jacket green, Mercedes, small bicycle, pink, young girl, road, fast, I go car, boy go fast, go Montefrio, *delincuente*,' he told her.

I thought that this report would be too difficult to understand, even by the keenest of listeners, and so I interspersed it with a few verbs. When he finished his tale of theft and pursuit, he seemed stuck and was searching for words. He turned to me and asked:

'How do you say: *If I hadn't caught him, he would have taken the bike to Montefrio.*'

I had no idea.

'I don't know how to use the past tense correctly, and you want me to use the subjunctive,' I gave him a long, pensive stare.

Encarna did not understand a word of what we were talking about but could see that we were having a disagreement about something. She decided to fill in the gaps in Robert's tale.

'They live close to my house. The father went to prison for selling drugs, but he's back now. The Guardia Civil go there every week to check on him,' she told us. 'The boy lives with his mum in Montefrio. She has five children, each from a different boyfriend, so he comes to the *campo* sometimes to be with his dad.'

'Is he still selling drugs,' Robert asked.

'I don't know, but I see a lot of strange cars stop outside their house on Friday and Saturday afternoons. I think he's growing marijuana somewhere. There is a yellow car that goes there all the time. Sometimes it's by the postboxes for a long time.'

'Who is it?' I asked.

'I don't know, but I think he's selling drugs for the *delincuente*.'

As she told this story, I realised that I had seen a beat-up lemon-coloured Citroën go past our house a few times in the last two months. I assumed it was a friend visiting someone down the valley because I didn't recognise the car.

'Do you know Isabella's fiancé, Daniel?' she asked, changing the subject.

'Yes. I'm a nice boy. I come here sometimes for a small beer,' Robert said in Spanish.

I saw Encarna's baffled expression and explained that it was *Dani* who sometimes drank beer with Robert. Despite our weekly Spanish classes in Alcalá, and our teacher's never-ending efforts to make us conjugate the Spanish verbs correctly, Robert insisted on using the first-person singular verb form no matter whether he was talking about other people or himself. This was inevitably very confusing to even the most patient of his interlocutors who had to deduce whether he was telling them something about himself, another person, or perhaps asking them a question.

We knew a little bit about Dani because he sometimes stopped by our house in the evenings on his way home from work. He and Robert would drink a couple of small beers and chat in English — he was the only neighbour who spoke English. Dani had studied computer science at Granada University but was now back in his home village of Montefrio doing mindless office work. It appeared that the only reason he had originally returned was that his girlfriend had fallen pregnant. The child was now six years old and seemed to be the only reason why Dani had come to live on the *campo* at his girlfriend's parents' farm. Not being a farmer, he must have had little to talk about with Isabella's father, Paco, who was all about the countryside and olive farming. I didn't think Dani felt at home here.

'Well, last week, his brother committed suicide,' Encarna told us.

'What did she say?' Robert asked. I didn't know what *se suicidó* meant, and Encarna could see from our blank expressions that we had not understood.

'You know Iglesia de la Villa?' she asked.

'Yes, the church. It's very beautiful,' I didn't know where her story was going, but I felt it would be polite to compliment the local architecture. She seemed slightly taken aback by my enthusiastic comment but continued.

'He threw himself off the rocks by the church. Some teenagers found him at the bottom of the cliff,' she explained.

With the context of the rocks and death now clear, I suddenly understood what *se suicide* meant. Robert was still confused about what had happened, so I translated Encarna's story.

'It is not the first time that someone has jumped off that cliff,' she continued once I had finished translating. 'Last year, another young boy jumped. His neighbours say that he was a bit strange though; he didn't have any friends. He never went to church or the local fiestas. The town hall should really put up some barriers around that cliff.'

As she told us the tragic story of how several young men had thrown themselves off the ridge outside the iconic Montefrio church, I had a clear recollection of the place. Iglesia de la Villa, which from a distance appears to be hanging off the side of a steep escarpment, is the emblem of Montefrio. It was built in the fourteenth century to replace the old Moorish fortress that had stood at that strategic position for centuries, defending the borders of the Caliphate.

The ruins of the old castle can still be found around the church. A few metres of fencing protects tourists from falling down the rock face by accident, but the fence does not cover the whole perimeter of the church area. There are several places where horizontal rocks jut out from the cliff, like diving boards. One can easily access these rocks, look down at the sheer drop of twenty or so metres, and take a final, fatal dive. Death would be instantaneous.

'It's the suicide triangle,' she said.

'The suicide triangle?' I repeated the Spanish expression.

'Yes. It's between Alcalá la Real, Montefrio and Priego de Cordoba. A lot of young people kill themselves here, especially in the spring. It's a *maldición*.'

'*Maldición?*' I echoed the Spanish word that I didn't understand. I looked it up later and found out that it means 'a curse'.

But Encarna did not stop to explain any difficult words. She noticed that she had my full attention and continued the story.

'My friends in Venta told me that their neighbour's son hanged himself on a cherry tree. It was two years ago in April. An English woman was walking her dogs early in the morning and found Adrian's lifeless body. They say that he did it because his girlfriend broke up with him.'

It was all sounding very sinister. Was there really something in the landscape that made people commit suicide. I thought of Van Gogh and his death. Did the almonds and irises bring forth melancholy in one's soul? I wasn't convinced.

That evening, I went online and 'researched' the topic. There is, in fact, a great deal of data that shows that the number of suicides among young people in rural Andalusia is much higher than in other places in Spain, including urban areas. But, unlike Encarna, who blames supernatural forces, sociologists blame a lack of awareness or ignorance of mental health issues as part of the problem. The stigma attached to anyone who might seek the help of a psychologist, never mind a psychiatrist, is so pervasive that people in need are reluctant to use these services. I found this sociological explanation much more menacing than the idea of a curse.

I imagined a lonely young person walking the narrow streets of Montefrio (the same stone-paved medieval passages that I find so charming and welcoming) and feeling that they did not fit in — seeing only evil stares and unfriendly faces. I had not considered this side of rural living before, not because it doesn't exist, but because I came here with a strong sense of who I am.

Unlike many young people, I didn't need to ask for permission or approval to be who I wanted to be. I thought that if I were a teenager growing up in Montefrio, I probably would have hated every single minute of it. After Dani's brother's funeral, we saw him a few more times, but his visits became rarer and rarer. A year later, we heard through the grapevine that he had left Isabella and their baby and had moved out of the village for good.

SEVEN
A LITTLE BIT OF LEARNING

'There's a small white dog by the postboxes,' Robert informed me while bringing the shopping bags from the car to the kitchen. 'Is it one of Paco's?'

'I don't think so. Potranca is black, and Nano is small and brown.'

'I gave it some bread because it looked hungry.' I noticed that the end of one of the baguettes had been ripped off.

'I'm sure it will find its way home soon,' I said. 'It might be lost or waiting for someone.'

It was the first week of June, and we had just finished installing the kitchens in the two rental apartments. The end result was good. The varnished pallet wood had a lot of character. It was warm and cosy and contrasted nicely with the exposed granite walls that Robert had repointed and painted with stone varnish the year before. I was now able to take some artistic photos of the kitchens and use them to promote the apartments online for self-catering visitors.

I spent a day setting up faux dinner parties in both apartments, with fresh artichokes, fennel, and other fresh vegetables from the garden decorating the tables in an effort to convey the idea of a rustic retreat. I set up wine glasses and polished cutlery, hoping they'd capture the spirit of having fun with friends. When I had finished the photoshoot, I stood back to admire the tableau and decided that it was time to host a real dinner party.

But back in our own kitchen, I sighed in despair on seeing the contrast. While the rental accommodation was fresh, modern, and inviting, our own headquarters were worse than they were when we first moved in. What we referred to as 'the kitchen' was a tiny corner in the living room. There was about half a metre of countertop space, a sink, and a stove. We bought a fridge as soon as we had moved in because the old one could barely keep the butter from melting. The refrigerator was the only new thing in that 'kitchen'.

The living room contained a small sofa that we had inherited with the house and a large wooden table for a family of six, which served us as a work table, dining table, and entertainment centre in the evenings. There was also a traditional Andalusian fireplace to heat up the place in the winter. The living room was crammed with our belongings, decorative bowls, photos, books, travel souvenirs, and other things that made it ours, but, as a result of all the clutter, there was barely an inch to move around in.

'We can't invite people here,' Robert agreed with me.

'Let's have a barbecue outside on the patio,' he said. 'We can invite some people from the class. What about Roy and Amy?'

Roy and Amy were an English couple we had met in our Spanish class. They were both in their fifties and had taken early retirement from the British army. Like us, they owned and ran a couple of holiday apartments in Mures, a village outside Alcalá la Real.

'I hope he doesn't bring his falcon,' I said.

In this new post-work life, Roy had become a falconer. He owned a hawk and a falcon, which he kept in an enclosure next to his cottage. That he loved his pets was evident from the fact that he took at least one of them wherever he went. In addition to outings to the countryside where they could soar over the mountains and hunt pigeons and rabbits, Roy even took his pets to parties and fiestas.

One summer, he took his pet falcon, Loki, to the medieval festival at the castle in Alcalá. Everyone wanted to have a photo taken with Loki. The pictures of grey-haired Roy dressed as a medieval falconer with his pet sitting calmly on his arm appeared the next day in the local newspaper. They were reported as one of the festival's highlights. Since then, everyone in Alcalá and the surrounding villages had known Roy as 'the Englishman with the falcons'. But Roy's enthusiasm for his birds did not end there.

As one of the assignments in our Spanish class, our teacher, Blanca, asked us to prepare a presentation about a topic that interested us. Céline, a Belgian woman in her 60s, volunteered to be first and spoke at length about *galgos*. It was the first time I had heard that word, but from the photos that she showed us, I guessed that a *galgo* is a type of Spanish greyhound. She told us about an organisation for which she volunteered, *Galgos del Sol*, which rescues Spanish greyhounds and finds them new homes all over the world.

Despite Céline's usually cheerful attitude, it was a somewhat dark presentation. I didn't understand every word, but the gist was clear. She reported that *galgos* were used for hunting, but once the hunting season was over, only the best ones were kept to breed. Thousands of *galgos* in Spain were being shot or left to die every year, often abandoned in the olive groves or forests far away from 'home'. The dogs that were spared death did not go home to a bowl full of food and a warm place to sleep. They were usually kept in horrific conditions, sleeping on cold concrete in a barn, chained to a barrel or another makeshift dog house, and fed just enough to keep them alive.

This was getting increasingly upsetting to the listeners, so to end on a positive note, Céline showed us photos of the *galgos* that she and her husband had fostered over the years. They were now in safe hands with their new families in Belgium and the Netherlands. I didn't know anything about *galgos* until Céline's presentation. It changed my attitude towards the hunters who sat on the hill opposite our house every August and spent each weekend trying to shoot turtle doves.

Each time I'd see them drive past our home during the hunting season with trailers with dog cages — each cage filled with *galgos* of various sizes — mean thoughts would come to my mind, wishing them only the worst. They'd come to our area to hunt for rabbits in a *barranco* a few kilometres down the road. I don't care for hunting as a hobby — it makes no sense to me. The dogs are mistreated, the turtle doves are now endangered in Europe, and the rabbits are not worth hunting — they have enough natural predators in the forest to keep their population down.

Roy must have been inspired by Céline's presentation because he volunteered to be next. The following Wednesday afternoon, as soon as we were all seated in our tiny space that was used as a classroom at the back of Fred's shop, Roy asked us to wait a minute. His wife, Amy, was sitting next to me and giggling quietly. Her freckled stubby nose and the blond ponytail made her look decidedly mischievous. I could see that they were up to something. Roy went out and quickly returned with his pride and joy, Loki.

Just in case Roy wanted us all to stroke his baby, I decided that it was time to confess to Amy that I suffered from ornithophobia, or an extreme fear of birds, as I expressed it in plain English. Ever since a childhood encounter with a vicious rooster, I have made it my life's mission to avoid any contact with pigeons, parakeets, or sparrows, never mind birds of prey with their ginormous talons and razor-sharp beaks. Amy started to apologise and said that they wouldn't have brought Loki if they'd known. I told her not to worry, but I did ask her to keep Loki as far as possible from me.

The truth was that I was used to sharing enclosed space with falcons. During our nine years in the UAE, I would encounter them regularly since they are the most beloved pets of the Gulf Arabs. Whenever I visited the vet's clinic in Al Ain with one of our cats, I had to share the waiting room with peregrines perched in the middle of the room on a specially designed, velvet and leather-covered shelf with fake grass at the bottom to serve as the falcons' toilet. The good thing was that when transported or taken out of their usual environment, falcons wear tiny medieval-looking hoods. This keeps them calm and collected — it also keeps me calm and collected. Without the headcover, I would not have been able to tolerate their killer stares.

Like the falcons that I had encountered in the Middle East, Loki, too, had his head covered. I didn't hear much of Roy's presentation because I devoted all my energy to being as still and quiet as was humanly possible. I was worried that Loki might detect my fear and decide to do some impromptu hunting of his own. Loki must have sensed something, all right, because five minutes into his owner's talk about falconry and peregrines, he suffered from a massive bout of diarrhoea. Falcon diarrhoea, I knew this fact from my days in Al Ain's vet's waiting room, is of the colour and consistency of yoghurt.

The first squirt went straight onto Blanca's whiteboard. Roy hadn't finished apologizing and asking Amy to bring some paper towels from the bathroom when Loki had another go, this time directly onto Blanca's desk and pencil case. Amy had just returned with the paper towels and gasped in horror on seeing Loki's work. The atmosphere in the room was getting somewhat tense. Since no one knew whether Loki was done redecorating the room or not, Blanca announced a short break. We all jostled for the door to get some air.

This memory of Loki's antics was still fresh in my mind when Robert suggested that we invite Roy and Amy to a party at our house.

'So, we have Roy and Amy, Céline and her husband,' we were going over the students in our Spanish class one by one.

'What about Bryan?'

'Yes, he's OK. He can come. And Agatha?'

'She's a bit posh but can be fun.'

'I suppose they will both bring their spouses,' I said, as I was making a guest list and wrote *plus one* next to Bryan and Agatha. 'It's eight,' I counted. 'Anyone else?'

'What about Max and his wife? What's her name?' Robert asked.

'Gwen,' I said. 'I thought you don't like them.'

I didn't care for either of them myself, so I was surprised to hear Robert mention them.

'Yes, but they're in our class; if we invite everyone else, it will be strange the next time we go to class.'

I had to agree. It reminded me of high school politics, which I never cared for.

'Then we need to invite everyone from the group,' I decided. 'If they come, they come; if they don't, that's even better.'

Personally, I didn't mind Max, even though he was one of the most pompous people that I have ever met. It was his wife who had become my arch-enemy over that year. It was strange because, on paper, they should have been a perfect match for us. Like us, they were educated and had successful careers. They had travelled outside Europe and even lived in the same emirate, Abu Dhabi, for some time. Despite these superficial similarities between our life experiences and paths, Max and Gwen had rubbed both Robert and me the wrong way.

Max, true to his name, was always 'one up'. When we first met in class, I mentioned that we were doing up a cottage to rent out to summer visitors. He was renovating *two* large cottages. When I said that we had lived in Abu Dhabi, he told me that he had lived *all over the Middle East*. When I mentioned that we had been university professors, he said that he had *managed an oil rig* in the Gulf. Because I was immune to his self-aggrandising innuendos and was neither impressed nor envious, Max quickly found new victims in Robert and Roy, whom he tortured with his tales of supremacy and one-upmanship. While I managed to ignore Max's arrogance, his wife gently got on my nerves during the Spanish classes.

At first, I felt sorry for Gwen. Our teacher, Blanca, had the idea that every other week, we would participate in a 'discussion club'. She would assign us a topic and would ask us to look up some useful phrases and expressions in preparation for the meeting. I really had to admire her enthusiasm. On a good day, some of us could describe our house or list our family members. That was the peak of our linguistic prowess. I often wondered how she expected us to make the leap from *There is a table and six chairs in my living room.* to *In my personal opinion, Britain shouldn't leave the European Union because it will have a detrimental effect on its future economy.*

Furthermore, she expected someone who could barely explain how many brothers and sisters they had to reply: *I'd have to disagree with you because the European Council is corrupt, and it costs a lot of taxpayer's money to pay for their salaries.*

But our teacher wasn't deterred, and every other week, she chose a hot topic from the news and called on us to debate it. While most of us prepared a couple of sentences expressing our particular stance on the assigned topic, Gwen wrote out a miniature treatise on each topic. When she was asked about her opinion about a recent bombing in Brussels, she searched her folder for a few minutes and then pulled out a neatly folded piece of paper.

She ceremoniously unfolded the precious piece of writing, and with her hands and voice shaking, she read from her paper for about seven minutes in a monotone voice. She occasionally stopped and asked Blanca to correct something *in situ*. I didn't envy Blanca because this performance really put her on the spot; no one else could understand what Gwen was reading — the vocabulary and grammar were too complex, obviously google-translated, most words were mispronounced, and the delivery itself was sleep-inducing, to say the least. At first, I felt sorry for Gwen's quivering voice and her meticulously-prepared papers rustling in her trembling hands. She was in her sixties, and in those moments, she looked exceptionally frail and pitiful.

'She always does it,' Amy leaned towards me and whispered while Gwen continued with her droning soliloquy.

Amy had taken a beginner's Spanish class with Gwen the year before, and she had sat through many of Gwen's drawn-out recitals. I rolled my eyes at Céline, and she gave me an understanding look back. At least I wasn't the only one stuck in this Bizarro Class. When Gwen finished her oration, the class was silent. We were not able to add anything to what had just been read out to us, and Blanca herself seemed to have just woken up from a bad dream.

'OK. *Muy bien.* For next week, please prepare something about the protests in Brazil,' our teacher remained undefeated.

Despite her nervous predisposition to public speaking, Gwen had a spiteful and gratuitously fussy personality. She liked to correct poor Céline and Bryan, who struggled with their Spanish pronunciation, or

Robert's poor grasp of the verb conjugations. But most of all, she enjoyed conducting private conversations with Blanca — while we all sat confused and left out — about the nuances between Pretérito Perfecto, Pretérito Indefinido and Pretérito Imperfecto. I found that incredibly infuriating, mostly because I had no clue what they were talking about.

But above all, Gwen loved to find fault in others. Now and again, Blanca would send us a passage or a story for us to read and answer some reading comprehension questions. We would correct this exercise in class — each person would read a paragraph, and then we would go round the table and answer the questions, one at a time. It was tedious and a bit boring, but since we only paid twenty-five euros a month for these lessons, we didn't argue with Blanca's methodology.

Since the pace was slow, I had ample opportunity to watch Gwen hunched over her papers and see her face transform from that of an ordinary woman in her sixties to a nasty, conniving rat. Each time someone made a mistake, she would scrunch her long nose and squint her eyes — giggling quietly to herself at the others' mistakes, delighting in these mistakes deep in her soul.

While she managed to hide her true nature from the others in the class who were too busy searching for answers and putting sentences together in their heads to notice, she showed me her spiteful character in all its glory one day when we were reading a text about geography. We went around the table, answering some follow-up vocabulary questions. Mine was *How many continents are in the world?* I read out my answer in Spanish:

'*Hay seis continentes en el mundo,*' there are six continents.

'No! No! NO!' I heard a crescendo squeal in front of the class and looked up to see Madam Know-it-all with her hand up in the air and her beady eyes just overflowing with supercilious pride at my seeming ignorance.

She was so overcome with *schadenfreude* that she could barely control herself. Her skinny arm was still quaking in the air when she explained to the whole class:

'Of course, there are *five* continents. We learned *that* in primary school. It's common knowledge.'

She was so excited to prove me wrong that she didn't even try to speak Spanish.

'I thought there were seven,' Blanca looked confused. 'I was just revising for a geography exam with my daughters, and their textbook says seven.'

The lesson quickly turned into a scholarly summit where everyone tried to tell the rest of us what *their* geography teacher in primary school had taught them. An impromptu, spirited debate broke out — albeit in English as no one could contain themselves. It appeared that everyone had a strong opinion about this topic. I sat back and admired Gwen's work.

Mind you, the average age of my classmates was fifty-five, so we were given a good insight into the British educational system of the 1960s and 70s. This led my classmates to reminisce about the 'good old times' in primary school. Robert told everyone how his Scottish headmaster used to beat him with a Wellington boot for being naughty at school. Agatha, who was twenty years older than Robert, also became nostalgic about the different objects that her headteacher had used to enforce discipline, from wooden rulers to bamboo sticks. Some of this discussion was in Spanish, but most was in English — that was how most of our classes went.

EIGHT
A WHITE DOG BY THE POSTBOX

'So, we're just going to invite people from our class?' Robert looked at my guest list.

'Yes. Let's not mix people from different circles. They may not have much to talk about.'

The next evening, Dani stopped by for a small beer with Robert. It was several weeks since his brother's suicide, and we had not really approached the subject apart from our initial condolences. While Robert and Dani sat outside on the patio, I remained in the kitchen, preparing supper. Even in this day and age, it is common in Andalusia for men to socialise with men and women with women. This arrangement suited me well, as Robert's conversations with other men tend to centre around topics like motorbikes, Tesla cars, or bitcoin, all of which I find hard to muster any enthusiasm for. I was content to stay inside and mind my own business.

'Have you seen the white dog by the postboxes,' I overheard Dani ask Robert.

'Yes. I think it's lost. I gave it some bread yesterday.'

'I've also been giving him food. When I go to work and when I come back. He's very cute.'

'How long has he been there?' I stuck my head through the fly curtain and onto the patio.

'Since Saturday,' Dani said. 'We think it belonged to the driver of the yellow car.'

'The yellow car that goes to the delinquent's house?' Robert asked.

'Yes, that one. He used to park by the postboxes and wait for 'clients' there. Anyway, he killed himself.'

'What?' I came out onto the patio now.

'He crashed his car on Friday night outside Pedriza. He didn't make the corner and drove off the road into a tree. You can see where it happened.'

'He must have been going very fast.' Robert said.

'Possibly, because he was dead when the ambulance arrived. We think that he was the owner of the little white dog because the dog has been sitting by the postboxes since Saturday morning as if he were waiting for someone.'

'It seems that everyone is feeding him,' I said.

'He's very friendly, but we already have Potranca and Nano. I'll ask my friend in Montefrio if he can take him before it gets too hot. He can't sleep outside in the summer — there will be no water in the *arroyo*.'

I agreed. At the moment, it was the first week of June, and sleeping outside was not a big problem for man or beast — our cats only came home for food and would disappear for days and nights in the surrounding fields. But it wouldn't be possible for an animal to survive without water in the heat of July and August.

'I hope your friend can take him,' I said.

'Why don't you take him?' Dani asked.

It was a good question. As a child, I had grown up with dogs. Even though we lived in an apartment, we had two dogs. I didn't particularly miss the responsibilities of dog ownership. I found our two cats much easier to deal with — they didn't require regular walks, constant attention, and pet sitters. If we were to go away for a night or two, we'd leave the small bathroom window open, fill up their feeders and water containers, and they wouldn't even notice that we were gone.

With a dog, this would change. We'd have to walk it several times a day, make sure it wasn't left alone for more than a few hours, and we'd have to plan our holidays well in advance to get a good pet sitter. I wasn't convinced. Robert, on the other hand, had been sent off to boarding school as a child and had never had a pet to look after. Now that we lived in a cottage in the countryside, he bombarded my Facebook feed with posts about dogs looking for a home.

'I'm not sure,' I answered Dani's questions.

'Did you know we found our Potranca in the same *arroyo?*' Daniel mentioned. He was referring to the small riverbed by our postboxes, which was dry for most of the year. Both Robert and I shook our heads.

'One morning, Isabella was waiting for the school bus by the postboxes when she saw a plastic bag in the ditch. She thought that someone had thrown their rubbish into the ditch. But then, when she came in the afternoon to collect our daughter, she noticed that the bag was moving. She thought it was very strange, so she got out of the car and went down the *barranco* to check it. Inside the rubbish bag, she found a puppy with its mouth tied shut with some tape.'

I gasped in horror.

'Of course, she took it home. By the time our daughter got off the school bus, Potranca was crawling around on the back seat.'

I was glad to hear the happy ending. Rural Andalusia is a cruel place for animals. Driving through villages, you will unavoidably see mangy Alsatians and doleful Mastins tied to a metal barrel which is meant to protect them from rain and snow. The lucky ones get to sleep in a cold garage. In the village supermarket, you'll find huge bags of dried bread, which the owners of these miserable creatures buy to feed them. Dog-chaining and a general lack of empathy towards cats and dogs are part of the Andalusian culture that many foreigners find difficult to understand and live with.

Even if they are not tied by a chain to a dirty dog house, many dogs rarely receive medical attention when sick. In a country where abortion is legal, pet sterilization, for some reason, is a divisive topic. As a result of this backward thinking, every spring, litters of unwanted puppies and kittens are left in cardboard boxes outside animal rescue centres, by the municipal bins or sometimes *inside* the containers. Our plumber found his dog, a beautiful black Belgian Shepherd, crying in a cardboard box inside a rubbish bin.

I don't think that people who live in the countryside are in themselves particularly prone to inflicting animal abuse. Perhaps living in a remote place where money is scarce has made them immune to the suffering of animals. I can only explain it by centuries of poverty and hardship, which might have made Andalusian farmers indifferent towards animal suffering.

Many of our neighbours were born after the civil war in the late nineteen-forties, and *Los Años de Hambre*, literally, the Years of Hunger, a decade when an estimated two hundred thousand people died of starvation, are in living memory. Perhaps for them, having a roof over one's head, no matter how perfunctory, and some dry bread to chew on was considered good enough in the yesteryear. Many people had little more themselves. For decades, local olive farmers worked like donkeys, day after day, for a handful of bread and a bowl of bean stew. Perhaps it's a mark of established consumerist societies to feel more empathy for a mistreated dog than a mistreated human.

I was glad to hear Potranca's story because it meant that these attitudes were changing. As people's quality of life improves, so does their pets' quality of life. As long as people don't turn a blind eye to cruelty, there is hope for Andalusian animals. We were soon to rescue one poor soul from the brink of death.

On the morning of our barbecue, Robert went to Montefrio to buy some drinks for the party.

'The white dog is still by the postboxes,' he told me when he came back from the shops. 'I got him a pig's ear in the shop, but he looks very pathetic.'

I had hoped that by now, someone would claim the dog or take him home, but it hadn't happened.

'OK. Let's go and see him,' I said. 'He can't sleep in the grass forever.'

I didn't know what our endgame was. I thought that we might keep the poor thing for a few days until we could find him a new home. When we arrived at the postboxes, I saw a skinny bundle of misery with a filthy, worn-out collar strapped very tightly around its neck. I took the collar off to check for a name or a phone number, but there were no markings on it, so I threw it away into the bush. By now, the dog was sitting by my leg, waiting for directions.

It was a medium-size dog, primarily white in colour, with a brown head and ears similar to an English Jack Russell. I wish I could say he was handsome, but his ears and neck were absolutely crawling with ticks, some filled with blood. I could see his ribs, and he was covered in dirt and grass. It wasn't a pretty sight. Since he was trying to jump up on my leg, I said *sit,* and he immediately sat down. *I can work with this dog*, I thought. He seemed obedient and eager to please.

'Do you still want a dog?' I turned to Robert.

'Ehhh,' there was hesitation.

'Well, here's a dog. He's for free, and you don't have to drive from one shelter to another looking for a dog. Let's get him into the car,' I decided.

Robert opened the back door of the four by four, and the dog jumped inside without us having to ask him.

'Where are we going to keep him?' Robert asked on the way home.

Obviously, we could not bring him home with the scores of ticks hanging off his neck and ears.

'He can stay inside the dog pen until you can take him to the vet.'

There was a dog pen on our property adjacent to the main gate. It had been used by the previous owners to keep a guard dog. We knew its purpose from the metal barrel that was inside the pen and from the remains of several desiccated pig jaws and hip bones that the poor animal must have chewed on for weeks. It wasn't a cheerful corner, but there was nowhere else to keep our tick-infested pooch. We had thrown away the rusty barrel long ago, so I started to think of some sleeping arrangements for the poor thing.

'He'll need a house or something because it gets chilly there at night,' I said. 'Do we have anything?'

'Maybe,' Robert sounded vague. 'What shall we call him?'

'Freddie?' I suggested.

'No, that's Keith's dog.'

'He doesn't have a proprietary licence for that name. It's a good name.'

'We need a different name.'

'What about *Bobby*? You're Robert, so he can be a *Bobby*. I think it works.'

'I'll think about it.'

As soon as we stopped by the gate, I opened the pen, and the dog jumped out of the car. I didn't want to touch him, so I threw him a piece of bread inside the pen and tied a piece of string to secure the pen's gate. We stood outside the enclosure for a few minutes looking at the wretched soul.

'I'll make him a little house,' Robert said.

'OK. I'll bring him some food and water, but then I need to prepare for the barbecue.'

We drove up to the house. Robert went into his workshop, and I went to the kitchen. When I came outside an hour later, I was surprised to see dark skies. The morning had been so sunny and clear. I didn't expect any rain; not in June. I went to the garage and saw that Robert had just built a little dog house from scrap wood.

'It's almost one o'clock,' I reminded him. 'The guests will be here in an hour.'

'OK. Help me with this roof, and then we can take it down.'

I helped him attach the roof. The little dog house wouldn't have been suitable dog accommodation in the freezing winter, but it was June, so it was enough to keep the dog warm at night and shaded during the day. I went into the house and grabbed two old blankets for bedding. When I came back, I saw that Robert was attaching a wooden plaque sideways over the entrance to the house. He had roughly engraved 'Dog! No Cats!' onto the plaque with his router. It was pretty adorable in a Hanna-Barbera kind of way.

We transported the dog house and blankets down to the pen. Bobby was delighted to see us, but he was also trembling a lot. Back then, I didn't know much about abandoned or scared dogs, and I thought that he was cold, so I laid the blankets nicely inside his new house. In hindsight, I realise that he must have been scared to death by his unknown future. Once Bobby was all set in his new home, with water, food, and blankets all laid out for him, we went back up the driveway to get ready for the guests.

As soon as we were back at the house, I heard a horrendous thunderclap. Lightning was repeatedly striking an olive hill not far from us. We ran under the patio. Outside the confinements of the roofed patio, a torrential spring shower began to fall.

'We can't sit outside,' I stated the obvious. 'Do we cancel the barbecue?'

'We can put the barbecue under the roof here.'

'Yes, but where is everyone going to sit?' I looked around.

On a sunny day, we could sit a good number of people on the patio, but in the rain, everyone would have to squeeze in one corner to avoid getting wet. There was only one solution.

'Let's move the party to the *granero*,' I suggested.

That's what we called one of the guest apartments, which in its previous life was used as a barn for donkeys and goats.

We carried the garden tables and chairs from the patio to the *granero*. Then we moved all the plates, glasses, drinks, and salads. It was still pouring with rain when we finished. We were both soaking wet. I checked my phone on the way to my bedroom to change into dry clothes. There were at least ten messages. The gist of all of the messages was: 'OMG, it's just started to rain all of a sudden!' and 'Are we still having a barbecue?' I typed 'Yes!' to those asking if we were still having a party. I figured that most guests would have made up their minds already if they were to arrive on time. It was just before two o'clock. As soon as I put on a dry T-shirt and a dry pair of jeans, I heard a car hooting outside.

Robert was first outside to greet Céline and her husband, Leon. He must have grabbed an umbrella on the way out because he gallantly escorted them under the umbrella from the car to the roofed part of the patio.

'I didn't know you had a dog,' Céline said as soon as we were done with greetings, and I handed her a glass of wine.

'We didn't, until a few hours ago,' I said and told her and Leon the whole story. Soon, more people arrived, and we moved to the *granero,* where we had drinks and snacks. As soon as it stopped raining, Leon offered to go to the dog pen to check on our latest acquisition. I went with him in case he had some advice about the ticks.

'Do you have tweezers?' he asked me while we were standing outside the dog pen. Since I had never acquired the habit of plucking my eyebrows, the answer was no.

'If I had known, I would have brought ours,' Leon said. 'I once pulled over a hundred ticks from a dog we rescued.'

While I didn't want poor Bobby to suffer from ticks, I wasn't sure I wanted Leon to sit in the living room pulling ticks all afternoon.

'What can we do?' I asked.

'When you take him to Lorena, she'll give him a pill, and they'll all fall out in a couple of hours.' Lorena was the vet that we both used.

I felt relief on hearing that. I suspected that tweezers might be involved, but I wasn't sure if either Robert or I would have enough strength of character to remove all of Bobby's ticks. Leon reached into his jacket pocket and took out some dog treats for Bobby, who was still shaking like a leaf.

'It's a good looking *bodeguero.*'

'What's that,' I didn't understand.

'It's a wine-cellar, rat-catching dog. It's called *Ratonero Bodeguero.* It's a type of terrier from Andalusia. It's kept by wineries and on farms to catch mice and rats.'

That's great.

We did have some mice and rats around the property, and several of them had tried to take up residence inside the house each winter. As we were to find out in the near future, our Bobby was a great hunter of rabbits but a lousy *ratonero.* Many a night, he would wake up the whole household barking incessantly because a mouse had run across the living room. I'd go downstairs to check what the ruckus was about, only to see him sitting on the sofa and looking in the direction of where the mouse must have disappeared.

He didn't even bother to get off the cushions. I suspect that deep down, he was a little afraid of mice because he hardly ever slept on the floor and always favoured the sofa or the armchair. On one winter evening, while watching TV, we all heard a mouse squeal behind a cupboard. Bobby just looked at me indignantly as if it were my job to rid the house of the rodents.

'Why can't these people keep their place pest-free? Really! It's not difficult!' the look on his cheeky face said. Then he would hide his face under a blanket and go back to sleep.

But that was yet to come.

Leon and I went back to the party and saw Roy and Robert attending the barbecue. It had stopped raining, but we left the grill under the patio roof out of precaution.

'Do you like shooting?' Robert asked Leon.

'Shooting what?'

'Targets.'

A week before, Robert had bought himself an air rifle — I didn't remember the excuse under which it was purchased because our budget was tight, and an air rifle didn't seem like a necessity. It may have had something to do with getting rid of the fat rat that we sometimes spotted scoffing at us from the top of the woodpile or chowing down almonds on a tree. In reality, it had only ever been used to shoot beer cans perched on the wall. The proposition of shooting cans off the wall got most men out of the house. I looked at the tableau presented to me as I went from our kitchen to the *granero* a couple of times to bring bread, olive oil, and other condiments.

Our transition to hillbillies is complete, I thought to myself as I watched the men laugh and guffaw at each other's marksmanship. But it didn't bother me. I've always had a soft spot for Appalachian moonshiners and other outlaws.

Soon the meat was ready, and we all sat at two garden tables that we pushed together inside the *granero*. A lively and warm atmosphere permeated the room — with constant chatter and laughter. People passed the plates of food and salads across the tables and seemed to thoroughly enjoy this somewhat improvised gathering. With the exposed stone wall as the backdrop and a cosy fireplace in the corner, the *granero* had become a comfortable place. I was happy to have found this group of people. They were easy to talk to and quite unpretentious in their ways.

We were going to be good friends, I thought as I finally sat down between Amy and Céline and had a long sip of red wine.

'Max and Gwen couldn't come?' Amy asked me.

'No. He has sent Robert an email that he's having a big party at his house today. Apparently, the whole of his extended family have arrived from Scotland, and they are having a huge barbecue at their cottages.'

'Of course,' Amy and I laughed.

On Monday morning, as soon as the vet was open, Bobby von Dazzler — for this became his official title in his passport — was rid of his multiple ticks, dewormed, chipped, and scheduled for more treatments. By the end of that week, he squeezed himself onto the tiny sofa next to Robert as if the spot had always been his. However, unlike us, the cats did not care for Bobby's company and thus dedicated all their energy to avoiding him. Most days, they'd lounge on the terrace above the patio and hiss at him from the grapevines above to let him know what they thought of his canine existence.

NINE
THE TASTE OF LIQUORICE

R enovating the cottage and preparing our rental apartments for guests was a long, nerve-wracking process. Once the holiday suites were ready, the wait for summer bookings was almost intolerable. We had put so much time, work, and money into the whole project that to see the weeks go by without any bookings was very upsetting. Neither Robert nor I had much experience running a small business, so in our naivety, we expected customers to start knocking on our doors as soon as we put the 'vacant' sign up in the window.

I advertised our little cottage everywhere I could, but instead of couples and small families wanting to relax in nature, we received enquiries from large groups who were obviously planning to have wild pool parties at our house. I rejected these requests but was, in turn, left staring at an empty booking calendar. There are few things as disheartening to an aspiring innkeeper as an open calendar.

That June, I spent my time staring at the white squares of my calendar, trying to will them to change colour to indicate a booking. I got so desperate that I considered booking the place myself, which would allow me to write an 'honest' review and, more importantly, would leave a little automated message next to our listing encouraging prospective travellers to book as soon as possible lest they lost the opportunity to stay here. The automated message used to say:

'This place has just been booked. Only one room left!'

Or something in that spirit — the practice of flashing 'Book now or else!' messages on booking websites has since been banned in Europe since it is misleading. I could understand why. I was losing my mind delineating our advertising performance on each booking site and not being able to draw any meaningful conclusions from it. I looked at other properties nearby. They all seemed to be getting sold out. I didn't know why we weren't. As the days went by, I relied more and more on magical thinking — I'd change the photos, redo the descriptions, and add travel guides. Each of these ideas was supposed to have a magic-wand effect and attract immediate bookings. I felt that I had no idea what I was doing and needed some guidance. In desperation, I decided to visit Emma and Stefan to snoop around and seek their advice.

Emma and Stefan were Belgian and had a small B&B on the other side of Montefrio. They had been running their guesthouse for eight years by the time we made contact with them. We first met when an Austrian couple who were staying with us wished to rent a pair of mountain bikes. I did a quick internet search and found Emma and Stefan's place, which rented bicycles in addition to hosting visitors. I wrote to them, and they came over to say hello and to tell us about their bicycle rentals. It was comforting to talk to other amateur hoteliers.

They were both in their late fifties. Emma was small but energetic, while Stefan was a friendly geek. It was clear that she was the head of the operation. They gave us a lot of great tips about cleaning and running the rentals, but most of all, they gave us a lot of encouragement. It turned out that the Austrian couple had sent me on a wild goose chase since they changed their mind about renting bicycles at the last minute, presumably after they drove up and down the steep hills around Montefrio. But at least, we made acquaintance with someone who could guide us through the first steps of the holiday rental business.

As I was fretting over whether we would get anyone to stay with us that summer, I sent Emma a message and invited myself over for coffee at their place. When we arrived, Emma and Stefan showed us around their property. Their guesthouse is located among the olive groves and overlooks Parapanda Mountain. They didn't have any guests at that moment, so we inspected their lovely rooms and talked about our experiences with remodelling and DIY projects. When we finished the tour, we sat at a large table on their patio, and Stefan brought us all coffees.

'Do you have a lot of guests in June?' I didn't want to beat around the bush.

'It's difficult to say. Really. Every season is different. Sometimes we have a lot of customers in June and sometimes very few.'

I felt better after hearing this. It wasn't only us who didn't have many clients that month.

'When is the busiest time?' I asked.

'For us, it is in spring. May is very busy. Then August is always booked. In autumn, it's different every year.'

'It also depends on the weather in the rest of Europe,' Stefan interjected, placing cups of coffee on the table. 'If there's a hot summer in the Netherlands and Belgium, we don't get many customers. They stay home. If there's a rainy summer in northern Europe, we are fully booked.'

'That's true. It's impossible to predict. Some seasons are excellent, and others are not. There are many factors.' Emma explained as she stirred her coffee. 'By the way, these are *stroopwafels*,' she pointed at a plate of caramel-coated cookies.

'We know *stroopwafels*. They're delicious. We used to eat them all the time when we lived in Nijmegen,' Robert explained.

'You lived in Nijmegen!' Emma was excited. 'I have family in Eindhoven. That's not far from there.'

We then spent half an hour talking about the Netherlands and the year Robert and I lived in Nijmegen when we were both students at the university there. We went over the peculiarities of Dutch cuisine that were still deeply embedded in our memories, such as putting *pindakaas*, peanut butter, on French fries and the custom of swallowing fresh herrings covered in raw onion. We then moved on to praise Belgian beers and chocolate.

The conversation must have made Stefan feel homesick because he went to the kitchen and returned with a bowl of sweet and salty *liquorice*. It would have been rude not to eat any, so I helped myself to a small piece. I wished he had served us some peanut butter fries instead. Even raw herring would have been better than Satan's sweets. If you have never tried Belgian sweet and salty liquorice, the taste and smell are impossible to describe; they're like nothing else on earth. According to experts, liquorice has all the flavours; sweet, sour, salty, and bitter. That may be true, but instead of complementing each other, they fight in your mouth and create a most unpleasant experience, making you want to gag and spit it out immediately.

Because liquorice is usually served at parties and small gatherings, it's not always possible to get rid of it once you have made the mistake of putting the black candy in your mouth. Even if you're lucky enough to be able to discreetly place it inside a serviette, the aftertaste will linger in your mouth for hours. And while the taste of liquorice is unpleasant and long-lasting, its texture is that of Arabic gum, namely chewy, yet hard, and, thus, distinctly unpalatable. Chewing on a piece of softened asphalt might be more agreeable than eating liquorice. But I didn't share these views with my hosts, who were convinced that they had just served us the best confectionary that Belgium had to offer, and decided to get back to the topic of holiday rentals.

'Do you use Airbnb?' I asked, moving the vile piece of candy from one cheek to the other.

'We stopped using them because we were getting a lot of silly requests,' Emma said. 'Someone would make a request to book as one person but then admit that they were planning to bring the whole family but didn't think that they should pay for the extra guests.'

'The first year we started, we made a big mistake,' Stefan said. 'We really needed money, so we agreed for three couples to have a New Year's Eve party at our place. We checked them in and went away to a friend's house for drinks. When we came back after midnight, there were at least twenty people in the house. They were smoking inside the house and leaving cigarette butts everywhere. Everyone was drunk, so we were afraid to confront them. We locked ourselves in our bedroom and waited until the morning.'

'You won't believe it,' Emma was getting angry at the memory of that event. 'We spent almost a week cleaning and fixing things after they'd left.'

'We had to repaint some of the walls, fix broken doors, lots of things were damaged.'

'Never again. The money and the stress were not worth it.'

'It's funny you say this,' I had finally managed to swallow the liquorice. 'Just last week, we had a guy from Madrid requesting a booking for him, his wife, and one daughter. I accepted, but then he asked me where he would collect the keys to the house. When I told him that we live on the property, he cancelled immediately and wrote a complaint to Airbnb about us.'

'Unfortunately, that's what some people do,' Stefan added. 'They book a remote cottage or house, one or two people go and collect the keys and meet the owner, then they go back to a restaurant or a petrol station where they have left the rest of the guests and then bring them over to the house behind the owner's back. It happens all the time.'

'Really?' Robert couldn't believe it. With his low tolerance for scammers and cheats, I could see that he was having a hard time digesting all this new information.

'And how is the bicycle rental business?' I decided to change the topic as it all resembled doom and gloom.

'It's not easy,' Stefan was honest. 'We bought expensive bikes to make sure that they don't break going downhill and that they last a long time, so the return on investment is very slow.'

'We get some bikers from the Netherlands and Belgium who come specifically to ride here, but as far as the average B&B guests are concerned, hardly anyone ever rents the bicycles. People like to muse about what they'd like to do on holiday. They message me months before their arrival, telling me how much they love hiking and how they can't wait to go up a mountain every day. But once they arrive, they seem to become literally glued to the sun loungers by the pool.'

'They'll also give you a lot of advice on how to improve your business,' Stefan interjected. 'One Englishman suggested that we should get donkeys.'

'Oh, yeah!' Emma laughed at the memory.

'*But we'd have to feed them and look after them*, I explained to him,' Stefan was reenacting the conversation for our entertainment. '*But they will attract a lot of customers*,' he mimicked the guest's whiny tone, which was quite entertaining and continued:

'I let him ramble on about it for most of the afternoon. People tend to develop great schemes while lying next to the pool drinking wine all day.'

'We don't argue with our guests,' Emma explained. 'Often, people book the bikes for a week and then ride for only one or two days. For the rest of their stay, they spin fantasies about their bicycle riding adventures.'

She didn't need to explain. I could understand why. In many parts of Central Europe, you can cycle from one city to the next without a significant change in elevation. It can give many born-again cyclists a false idea of their physical endurance and stamina. However, the hills between Montefrio and Alcalá la Real are really steep and long. The descents on a bike are breakneck and require brakes designed by the best German engineers. The ascents can make the most enthusiastic cyclist rethink their life choices.

On the way home, Robert and I digested the story of the wild New Year's Eve party that Emma and Stefan told us about. Robert was raging on about how he would have dealt with guests misbehaving or using our place for a party — some of his solutions involved throwing their suitcases over the fence. Little did we know that in less than a month, we would indeed be throwing guests out of our *casa rural*.

In light of Emma's insights about the irregularities in booking patterns and how it was impossible to predict the tourist season, I decided to reduce our prices in a desperate hope to attract more visitors. Following the same principle by which a busy restaurant has a queue round the corner while the empty one next door remains inexplicably void of patrons, I trusted that the more reviews we had, the easier it would become to convince travellers to stay with us. The price reduction had an immediate positive effect on the number of bookings. Still, the parade of riffraff and cheapskates that we had to endure that first summer made me question my business acumen.

Riffraff are not always easy to describe, but you know them when you see them — they bring their own boombox to the pool and play a selection of summer hits for everyone to enjoy at full volume. They stuff empty crisp packets under the sun lounger mattresses, spit chewing gum onto the tiles, throw cigarette butts onto the white gravel, empty brine from tuna tins into flower pots, break toasters and water kettles and keep schtum about it, make barbecues at one a.m., and ask to rent noisy quad bikes to explore the local nature. While the riffraff are a nuisance, they don't work their way into your mind. Their existence is similar to that of an annoying fly that you might swat away from your face, never to give it a second thought. It is the cheapskates that leave an indelible mark on your soul and make you question humanity.

Being a cheapskate is not a question of wealth or class — it's a personality type that transcends a person's social and financial status. The cheapskate's sole aim in life is to suck the fun and spontaneity out of every activity. A typical holiday cheapskate never books directly — they spend days trawling the internet for the best price for a place. They stack up all the discounts, promotions, and special deals, and then they contact the host directly to inquire whether they'd calculated the right price and whether you could improve on the already discounted price. They often lie and tell you that they plan to stay for a whole week just to get an additional discount, and as soon as you give in and lower the price to the absolute bottom, they change their mind and reduce the number of nights that they plan to stay.

'*We're very sorry. We've just found out that our plane leaves on*

Wednesday, not on Sunday,' one Swiss couple sent me this phoney excuse for shortening their stay at the last minute.

When they arrived, they seemed surprised that breakfast was not included in their rock-bottom price and whinged and negotiated until they got it.

'But I distinctly remember, on your website, I think it was your website or maybe the agent's site. Do you remember, Hubert?' the woman brazenly turned to her spouse to corroborate the lie.

'The website said that the breakfast is included. I can go and look for it now. But I'm not sure if it was your website or another website. But it said that breakfast is included,' she started to gently drill into my skull.

I'm not a wilfully stubborn person and don't like to argue about petty things, so I gave in, and even though I was sure the wife was wrong, I agreed to serve them breakfast.

'You what? You agreed to serve them breakfast for free?' Robert was fuming when he heard it.

'I don't know,' I admit. 'She bamboozled me. I've agreed, so I'm not going to go back on my word. Anyway, we need reviews so let's hope they give us a good review.'

The following day, I brought them their ransom. She had ordered a vegetarian breakfast that included homemade muesli instead of ham and *salchichón*, and Hubert had ordered an Andalusian breakfast that consisted of a selection of local meats and cheese.

'Oh, by the way,' the woman started to whimper as I was setting up her breakfast on the terrace. 'Do you serve fried eggs?'

If my eyes could roll around in their own orbit, they would have. Instead, I put on my best fake smile and asked:

'How would you like your eggs? With runny yolk or hard?'

'Not runny, please,' the delicate flower was adamant. 'Thank you so much. It's so kind of you. You know I need to eat protein.'

She kept on telling me about her dietary habits in the grating, feel-sorry-for-me voice that only brings out the best in me. Ten minutes later, I came back with her special order. I wouldn't normally serve a cooked breakfast. Because our guests got up at various hours in the morning, with Germans and Dutch getting up at the crack of dawn and Spanish and French guests only starting to feel hungry at around eleven, I would be sitting by the stove all morning waiting for orders.

Instead, I offered them a generous spread of local food, with fresh baguettes, fruit, pots of yoghurt, homemade marmalade, and muesli made from our own almonds and walnuts roasted in the oven and mixed with oats, honey, and other seeds. I thought that was enough food to satisfy even the pickiest of eaters, but I was wrong. Nothing is too much for the holiday cheapskate.

'Oh, thank you so much,' the Swiss lady said as I put her eggs next to her plate on which she had already buttered half a baguette and which was now covered in *salchichón*, which is a delicious, peppery dry sausage.

'I'm sorry,' I said without thinking. 'I thought you wanted a vegetarian breakfast?' I was confused by seeing both of them covering their bread with *jamón* and *salchichón*.

'I like to try different food. It's important to have variety,' she said as if this explained why a vegetarian would eat half a pork loin before noon.

'All right,' I said, biting my tongue. 'Enjoy your breakfast, and let me know if you need anything else.'

I was on my way out, not expecting any more special requests, but for a cheapskate, the magical words: *Let me know if you need anything else* is a clear invitation to ask for more. They always want more.

'Do you mind if we keep the muesli to eat for lunch?' Mrs Scrooge asked. 'It's too much, and we can't eat it all.'

It's not a competition, lady. You don't need to eat it all, I thought, but I put on a smile and told her to enjoy the muesli later.

'And the yoghurts?' she had no limits. 'Can we keep them too?'

'Keep the yoghurts. No problem.' I chewed the inside of my cheeks as I turned my back, making a mental note not to ask her again if she needed anything.

When they finally left after a three-night stay, both Robert and I were exhausted. Once we waved them goodbye and saw the dust cloud follow their car, we sat down on the patio.

'I feel as if they'd sucked the life out of me,' I said. 'I need a beer.'

'How long were they here?' Robert was sitting by the table with his head resting on it.

'Three days,' I said.

'It can't be! It felt like two weeks.'

That's the true nature of the holiday cheapskate — they drain you of money, resources, emotions, and energy. Once they're gone, you're left an empty shell.

'When are the next guests coming?' Robert asked while yawning.

'Next week. It's a couple from Sevilla.'

'Hope they're ok?'

'We'll see. They asked me to check in at nine a.m.'

'Nine a.m.?'

'Yes. I told them that the earliest that they could check in was at eleven. They're coming on the same day as Ula and her family.'

Ula was a friend of mine from high school, and we hadn't seen each other since we were seventeen. Thanks to the growth of social media sites, we had managed to get back in touch with each other a few years earlier when I was still in Abu Dhabi, and now that I was back in Europe, she had decided to visit us. Ula had been a massive supporter of our adventure of restoring the cottage and moving to Spain, and I was excited for her to see the place with her own eyes. I hoped she wouldn't be disappointed.

TEN
GUESTS FROM SEVILLA

The following week, the guests from Sevilla appeared on our driveway precisely one minute before eleven. I looked inside the car, and my heart sank. There were three people in the car even though the booking was for two adults. The driver's door opened, and a middle-aged man wearing tracksuit pants and a football T-shirt came out and shook my hand as if we were long-lost friends. His wife came out of the passenger door.

She was wearing my least-favoured type of female garment, which is rompers, or shorts and top combined into one outfit. She threw her fake hair extensions to the side, bent down, and extinguished a cigarette in a convenient flowerpot. She then greeted me by showering me with kisses which is the traditional way of greeting complete strangers in Andalusia. The husband opened the back passenger door to reveal a tween boy with a Gameboy permanently glued to his hands. I was a complete novice in the hospitality business and had no idea what to do with the unexpected extra guest.

In hindsight, I should have informed them then and there that they needed to pay for their child, and if they refused, I should have let them return to Sevilla. But again, we were struggling to get customers, and it was a booking for five nights. I also have a soft spot for children who are accompanied by scummy parents. I could see from the way the child was clutching the Gameboy, concentrating on his game and avoiding any eye contact with me that it was not the first time that he was witness to his parents trying to con establishments by having him stay for free. I didn't know what to do, so I led them to their apartment and told them about the locale.

'I know this area,' the father said. 'I have friends in Montefrio.'

'That's nice,' I opened the sliding door from the terrace to the living room.

'*¡Que precioso!*' the wife gasped.

'*¡Muy bien!*'

As the patriarch gave his seal of approval, I gathered some courage to address the elephant in the room.

'Your reservation was for two adults only,' I said in Spanish. 'It doesn't include the child.' By now, the boy was sitting on the armchair in the living room and appeared to be blocking out the inevitable confrontation.

'What! That's not possible! I typed in two adults and one child. I'm sure of it.' The wife began shouting at no one in particular. This incited the husband, who appeared to have the shortest fuse in the world.

'It's not possible! For sure! We've made the reservation for three people,' he was agitated too. They went back and forth for several minutes. I wasn't able to get a word in edgeways. My Spanish was not good enough to argue with these two ruffians.

'It's OK,' I said. 'There must be a mistake in the booking.' They seemed relieved.

'He can sleep with us,' the wife offered a solution. 'This bed is very big.' She pointed to the king-size bed.

Since I didn't have to prepare an extra bed, I felt that I had won at least half the battle. I wished them a great stay and went away. Ten minutes later, they were by the pool with plates of snacks, bottles of beer, and their portable radio blasting the latest Spanish summer hits.

'I have a question,' the husband turned down the volume when he saw me walk across the patio by the pool.

'Yes.'

'Is it OK if my daughter and her boyfriend visit us?' he asked.

I wasn't sure if I had understood correctly, so I asked him to repeat what he had said.

'Do you mean to sleep in your apartment?' I asked.

'Yes.'

His audacity took me by surprise.

'But there is no place for them to sleep,' I tried to reason.

'They can sleep on the floor. It's not a problem at all,' he assured me as if it were *me* who was planning to put extra guests in his accommodation and have them sleep on the floor.

'We don't allow guests to sleep on the floor,' I said, not really knowing what else to say. If we defined the apartment's capacity by how many people could sleep on the floor, we could easily put thirty people in there; with sleeping bags and yoga mats to lie on, it would make a great dosshouse.

'But really, it's not a problem. They're young,' the wife chirped in from the adjacent sun lounger.

'I'm not sure,' it was a British *I'm not sure,* which was meant to imply a polite 'no' but translated into Spanish, it only encouraged them.

'But can they come for a day visit? To have a barbecue and a swim?'

I really couldn't believe my own ears. I found the proposition so outrageous that I had to ask them to repeat it again.

'When do you want them to come?' I asked.

'We don't know. They're in Sevilla. My daughter has to work today, so maybe tomorrow. I'm not sure,' the man was vague.

'Yes, they're busy now. But it would be nice to see them while we are on holiday,' the wife was bargaining.

I was confused by the whole conversation. We went back and forth like this a few more times. I didn't want to upset them, and I was too green a hotelier to say 'no' directly to their faces.

'Let me know when you hear from them. OK?' I thought that leaving the conversation undecided would imply a negative answer from me. But I was wrong.

The same afternoon, Robert and I went to Malaga airport to collect my friend and her family. We were near our house, driving back home, when we saw the husband travelling in the direction of Montefrio, alone.

'He's one of our guests,' I told Ula. 'I think he's going drinking with his friends in Montefrio.'

My assumption was confirmed by the wife, who was by the pool when we arrived and told me that her husband had just gone out to meet his friends in Montefrio. We all had a pleasant afternoon. It was a lovely July day. We made a barbecue for Ula and her family and had drinks on the patio. At some stage, the wife brought us a bowl of homemade snacks that she had brought from her home.

'What is it?' Lukasz asked.

'I have no idea,' I admitted. The dish looked like cured vegetables, but I could not identify the plant. They consisted of small green stems with round ends. We all took one each and were surprised by a taste similar to pickled cucumbers.

'These are wild capers,' Robert informed us as he returned to the table with another round of cold beers.

Now that he had identified it, I realised that the green snack tasted very similar to store-bought capers, but these ones were much bigger and had a small stem attached to them, making them perfectly practical as finger food.

'How do you know that?' I asked.

'I helped Rafa collect them in the field last spring.'

'We have capers growing in the field?' I was astonished. I couldn't recall any plant looking like capers.

'You have seen them yourself — the pink and white flowers that grow close to the ground and have a lot of thorns. Rafa collects the flower buds before they blossom, and then Loli marinades them.'

'Why don't we do that?'

'Because it takes forever to collect a handful. I helped him for half an hour, and we had just enough to fill a small jar.'

It reminded me of the time when I cured olives and told Ula and Lukasz about my forays into Andalusian food preservation. They refused to believe me that you can't eat olives straight from the tree and thought that I was exaggerating. Lukasz went over to a tree at the edge of the patio and picked a juicy looking green olive, only to spit it out a second later. We all laughed.

'When we were in the shop on the way here, I told him not to buy any olives because they grow on the trees here,' Ula admitted.

Around ten p.m., the Sevillian wife stopped by our patio again and asked Robert to help her set up a barbecue for her family. She wasn't sure what time her husband would arrive. She hadn't heard from him in several hours. Robert got her some firewood and helped her light the fire. Another hour passed. We were still sitting outside with our Polish guests when we heard a car drive up.

'It's not the husband,' I told Robert. 'It's a different car.'

'Maybe he had too much to drink, and someone drove him home,' Ula suggested.

'Let me see,' Robert went around the house to see who was in the car. He came back soon.

'You need to go there and sort this out,' he told me.

'Sort what out?'

'I don't know who these people are. The wife tells me that you know.'

I couldn't believe it. They actually thought that I had agreed that their daughter and her boyfriend could come and sleep over. I tried to gather my thoughts as I went to see what was going on.

Around the corner under the terrace of the rental apartment was the lit barbecue and a beaten-up Ford Fiesta. A young man in his twenties was nonchalantly leaning against the bonnet and staring at his mobile. His girlfriend was taking care of the barbecue. I was about to speak to them when the wife came down the steps from the terrace with meat for the barbecue.

'Are these your visitors?' I asked her.

'Yes, this is my husband's daughter and her boyfriend.' The two in question ignored me.

'But it's eleven o'clock. Where are they going to sleep?' I asked.

'On the floor, it's not a problem.' Once again, I could not believe my ears. I thought we had gone through this in the morning, but obviously, I was misunderstood. I turned around and went to report to Robert.

'No, they aren't,' Robert told me on hearing my news that the additional guests were planning to sleep in the same apartment. 'Where's Bobby? I want to put him on his lead.'

Bobby was sleeping under the table, heavy after a long evening of snacking on cheese and barbecue scraps. Since he was a medium-sized dog, I wasn't sure his presence would intimidate the unwanted guests, but he was better than the two lazy cats who were sleeping on the terrace above the patio. Robert put Bobby on his red lead, and they went around the corner to talk sense to the guests.

Arguing in a foreign language is an art that takes many years of studying and using the language to master. That's one of the reasons why most non-native speakers lose in an altercation with a native speaker. I could only admire Robert's determination to argue in Spanish as he disappeared behind the corner of the house. Soon voices were raised, and I was called in to interpret.

'Tell them that they need to go now,' he said in a calm but determined tone.

I dutifully translated the sentiment.

'What about the money,' the wife asked. 'We've already paid for five nights.'

Since I really wanted them to go away, I wasn't prepared to argue that they were not eligible for a refund because they had broken the rental rules. I went back to our living room, past Ula and Lukasz, who just looked at me wide-eyed, and recovered the cash I had been given earlier that day. It was untouched. I went back and handed her the money.

'Now, you need to go,' I said.

My hand was shaking as I was furious. They embarrassed me in front of my friends and made us look like fools. This could not have happened at a worse time, but on the other hand, it was comforting to know that we were not alone in the house and had witnesses to these events.

'It's the middle of the night. Where are we going to find a place to sleep? I need to call my husband,' the woman tried her mobile, but there was no answer.

'Tell her that they need to pack now and go,' Robert was not giving in.

It took fifteen minutes for the family to carry all their food and clothes into the step-daughter's car. The boyfriend continued leaning against the car and disconnected himself from the palaver by blindly staring at his phone, pretending to be oblivious of what was going on. The mother alternated between shouting at everyone, threatening Robert, and pleading with me. Once the step-daughter's car was loaded, they got in and drove away. Robert went down to the gate and locked it behind them. As soon as he returned to the patio, Ula and Lukasz looked at us quizzically. Any romantic ideas that they might have had about running a rural guesthouse had vanished in that instant. I poured us all generous glasses of wine. I could see the guests' car was still parked outside our house on the track with its headlights on. It was almost midnight.

'Are they going to sleep there?' Ula asked.

'I hope not. They must be trying to reach the father or looking for a *hostal* where they can sleep,' I guessed.

I had to explain to Ula and Lukasz what had happened. But before I could open my mouth, I heard a car on the dirt track coming up from Montefrio. Robert switched off all the outside lights. The four of us sat in total darkness and listened. Sure enough, this other car stopped at our gate. It was the father. We could hear doors open, followed by a lot of drunken shouting and arguing. It went on for ten more minutes until finally, the two cars drove away.

'Ufff,' Robert sighed as their flickering rear lights disappeared around the corner. 'It's good we got rid of them before the father came home.'

We all agreed. Throwing out a woman with two kids and an adolescent man was one thing, but I'm not sure how things would have turned out if we had to argue with a drunken macho man. The last we heard of them was two days later when they posted their 'review'.

'Two out of ten,' I told Robert. 'I don't think you can score lower than that.'

'Did they say that we kicked them out?'

'No, they don't mention that at all. It says that there were spider webs everywhere.'

There was nothing else to say. I was gutted. The booking site refused to remove this 'honest review'. And so, we inaugurated our first summer as hoteliers with a review of Miss Havisham's house for the whole world to see and admire.

ELEVEN
WATER WORRIES

Three days into my friend's stay, our well dried out. I informed Robert of the fact, and he took it rather stoically. It was not really news. We were expecting it. Each time that summer when I turned on the water pump in the well, it was a game of Russian roulette — will it go off or not? I stopped lifting the lid of the well to check the water level in early June because the sight of the rapidly dropping water level was too demoralising.

Instead, I engaged in a game of luck and chance, generally described as 'hope-for-the-best'. A great sense of relief would come over me each time I pushed the pump button and heard the water gush through the pipes and up the hill to the house. Until one day, the pump remained silent. I pushed the pump button a few more times, hoping that there was an electrical error, but it was pointless. It was time to face the music.

'How much water is in the white tank?' Robert asked when the inevitable happened.

'I think it's enough for two or three days,' I said calmly, but in my head, I was panicking: *What are we going to do? We have lots of guests booked for August. I don't want to cancel now after all the work has been done.*

We were not the only family in Andalusia suffering from the drought. In the summer of 2016, water was on everyone's mind. We had barely seen any rain that year, which meant that all the water tanks and wells in the area were either dry or inches from drying out. Our cottage is located not far from Montefrio but too far for us to be connected to the municipal water supply. The families in our valley have independent water supplies, which are either wells or boreholes. A few lucky homes are near a *fuente*, or a spring, where water miraculously flows from the rocks all year round. We had neither a borehole nor a *fuente,* and our well was only seven metres deep, which, as we learned from talking to our neighbours, was not very deep.

Most summers in Andalusia, it's considered good manners to start a conversation by exclaiming the obvious: *'¡Qué calor!'*, *What heat!*. With the average temperature around forty degrees Celsius, which is one hundred and four Fahrenheit, on any July or August afternoon, it's as good a greeting as the textbook *¿Qué tal?*. But in the summer of the drought, the polite greeting: *¡Qué calor!* was replaced with: *¿Tienes agua en tu pozo?* or *Do you have water in your well?*.

Whenever we met our neighbours, instead of *How are you?*, we'd ask each other about the state of our wells. It was a common concern. While people in the countryside had been fretting about the drought for months, people in nearby towns and cities did not seem perturbed by the water shortage. Many ran their taps every day, oblivious to how scarce the water supply was.

I realised that there was a huge gap in people's understanding of where the water came from one day as I was leaving my Spanish classes. Fred, the owner of the shop where the classes were held, asked me casually how we were doing.

'Our *pozo* is almost dry,' I told him honestly.

'Oh yeah,' he nodded. 'It's a problem when you live in the *campo*.'

I looked at him and feigned a smile. Anyone who had not been in a coma since spring should have been aware of the fact that the water reserves in all of the cities in Andalusia were low. Most municipalities had switched off the fountains in their parks and closed municipal swimming pools weeks earlier. Even the water features in Cordoba and the Alhambra had to be turned off to save water. In Montefrio, the village's water reservoir was so low that the chief engineer was reported walking around the bottom of the reservoir in his Wellington boots in disbelief. If they had half a metre left from the bottom, that was it.

I wondered where, according to Fred, his magical water supply in Alcalá came from? The writing was on the wall. Once massive, lake reservoirs all around Andalusia had now shrunk to the size of fish ponds. Some were so low that you wouldn't even be able to keep carp in them. The river beds had turned into Arabian *wadis*. Yet, many people in the cities still believed in their taps that provided them with an infinite water supply from Neverland.

In the countryside, folk were taking twenty-second showers, flushed toilets only when it was vital and washed their clothes only when they could smell each other from a distance. The city folk, on the other hand, kept to their routines of running taps while brushing teeth, using washing machines with a single pair of socks inside, cleaning their cars with a hosepipe every night and generously watering their gardens twice a day to keep them lush and green. It was as if we lived in parallel universes. Us, country bumpkins, in our stinky clothes and vehicles covered in heavy layers of dust, and them, soap smelling city-dwellers in their shiny cars and spotless garments.

I was chewing on the unfairness of this on the way home. I could not believe the ignorance. The reason for my anger was that Fred was not the first person I had met that summer who seemed oblivious to the drought and water shortage in Andalusia. As a host, I didn't want to overwhelm guests with instructions and warnings. That's why I kept these to the bare minimum and chose to prioritise whichever rule I felt was the most important to share at the moment. If they got out of the car with a cigarette in hand, I'd ask them not to smoke inside, and if they seemed in a party mode, I'd mention not to use glass bottles by the pool.

But in the summer of 2016, the first thing that we'd emphasise after introducing ourselves and showing the guests around was the need to save water. Our Dutch, Danish, and Polish guests understood how to save water and did indeed limit their ablutions to a quick rub and a rinse. It must have been because water is indeed quite expensive in northern Europe, and many households in Northern and Central Europe try to control their own use. It was the Spanish guests who seemed the most resistant to following the simple rules of water conservation. And not the Spaniards from Madrid or Barcelona who generally live in a different world than the rest of Spain, but Andalusians from Seville and Malaga.

One couple, in particular, used enough water during their one-night stay to keep a small agricultural estate running for a week. When they checked in, I asked them to conserve water because of the shortage, to which they nodded their heads and pretended to understand what I was talking about. I assumed that as a couple of adults who had managed to get so far in their lives that they could afford weekend getaways, they would know how to limit their water usage without a long lecture with charts and illustrations.

The couple settled in quickly and enjoyed the afternoon by the pool and on the terrace. Around seven p.m., they started preparing to go out for their evening meal, and the water began to flow. I could hear the water pump hum in the room behind our kitchen. The threat of running out of water was so deeply seeded in my mind that as soon as I heard the pump start, I looked at the clock. After ten minutes, I started to worry that they had left a tap on by mistake, which had happened in the past.

A month earlier, an older gentleman had left his shower tap half-open through the night and emptied all the water from the three thousand litre water tank that supplied the house. He woke us up at the crack of dawn by knocking on the door and demanding to know why there was no water in his bathroom. Since that accident, I became super vigilant. As soon as I heard the water pump turn on, my ears would stand up like those of a hyperactive terrier's. This time, I listened for five more minutes and started to worry. *Why would someone take a fifteen-minute shower during a drought?* I wondered. I went outside to see if the guests' car was still there, in case they had gone out and left a tap open, but the car was still there.

In desperation, I went behind the house to check how much water was left in the tank. Standing next to the water tank, I watched the water pump working and reflected on the pointlessness of whatever it was I was doing, but I could not stop my compulsive behaviour. I could see that the water heater was on, so I knew that someone was taking a shower. I stood in the pump room for another ten minutes, not knowing what to do exactly.

Had I not explained it clearly enough? I asked myself.

There was also a flyer in the room stressing the importance of saving water during the drought. I felt speechless and defeated. The water had now been running for almost thirty minutes nonstop.

Surely their skin must be peeling off them by now, I thought.

I considered switching off the water supply but weighed it against receiving a bad review. I walked away and decided to work in the garden for some time so that I would not hear the water pump running.

I didn't see the guests that evening. They returned when I was asleep. In the morning, they slept in until around eleven, when I heard the ominous sound of the water pump turning on. After another almost forty-minute-long shower, they were ready to check out. We bade them farewell in an amicable way and shouted *gracias* and *adios* as they drove off. I then went to check the water tank to find out that during their very short stay, they had used over a thousand litres of water. I was a little upset about it, but I couldn't be angry. I knew precisely why they behaved in this manner because I was the same type of thoughtless traveller who, when I stayed in a hotel, expected unrivalled luxury and comfort.

Once I enter a hotel room, I demand that my towels be fresh every day and my sheets be ironed. Nothing but the best will do when madam sojourns in an establishment. The same person who doesn't change her own bedsheets for weeks on end and only washes her towels when they can no longer be distinguished from floor rags demands the utmost level of cleanliness when travelling abroad. Her own bathroom floors may be covered with all types of human hair, but should she find a lonely strand in a hotel bathtub or on a bathroom floor, all hell breaks loose, and the holiday is spoilt.

'How filthy!' I exclaim. From now on, that single offending curl is all that I can remember from my stay.

Loved the friendly staff and the stunning views. The breakfast was out of this world, but the place needs a good clean.

I hoped that, like me, the couple had double standards. And that once in their apartment in Seville, they did save water and did something to prevent our province from drying out completely.

As for our little guest house, we ran out of water in the first week of August. With the calendar now filled with summer visitors, I had no idea how we were going to pull it off.

'I can't go to Montefrio every day to get water,' Robert said as we were sitting on the patio trying to solve the water problem. 'It will take two hours every day to get a thousand litres, and we'll destroy the car by the end of the summer.'

It was true. Taking the trailer with the water cube to Montefrio each time a client took a long shower was not a solution for a holiday home. The year before, we had brought cubes of water from Montefrio, but we were alone in the house and had cut our water consumption down to the absolute minimum. This summer, we had guests who not only expected to be able to freshen up, wash the dishes, and do their laundry but also swim in the pool, which needed topping up every few days. To meet their needs, Robert would have to go to Montefrio at least once a day to keep a steady supply of water and going up and down steep hills while pulling a thousand litres of water in a trailer was a job that would definitely affect the car.

'I can ask Jaime if we can use his water,' Robert suggested.

'We'd have to pay for it,' I said.

'How much shall I offer him?'

'I have no idea. Five or ten euros per cube,' I guessed.

'OK. We'll see. Come with me.'

It was a clear signal that I was going to have to do most of the talking and negotiating. Robert was still using the first-person present tense conjugation on all verbs, which was usually confusing to Spanish listeners.

'Do I have a chainsaw file?' I once heard him ask our neighbour Rafa. I knew what he wanted, but Rafa was clueless.

'That's very good,' our neighbour would congratulate Robert in Spanish.

Then, they stood for a minute in silence, looking at each other. Robert would then repeat the same erroneous question but this time demonstrate what he wanted. After a while, Rafa and other neighbours got used to Robert speaking in first person and relied on the context to guess whether he was talking about himself, them, or someone else entirely.

Since buying water from Jaime was essential to our business's success, we decided it would be best if I did the talking. While my Spanish was far from perfect, I had a good enough grasp of the conjugation system to give Jaime a clear idea of who wanted to buy water from whom. The reason why our resourceful neighbour had water while everyone else in the valley didn't was an ingenious system of collecting rainwater that he devised on the hill behind his house. He first cleared the slope of rocks, bushes, and any small trees and then covered the ground with heavy-duty black plastic. This gave him a substantial area to collect rainwater which was then funnelled into a gigantic water tank that he had built from corrugated steel. Even though it had rained for only a couple of weeks in February, it was enough to fill up his water tank. The tank was just a few hundred metres from our house, and taking water from it and bringing it to our cottage would be much easier and faster than hauling it all the way from Montefrio.

As we walked over to his house, I hoped he would be willing to help us. We stood on his patio for a few minutes and yelled his and his wife's names, but there was no answer. So, we walked up the hill to his barn. They were both there. The barn floor was made of concrete and was covered entirely by the black nets used during the olive harvest. His wife, Maria, was sitting on the floor with what looked like a giant needle in hand. They were both busy fixing the holes in the nets. We exchanged the typical greetings, and Jaime soon asked us about the state of our *pozo*, or well. This made it easy for me to broach the topic and explain the main reason for our visit.

'But how much water do you use?' Jaime was curious.

'We only take ten-second showers,' Robert explained and mimed watering himself down, switching off the shower to soap up and then rinsing.

Jaime did not seem keen on giving water to people who waste it, so he continued the interrogation.

'Do you wash your car?' he asked.

'No, we haven't washed our car since May,' I explained. He must have seen it; like all the other *campo* cars, it was covered in a thick layer of dust.

'Do you water your garden?'

'No, we stopped watering it last month. I only have agaves in the garden.'

'What about the swimming pool?'

'We need to keep it for the guests. It takes about one or two thousand litres a week,' I explained. 'It depends on the weather and the wind.'

As the interrogation ended, Jaime turned to discuss the topic with his wife. I could see she was not interested in our predicament because she kept her eyes on the floor and wouldn't look up. I realised we were putting her in a somewhat difficult situation.

Until now, our neighbours had always been generous with their time and resources; they would always bring us fruit and vegetables from their garden, homemade sausages after *matanza*, and share food and recipes that they made at home. But the water was essential, and we were asking them to share it with us at a time when there was almost nothing to spare. Jaime turned back to us and explained that he needed a lot of water for his olives. He explained that if he irrigated his trees during the summer, he would increase his harvest by ten or fifteen percent, which meant increased profit.

'We can pay you for the water,' I said. 'How much would a cube cost?'

Maria now looked up and seemed more interested in the proposition. They exchanged a few comments, but I could see they were not comfortable making a decision in front of us.

'Well, think about it, please and let us know. We're happy to pay for the water,' I reiterated.

Jaime agreed, and we waved each other goodbye and walked out of the cool barn back onto the scorching August sun. As we started to descend, Maria came out of the barn and called us back.

'*Vale*,' she said, meaning *okay*. 'You can take the water.'

We agreed on the price, and a huge weight was instantly lifted off my shoulders. I thought I might ascend to heaven at that very moment. We were going to survive the summer, and it would not cost us a fortune. We both showered her with *muchas gracias*. As Maria went back to sewing the nets, Jaime came out to show us the tap and the pipe that we could use to fill in the cube on the back of the trailer. Once we made an arrangement on how we were going to keep track of the water that we took, we skipped all the way home. It wasn't ideal having to bring cubes of water to fill our own water tank, but at least the journey was only a few hundred metres which saved us a lot of time and petrol.

That summer, Robert's main household chore was to bring water to our home. Even though our new supply was close by, it still took some time to fill up the cube on the trailer. He would then drive up the hill behind our house and use gravity to transfer water from the trailer to the water tank behind the house. In the weeks when we were fully booked, he'd have to do it every day. That August, it became apparent that we had to look for a more sustainable solution to our water problem.

'You should drill a borehole of at least a hundred metres,' Rafa suggested one day while we were chatting on the road waiting for the cube to fill up.

'But is there water underground?' Robert asked.

'There could be water. You need to ask in Granada,' Rafa advised us.

I wasn't sure who we would have to ask in Granada, and he wasn't too forthcoming with that information. I assumed there was some government office responsible for water.

'How much is a borehole?'

'You pay per metre. It's thirty-five euros per metre with no guarantee or fifty euros per metre with a guarantee.'

'What do you mean 'a guarantee'?' Robert asked.

'If there is no water when they finish digging, you get your money back, or they look somewhere else.'

'So, it's three thousand five hundred euros for the cheap option, but if there is no water, we lose the money or five thousand euros with a guarantee?' Robert asked.

'Yes,' it's better to choose the option with a guarantee,' Rafa suggested. 'I'll give you a number for a guy who made a borehole at my house in Algarinejo.'

I went over to the car to get my phone to record the phone number. I wrote down the contact details out of politeness because, in all honesty, we did not have a cool five thousand euros lying around. It might as well have been fifty thousand. The amount of money was out of our reach. While we had started making some money from the rental apartments, it was evident that we had to save every penny to survive the winter months when occupancy was low.

'We should build a steel water tank like Jaime's and collect rainwater from the roof,' Robert suggested as we were driving home with another cube of water.

'But how much will it cost?' I asked.

'Jaime's cost twenty-five thousand. He told me two years ago when he was building it.'

'Twenty-five thousand!' my heart sank. *We are never going to solve our water problems*, I thought.

'Yes, but his is huge. We need a much smaller one, for eighty or hundred thousand litres. I'll ask him next time I see him.'

According to Jaime's estimates, a steel tank to collect rainwater for our household would cost about three thousand euros plus cement and steel to make a foundation for the tank. This seemed much more feasible than throwing two thousand five hundred euros into a hundred-metre-deep hole that may or may not have water.

'We'd also need to install gutters and connect them to the tank. This will cost about a thousand,' Robert explained.

I wrote all these estimates down, and we spent most of August exploring options and searching for a solution to our water problem. But wherever we looked, our lack of finances was stopping us from moving forward. It was indisputable that we needed a steady source of income to be able to keep on living in the middle of nowhere.

TWELVE
BACK TO THE MIDDLE EAST

Since we had abandoned our old jobs as teachers in the Middle East, we worked from home as freelancers. Every now and then, I would pick up a textbook contract, and Robert would edit and translate academic articles. While these jobs suited our new lifestyle and allowed us to juggle house renovation and work, we never knew when the next project would come, and so our money worries were always in the back of my mind. And now that solving the problem of our water supply had become our primary concern, it became blatantly obvious that at least one of us had to go back to work.

'I can apply to my old university in Abu Dhabi,' I mentioned one afternoon. 'Julie told me that they're looking for a lecturer.'

It had taken me several weeks to consider this option as I loathed the idea of having to go back to the Gulf. It was a place that I associated with mental and physical imprisonment. Even though many expats see Abu Dhabi as a liberal and westernised city, I could not see past the bars of the gilded cage. In my mind's eye, I saw myself renting a small studio in Al Rafa or Reem island. After work, I'd go to this tiny apartment and while away long, lonely evenings watching TV and drinking wine. It was a sad prospect.

I could get a membership to the Fairmont or another resort, I thought, in an attempt to entice myself to this idea.

It would be nice to go to a spa again. I tried to convince myself that going back to the Middle East wasn't all bad.

But no matter how much I tried to spin this, I wasn't really buying it. To me, going back would be admitting defeat, and I saw it as a step backwards in my life journey. I also thought of Robert with the cats and Bobby all by themselves in the Andalusian countryside. There was no doubt that either the cats or the dog would have disappeared by the time I came back. Robert was not the most attentive of pet owners, and he would not notice if an animal wasn't around for a couple of days.

Whichever way I looked at the prospect of going back to the Middle East to earn money, it was all doom and gloom. Still, a steady supply of cash would mean we could solve the water situation, renovate our own living room and kitchen, which had been untouched since we purchased the house, and fix dozens of other things that would bring our cottage into the current century. The fact was that the downstairs of our cottage, where we worked on our laptops, cooked, ate our meals and entertained, was worse than it had been when we first bought the property.

Since we had moved to Spain in 2014, the old living room had been exposed to wind and rain and had been part of a building site for almost a year. What used to be a small guest bedroom next to the kitchen was now a dark and dingy room, covered in mould from the time when we were flooded by torrential rains two years earlier; the room was filled with unpacked boxes from the floor to the ceiling which made it impossible to clean the mould off the walls. It all needed renovation, but with no cash, there was little we could do about it.

'Maybe I can go with you and get a job too,' Robert was clearly not too enthusiastic about staying home alone.

'But what about the animals? And who's going to look after the house for that long?'

It seemed that we only had questions and no answers. I discussed our financial difficulties with a friend who had recently moved back from Abu Dhabi to Wales. Like us, she and her husband were constantly agonising about — what she called — 'cash flow' since they had left the Middle East.

I'll send you the contact details of a Chinese company, she wrote in her email. *They need online teachers. Mark and I trained to teach for them, but we couldn't get past the technicalities. Anyway, we're waiting for a reply from the British Council in Sudan, so we may be off in the next few months anyway.*

I didn't understand what she meant by 'technicalities', but I was soon to find out. After I passed the initial demo lesson on Skype, I had to go through a week of training. Every morning, I would teach for thirty minutes and receive feedback from my trainer. I was excited about the future possibilities. If both of us did some online teaching every day, I wouldn't have to go back to the Gulf.

I sent Robert's details to the recruiter, and he was to start his training after me. Before my first lesson, I received several very detailed PowerPoint presentations that I had to go through in order to prepare my lessons. There was new software to learn and a whole new suite of Chinese versions of common communication apps. From now on, we were not going to use Skype and WhatsApp, but apps that I had never heard of before but which, as I found out, were used by a billion Chinese subscribers.

I went through the endless PowerPoint slides whose content could easily have been summarised on two or three pages of a Word document. The slides were riddled with punctuation and spelling errors which made me worried about the whole enterprise.

What am I getting myself into? I scratched my head while looking at the word *english* written with lower case and *learner* spelt as *lerner*.

'Maybe it's a scam to steal your personal information?' Robert suggested when I vented my frustration about all the apps that I had to install and the conspicuous lack of professionalism in the training materials.

His words made me worried, and I didn't dare tell him that that very morning Karen had taken control of my laptop to demonstrate how the teachers' app worked. 'Karen' was my Chinese trainer's Western name. Her real name was never revealed to me, which added to my concern.

'Christine had done the same training with them, and they hadn't stolen anything from her,' I told him and, at the same time, assured myself. 'Also, I can't imagine them developing this elaborate scheme of teacher training to steal a few hundred euros from our bank account.'

The spelling mistakes in my training material were vast and furious, but the Google translation errors made some of the instructions simply incomprehensible — these, I had to underline and ask Karen for further explanation.

'What do you mean by *strength*?' I'd ask Karen.

'Where is that?'

'On the slide with the title: *How should I introduce myself to the student?*

'Aha.'

'It says: *You can tell your name, and hobbies as well as strength is also when the student asks,*' I read from the slide on my desktop.

There was dead silence. Karen was clearly as confused by these directives as I was.

'Anyway, let's move to teacher's conduct and dress code,' she changed the topic without answering my question. 'Did you read it?'

'Yes.'

'Do you have any questions?'

This time I was speechless. I wasn't sure what to ask. The conduct stipulated that the teacher shouldn't be playing on the phone while teaching, talking to other people in his or her house, yawning into the camera, eating, or conducting the lesson from his or her bed or from a noisy bar. The only question I had was *What kind of dimwit does your company employ that you need to write these out for them?* But I fought the urge to ask and said *no*. I didn't need any clarification on these rules of conduct.

'That's great,' Karen said. 'And about the dress code, please make sure you wear formal clothes because the parents are often watching the lesson, and it's important that the teachers look professional.'

'So, no tank tops, bikinis, or pyjamas?' I started reading aloud from the list of forbidden garments listed in my training materials when my eye caught the words *no shirt* listed as a look that would be frowned upon by the company. My mind wandered off as Karen went on paraphrasing the content of the slides to me as if I were an illiterate Neanderthal who had never lived among civilised people and was thus unable to make sense of these myself.

I was fascinated by these instructions. They were obviously not created out of thin air. At some stage in their company's history, someone must have appeared in the online lesson shirtless. I assumed it was a man, as a shirtless woman teaching online would have made it to the news. I imagined a backpacking doofus on the beach in Thailand, landing himself a cushy job that he hoped would extend his gap year indefinitely. He'd go to a bar to get free internet, order a spicy *pad thai* and a cold beer, take off his shirt, and commence educating. But I was hardly the one to judge. I looked around.

I was sitting on the floor by my bed. I didn't want to do the training in the living room because of the constant commotion and the possibility of Bobby barking or cats fighting outside. To make the best impression possible, I opted for the bedroom upstairs, which was quieter but had a weak Wi-Fi signal. That's why I had to sit on the floor right above the router to get the strongest connection. I put the laptop on the laundry basket and made sure the background was just a white wall and not the legs of the bed frame. I put on a nice shirt but kept to tracksuit pants and flip-flops. This appearance definitely reflected my attitude to the whole enterprise.

Once Karen read the slides to me, I delivered a series of lessons that she would assess. The company wouldn't risk having trainees teach real students, so every morning, I sat down on the carpet by my bed and taught a heavily scripted lesson while Karen pretended to be a Chinese schoolgirl.

It was a bizarre arrangement. She even changed her voice to a soft squeak which made me very uncomfortable. Should a stranger walk into my bedroom, they'd see me sitting on the floor in front of an open laptop, enthusiastically clapping my hands while singing:

There was a farmer who had a dog and Bingo was his name. Oh! I'd emphasise the *Oh!* And then clap-and-spell the name of the dog.

On the screen, a forty-something-year-old Chinese woman in a neat white work shirt and tight ponytail was imitating my actions, singing along in an uncanny child-like voice, spelling the dog's name: *B — I — N — G — O!* For someone who is certifiably tone-deaf and generally unenthusiastic, it was probably the lowest moment in my teaching career.

'You'd better show more encouragement,' Karen gave me her feedback after the first lesson.

I was silent. I wanted to tell her that for an Eastern European whose main occupation in life is thinking about death, I was as cheerful as they get.

B — I — N — G — O! the wretched song now playing on a loop in my head.

'You'd better send some stickers.'

Karen — who once again had control of my laptop — displayed the grotesque pastel pink and green stickers with kittens and rabbits that were part of the teacher's app.

'Did you know that my grandmother worked three shifts in Gdansk harbour when she was nineteen, spent her free time shovelling rubble because the city was bombed to the ground by the communists and had buried three infant children by the age of twenty-five because there was not enough penicillin to go around? *She* didn't get a sticker,' I wanted to explain to Karen my seeming lack of passion. *B — I — N — G — O!* I thought better of it.

'OK,' I said. I didn't care for her use of *you'd better* at the start of each sentence, but I knew it was a language error rather than a warning. She'd used that phrase throughout our training sessions instead of more neutral expressions such as, *you should,* or *you might consider.* I didn't correct her because I got distracted by dozens of hideous kitty and rabbit stickers — each striking a different pose, and *B — I — N — G — O!* still playing in my head.

'Also, you'd better say *well done* and *great job* more,' she continued.

The next day, I showered my fake student with stickers and exaggerated praise.

'You'd better correct the mistakes,' Karen advised me this time.

I wanted to roll my eyes, but I was on the video call and didn't want to appear rude.

If I were to correct all the errors that you made, we wouldn't go past the second slide of the lesson, I thought.

'The parents want to see value for money. You need to correct all the errors so that children don't repeat them,' Karen explained to me while mispronouncing *parents, errors, children*, and *repeat*.

The following day was my final lesson. I filled it with fake exuberance and undeserved praise. I corrected the obviously fake errors that my faux student made and sent hundreds of bunnies and kittens her way. I thought I was in the clear and ready to start earning money the following week.

'You'd better change your accent,' Karen told me in her own heavily marked Chinese voice.

'Aha,' I said while processing this feedback. She thought I needed time to think about it.

'You don't sound British or American. In fact, parents prefer an American accent. Can you do it?'

'I don't have a British or American accent because I'm Polish,' I told her. 'I think my accent is pretty clear and easy to understand.'

'You'd better speak American.'

I was done with this whole charade of keeping my mouth shut and pretending I had no idea about teaching. I was not going to be schooled anymore.

'Which American accent would you like me to imitate?' I asked rhetorically. 'New York? California? The South? I don't know what you're talking about. A person can't just change their accent. I'm not Meryl Streep.'

'Aha,' this time, it was her who needed time to process my outburst.

After a brief silence, Karen did not seem to have any more advice for me and told me that she would send her feedback to her bosses. We bid farewell. I knew I would never hear from them again. My instructor had lost face, and she was not going to recommend me for the teaching job.

I now understood what my friend, Christine, meant when she said that there were a lot of technicalities. There was no doubt Karen loved Christine's British accent, so it would not have been a problem, but I could not imagine my usually grumpy friend being on board with the sickening array of kittens and rabbits. While I was half-relieved for not having to sing and clap my hands every afternoon in front of a Chinese child and his or her fault-finding parents, Robert and I were back to square one.

Well, not entirely. To my surprise, Robert, who is predominantly a sulky and reluctant teacher, passed the training with flying colours. He was going to start teaching Chinese adults in a couple of weeks when he received an email from his old student from Al Ain.

'Samira is opening a private school in Sur,' he told me one morning while I was drinking coffee and reading the news on my laptop. 'She wants us to come and help her.'

'Who is Samira?' I asked.

'She was studying to be a teacher in Al Ain, but she's Omani. Don't you remember her? She was quite bright and very active.'

We used to teach at the same university in Al Ain for a couple of years, but I honestly couldn't remember any of Robert's students.

'*I need help to open a British curriculum school in my hometown in Sur,*' Robert read from Samira's email. '*If you and Sabina could come and help me, I can offer you half of the school.*'

I don't want to run a school in Oman, was my immediate thought.

'It's a kind offer,' I told Robert. 'But it's a lot of work, and we'd have to move there for several years. She doesn't give us any numbers. It's all a bit fishy. Is this for real?'

Robert agreed that the whole proposition was too good to be true. Samira came out of nowhere and was asking us to leave our lives behind and move to Sur to work on a project that we had little idea about. He wrote back and explained that we couldn't come. A few hours later, Samira replied.

'She asks if I can come for a month and help her open the school,' Robert informed me at lunch.

'When does the school open?'

'Next week — the first week of September.'

'When does she want you to be there?'

'As soon as possible. She seems overwhelmed.'

That day Robert and Samira exchanged several more emails. Since Skype was banned in Oman, it was the quickest way to communicate. They agreed on his pay and made arrangements for his accommodation. Moneywise, it was a godsend to us. That same day Samira transferred money so that we could buy Robert's plane tickets, and two days later, he was flying over the Suez Canal on his way to open a private school in Sur.

THIRTEEN
SUN-DRIED GRAPES

R obert's decision to travel to the Middle East was rather sudden, and so we had only a few days to prepare. Our friend, Keith, was to take Robert to the airport early on Thursday morning. We had to ask a friend for a lift because, in the first two years of our new life in Spain, I had not managed to transfer my driving licence. I had a UAE driving licence, which was not valid in Spain. Another reason why Keith had to take Robert to the airport was that even if I dared to drive without a valid license, I was not confident enough to go to Malaga in the 4x4 with a manual gearbox.

I had learned how to drive in a car with an automatic gearbox, which makes driving easy. I had no feel for a manual gearbox or the clutch and had consequently developed an inherent aversion and hatred of manual gearboxes. While I could drive a manual car in theory, I chose not to. Since I would be alone for a month and not be able to drive to town to get groceries, I asked Keith whether he would mind taking me to the shops once a week whenever he was going to Alcalá. He didn't seem to mind. The day before Robert's departure, we went to the shops and bought a supply of drinking water to last me a month. I also bought a good stock of groceries to limit my shopping trips during the following month to a minimum. The last thing to sort out was water for the house.

Driving a manual car in the Andalusian mountains sounded like an obvious nightmare. Driving it with a trailer to bring water to the house sounded impossible to me, but Robert was unusually optimistic about my abilities to do so. He spent most of the afternoon before his departure teaching me how to drive the car with a trailer, where to park it to fill the cube with water, and how to get it up the hill behind the house to fill up our water tank. In the process of educating me, he filled the three-thousand-litre water tank to the brim, and I swore to myself to be extremely careful with the water so as to not have to drive the car.

'Do you understand the low gear system?' he asked me about the 4x4 gears. 'You need to come to a complete stop before you disengage the gear; otherwise, you will break it. Also, don't drive on the road with it on because you will break it.'

It sounded that whatever I did, I was destined to break the gearbox.

'So when do I use '4x4 low'?' I was getting confused.

As he started to explain for the tenth time the difference between '4x4 low' and '4x4 high', my mind started to wander.

I'll ask Rafa to help me if I need more water. I cheered myself up and excused myself from listening but kept on nodding my head.

There are situations in our lives that foreshadow our future and allow us to rehearse what our lives might be like one day. The morning after Robert's departure, I placed a dirty coffee mug in the sink and stood in the middle of our living room.

What to do now?

I was overwhelmed by a feeling of emptiness and wondered how I was supposed to fill my day. It was only nine a.m.; I had already walked Bobby, drank coffee, and read the news on my laptop. I realised that I was being visited by the Ghost of the Future — the morning after my husband's demise. I couldn't understand what had happened. The day before, I was running around, doing errands, organising, cleaning, cooking, instructing, nagging, writing, and struggling to find enough hours in the day. Today, I stood paralysed by the void that confronted me. My mind was blank.

What to do?

Since Robert wasn't dead and was just 10,000 metres in the air somewhere over the Empty Quarter or the Hajar Mountains, I thought it might be an excellent opportunity to practice living alone in preparation for his inevitable but more permanent departure in thirty or forty years.

The more sensitive reader might think it was harsh of me to immediately start preparing for the worst, but you probably don't know that I come from a long line of 'preppers-for-the-worst'. As a child of a young single-mum in the 1980s, I spent most of my childhood shadowing my grandmother. Having been deeply traumatised by the Second World War in Poland and the subsequent imposition of martial law in our hometown, she left nothing to chance.

Big chunks of her mornings and evenings were taken up by fervently praying to God to spare her family from any of the imminent disasters that He was preparing to unleash on the long-suffering Polish population. She would list off all her family members one by one in her prayers, outlining our good qualities as if we were applicants hoping to get into a private school and needed a good word put in with the Divine Headmaster. When she wasn't busy making sure we would all meet again in Heaven, she devoted her every waking hour preparing for the worst.

Secreted away on the eighth floor of her two-bedroom communist-era apartment overlooking the river Motława, she had enough food supplies to open a small grocery shop. The most precious commodity consisted of huge bags of sugar, enough to last us a decade. Then, there was shelf upon shelf of homemade preserves — meats, fruit, vegetables, and lard. Should the Red Army strike again, we were ready to hide out in the tiny windowless bathroom for a year or longer. Since I was her secret apprentice, she'd explain to me where all the supplies were stored so that I could take over should she die. The idea of preparing for the worst stayed with me. Whilst I currently don't store vast supplies of highly calorific staples in preparation for a future catastrophe, I do like to be mentally ready in case of any unexpected calamity.

Now that I had found a new purpose in life, I felt a bit better. After a quick chat with Bobby, who had a questioning look on his face as if he were evaluating his mistress's mental state, I took out a piece of paper to write down a daily schedule that I would follow to fill my days with productive activities. I went out to the patio, had a good look around and sat down to make a list of things that could be done by one person. First on the list was something that was staring me in the face: *cut down the grapes*. I wrote it down and looked up at the grapes. I could not think of anything else to write and so I decided to start working on the grapes in the hope that the physical activity would help stimulate my brain.

A well-established grapevine shading the patio is the most iconic feature of any Andalusian cortijo. The lush, broad foliage provides ample shade and will cool most patios down, even on the hottest day in August. Our guests would often take photos of the green and purple grapes hanging over their heads. Juicy grapes that grow freely are a true sign of the Mediterranean and the only reason why we let the fruit stay on the vine most of the summer. The truth is that for most local people, the fruit of the grapevine is a bit of a nuisance. When the grapes first mature and are sweet enough to eat, things are great; but the situation can become complicated. Because the sugary fruit attracts wasps, many people cut all the fruit down as soon as they form and throw it away to keep the sugar-craving wasps at bay.

The problem with grapes is that their growth isn't adequately staggered to fulfil a simple supply-and-demand chain over an extended period of time. At the first sight of ripened grapes in early August, I get excited. I pick up a large bowl and go to the patio to cut down a few bunches for personal consumption. I stare for a minute or two at the homegrown grapes and feel smug thinking about all the poor schmucks who have to go to the supermarket to buy their grapes. *Look at me and my grapes.* I almost chuckle in my self-satisfied pompousness. Unavoidably, the said bunches of grapes end up on social media, carefully posed and filtered, to inspire awe in my enemies. As August turns to September, the need for the fruit diminishes drastically, but the vine itself increases its production to unprecedented levels. At that stage, I also have to deal with tons of figs that will have begun to rot on the trees.

Usually, by September, I feel sick to my stomach from eating grapes and figs and find myself in a position where I don't ever want to eat any more fruit in my life, but — waste not, want not. I grab another bowl and wander off to collect the figs before they all fall to the ground. As I approach the fig tree, I see black starlings stripping the tree of the fruit. Walking under the fig tree and picking the fruit, I can feel the squishy flesh under my flip-flops — there is now a thick layer of rotting figs on the ground that I am walking over.

I wish we had pigs, I think to myself. *They'd love it here. But then we'd need to house them, feed them, call the vet, and maybe eventually slaughter them.* This is too big a commitment and possible emotional challenge just to solve the problem of having too much fruit.

The curse of the Andalusian bounty is that all the delicious fruit and vegetables that grow here have a tendency to ripen all at the same time. On many an occasion in the late summer and early autumn, I'd find myself in the kitchen surrounded by containers of different provenance filled with grapes, figs, peaches, onions, peppers, tomatoes, and courgettes. At these times, it is a blessing to have a house full of summer guests who appreciate free fruit and vegetables. But even the most enthusiastic of guests can't eat *all* the grapes and figs that ripen during the summer.

Since it was the first week of September, it was time to cut down the grapes that were now rotting on the vine and falling onto the patio. I got two sizeable black plastic baskets into which I tossed the fruit. After an hour, I had filled both baskets to the brim with grapes. I should have tossed them over the fence into the dry river bed at the bottom of our valley. But I was determined to make use of them, and — more importantly — I had to fill the existential void that was looming before me. I really had nothing else to do at that moment in my life, so I decided to play a country housewife.

My first idea was to preserve the grapes the same way that I preserved tomatoes and figs, namely, sun-dry them. The production of raisins seemed like an easy enough job, but it took several days. I selected several succulent bunches of grapes from the baskets, cleaned them, and then placed them in the direct sun, next to the tomatoes and figs that were also in the process of being sun-dried. While the grapes were sun-drying, I decided to ask some friends on social media what else I could do with the remaining grapes — there was still a basket and a half left. The immediate response was, of course, to make wine. I considered it for a second and even searched online 'how to make your own wine'. However, after my superficial research effort, I was sure that it would be a futile endeavour.

To start with, I did not have the requisite equipment to make wine, including the giant jugs to store the wine in during its fermentation stage. Knowledgeable how-to-make-your-own-wine bloggers also listed funnels, airlocks, rubber corks, straining bags, wine bottles, sanitised corks, a hand corker, and a hydrometer as essential to successful wine production. The only items on the list that I could provide in abundance were recycled wine bottles. I had not seen any of the other listed items in the *ferretería*, or hardware store, where, in addition to DIY and farming tools, most farmers buy their kitchen and food-processing utensils. I'd have to drive all around Andalusia to find all the bits and pieces indispensable to wine-making.

'Making your own wine is a great conversation starter,' one of the wine bloggers had made a list of ten reasons why you should make your own wine.

I asked myself, while reading, *do you want to be the type of person who makes her own wine in order to talk about it incessantly at parties and social gatherings?*

Few things in life are as annoying as people who deliberate about their artisanal food-preparation techniques, the heirloom fruit and vegetables they grow, and craft beverages they brew. I wasn't ready to encourage this type of nonsense of haranguing strangers about my homemade Andalusian patio wine. I also had a strong recollection of the wine that our neighbours who live at the end of the valley make each year.

Every spring, Antonio brings us a couple of two-litre plastic bottles of his father's homemade wine. It is made by Old Antonio from his patio grapes and is dispensed in recycled Cola, Fanta, and Sprite bottles and distributed as gifts to his neighbours and friends. The transparent plastic bottle allows any wine aficionado to ascertain its exact colour, opacity, and viscosity, which I can best describe as muddy-orangey-pink-water — a 'poor man's rosé' is the best way to describe it. Whenever we are generously gifted one of Old Antonio's wines, I place it in the pantry next to the other cleaning products. But — despite my reluctance to drink it — it miraculously disappears each summer.

It's during the long summer evenings, when we entertain friends or guests, that we inevitably stumble onto the topic of wine-making. To prove to everyone that amateur wine-making is a potentially futile endeavour, I wander off to the pantry, hunting for the lonely Cola bottle hiding behind the bleach and window cleaning products.

'It's your chance to shine, my friend,' I encourage the debutante.

Once the shot glasses are set in front of the guests, the tasting session begins. As I pour it generously into the glasses, our guests don't have to bring them close to their nostrils to take a whiff. The initial aroma of earthy ammonia mixed with white spirits hits them in the face with brutal force. Fortunately, the subsequent anosmia, or smell blindness, is temporary but perhaps preferable for those who plan on actually drinking the wine. I advise everyone to keep Old Antonio's rosé away from their eyes as the damage to the cornea might be irreversible.

The actual tasting part of Antonio's wine should always be kept to a minimum. Instead of keeping it in your mouth to let your tongue and palate absorb all the flavours, it's best to chug it down your throat as fast as possible to avoid burning off your taste buds. Strangely, despite the horrible things I have said so far about craft wine-making being a terrible conversation topic and about Old

Antonio's rosé being undrinkable, the conversation flows, and the wine vanishes.

As I was sitting on the patio, reading hipster blogs about craft wine-making, I saw Bobby next to the grape basket vomiting blood. At least I thought it was blood until I realised that, unnoticed, he'd been stealing bunches of overly-matured red grapes and was now naturally intoxicated. I put the basket away in a safe place until I decided what to do with the grapes, but after a few days, I admitted defeat and threw them away into the *barranco*.

In those first two weeks of September, I turned our patio table into my workstation. I sat there each day listening to comedy podcasts while vacuum-packing tomatoes, figs, and raisins. I designed the website for the primary school that Robert was busy opening in Sur. The website he had created was perfect for a classy funeral home. The colour scheme that he chose consisted mainly of black and several shades of grey, which gave it a sombre and votive tone.

'Visual arts are really not your strength,' I wrote in my feedback after viewing his efforts. Instead of a rainbow colour scheme and stock images of children with oversized wax crayons and play-dough, his website seemed to have been inspired by *The Twilight Zone*.

'Leave it with me,' I told him.

Soon enough, I was filling the void. I had moved on from not knowing what to do with myself. I was now busy playing the role of the rural housewife, web designer, and social media marketer for a primary school. I was almost done processing my sun-dried figs, grapes, and tomatoes and so started to plan what to do next when a tiny figure appeared around the corner from behind the oak tree. It was my neighbour, Carmen. She was carrying two heavy bags. We greeted each other, and she put the two bags on my patio table.

'These are for you,' she said in Spanish.

'Oh, grapes!' I pretended to be delighted by this gift. 'How nice! I love grapes.'

'Perfect,' Carmen was delighted with her gift. 'These are delicious.'

'I'm sure they are.'

'I can bring you some more when you finish these.'

I really admired my neighbours' belief in how much fruit I could consume. I had just been given enough grapes to start a small fruit export business, and she was asking me if I wanted more. I'd have to eat nothing but grapes for two weeks before I would need more. Carmen was not the only one who loved to inundate me with fruit and vegetables that they couldn't eat themselves. One morning, I was walking Bobby past Rafa's house and seeing him by the side of the road tinkering with his trailer. I complimented him on the growth of his pomegranate trees.

'Your pomegranates are lovely,' I said, which was true.

Rafa's pomegranates are the size of ostrich eggs. They are rich in colour and glisten inside, in contrast to our pomegranate tree, which has yet to bear any fruit. I hoped to hear some helpful tips from him on how to grow such pomegranates, but instead, the next day, Rafa arrived at my patio with two baskets of pomegranates. He admitted that he hardly ever ate the fruit and that the trees were just left to grow wild.

I thanked him kindly and put the fruit away in the pantry, only to throw most of it away in a secret location — so that Rafa wouldn't find out — two months later. The same happens every year with kaki fruit or persimmon. An innocent remark made to someone in passing about how much I like kaki means that I am now the sole recipient of all the kaki that grows within a radius of one kilometre from our house. And so, as I cast my eye over the bags of grapes that Carmen had just placed in front of me, I knew that this was the precursor to an annual delivery. I could have said something to stop the avalanche of fruit that I continue to receive every autumn, but I didn't want to appear ungrateful. And deep within me, I was very grateful.

FOURTEEN
THE CURSE OF PERSEPHONE

I t was the second week of September when I found myself in the middle of the field, digging a hole big enough to fit a small coffin or a dead pet. Or rather, I was *trying* to dig a hole, but since the soil was rock hard after months of no rain, I was barely scratching the surface. Any local who might drive by would see that whatever I was aiming to do was clearly part of some amateur hour. First of all, it was past noon, and the sun was high above my head. No one in their right mind would venture out with a spade during the hottest part of the day. This type of work should be done first thing in the morning.

It was also noticeable that I hadn't prepared properly for the job, as I was digging in flip-flops, wearing shorts and a sleeveless T-shirt. Perhaps I was a holidaymaker who had been kidnapped from the Costa del Sol and told to dig her own grave. The pained expression would have confirmed this assumption. In the few days that we had to plan for my time alone at the house *sans* transport, Robert and I had focused on buying adequate food supplies and drinking water. But I had forgotten to plan how to get rid of the domestic waste. Keith would take me shopping once a week, but I didn't want to put my stinking rubbish bags in his car — it would have put a strain on our friendship. I briefly considered hiking to the municipal bins, but since they were about four kilometres, or two and a half miles, away from the house, I quickly abandoned this idea.

The heat was quickly making me angrier and angrier about the whole job. But I could not delay it any longer. I had two garbage bags full of domestic garbage that was almost a week old now and was stinking up the area around the house, including the patio where I liked to spend most of my day. At first, I thought of burning the rubbish, but there was a ban on open fires during the summer. The only solution was to bury it. As I continued digging, I imagined myself as a modern-day hermit.

I have always found the life of the recluse strangely appealing. Being brought up Catholic, I loved hearing stories of religious hermits, people who had decided to abandon society, take a vow of silence, and reside in some obscure location. David the Dendrite spent three years of his life in an almond tree. I looked up from my shallow grave at the almond trees at the top of the driveway and shook my head. It was not his particular lifestyle that I questioned but rather his choice of dwelling.

Most almond trees are puny and relatively small in size. The branches are thin, and the main trunk is often only as thick as a human leg. Were a grown man to abide within the branches of an almond tree, he would look comically oversized. Moreover, the almond tree does not lend itself to climbing to any great height. Their arms are usually twisted, and most of the foliage sprouts off thin vertical shoots. I mused while hacking away at the hard surface.

Were I to abandon society and take up residence in a tree, then I would definitely choose an old Iberian oak tree. They have thick and sturdy boughs, which often spread horizontally to allow space for one to recline. But perhaps Dave the Dendrite did not seek after life's comforts. Maybe he chose the almond tree for maximum ridicule and discomfort? Living in Greece, he could have moved into an olive tree which would have given him shade and some shelter throughout the year. Olive branches are thicker than those of the almond trees, and the way they are pruned allows for some room for one to adopt a variety of postures.

In early spring, David the Dendrite would be surrounded by beautiful almond blossoms. In autumn, he could satiate his hunger with as many delicious nuts as he wanted — he might even store some for the winter. But in the winter? Well, I dare suggest that on particularly cold and rainy winter days, he climbed down from the almond tree and hid under a rock. How would anyone know? Did his followers leave their warm and cosy spots by the fireplace and walk out onto the raging storm to check if their local hermit was still sitting in his almond tree?

As I considered the practicalities of the hermit lifestyle, I had to admire the hermit's perseverance in staying in one place for long stretches of time. The idea of not having to talk to anyone was very appealing too. Whilst I could not picture myself living in a tree, I could imagine living in a remote spot in the Northwest Territories of Canada or somewhere in Siberia. An odd journalist would appear on my doorstep once every five years to report on this freak of nature whose nearest neighbour was a day's drive away and who spent her time sharpening knives and polishing homemade skis.

I recalled a woman who I had seen in a TV documentary. She was living in the middle of nowhere in one of the coldest parts of Canada. She looked sixty, but she might have been only thirty; hard work and years of discomfort tend to weather one's face. With her long grey hair tied up into a thin and greasy ponytail, a sun-burnt face covered in deep ruts, and skinny arthritic fingers holding on to a shotgun, she was filmed leaning over the wooden fence outside her log cabin as she elaborated on her life's principles. It was discernible that the woman hadn't spoken to another human being in months.

She was so starved of talk that what came out of her mouth were the ramblings of a maniac. Her timeframes and points of reference were confusing; it wasn't clear whether she was trying to engage the cameraman in conversation or was going to shoot him for trespassing. The producer asked her if she ever felt bored being on her own, and she went off listing the things that needed to be done around her cottage from dawn to dusk in order to stay clean, fed, warm, and safe from wild animals; there were things that needed doing before heavy rains, heavy winds, or snow. The list was long and laborious. The woman was an embodiment of self-reliance but seemed to lack any social awareness.

It is easy to disparage and ridicule the hermit lifestyle, but I was also somewhat jealous of it. I felt nostalgic for its simplicity, a life without clutter and social baggage; life stripped down to its bare essentials. And while my situation was nowhere near as dire or desolate as hers, I felt some affinity with the crazy Canadian woman. I stopped digging for a minute and leaned against the spade to survey *my* empire of dirt.

The Canadian recluse had endless pine, cedar, and oak forest, mountains, and lakes to gaze upon. I had a sea of olive and almond trees, rabbits running across the road every few minutes, and foxes crying and wailing their mating calls on hot summer nights. To top it off, I had a small white dog who would bark each night from the comfort and safety of his sofa in his brave efforts to warn me of the presence of the foxes.

What did the Canadienne do with her rubbish? I wished I had paid more attention to the programme.

I giggled to myself and went to the house to grab the rubbish that I wanted to bury. Once the rubbish had been dealt with, I washed my hands and face and sat down with a glass of water to cool off. I was going to reflect more on this new lifestyle of mine when I noticed that there were several messages on my phone.

We're a couple travelling on a motorbike. We really love your house. Can we check in this evening? Susanne and Jonathan.

The first message was followed by four more, each with an increasing tone of desperation. I realised that I had forgotten to block all the calendars to prevent any online bookings while Robert was away. Because I was not confident that I'd be able to bring in the necessary water and food supplies for the guests, I had closed our listing on the two main booking sites. But this ingenious couple had somehow discovered that our listing was still open for bookings on one of the fringe websites I had long forgotten we had registered with. I weighed my options and decided to honour their request.

I checked the clock. It was almost two p.m. The apartment had to be cleaned, and the sheets had to be ironed. I also needed time to tidy up around the pool, but I felt I could do it all in time.

Yes, your apartment will be ready after 7, if that's OK. I'll send you the directions soon.

I sent them written directions to the house and went to work. As I was ironing sheets at the speed of light and going over the to-do checklists in my head, I remembered that I had invited Keith and his workaways that afternoon for tapas and drinks. I cursed under my breath since I did not take this into account when I agreed to host paying guests.

Workaway is one of those organisations that, on paper, looks like a good idea. Its aim is to connect people who need help with light housework, such as gardening, babysitting, pet sitting, cleaning, painting, cooking and so on, with people who are willing to do these things for temporary accommodation and some food. The only difference between the Workaway system and legitimised slavery is that 'workaways' — the individuals who take on these assignments — put themselves in oppressive circumstances by choice. But the reality is that many workaways are very vulnerable. They have neither the money nor the transport which is needed to run away if the job that they signed up for turns out to be Herculean labour. At least, these were the stories I had heard from numerous workaways who stayed with Keith.

From their tales, I got the impression that most hosts were in the business of luring innocent souls with a photo of a pretty rose garden that needed light weeding to then confront them with a landscaping project which required carrying Stonehenge boulders across the property. Keith was a serial workaway host. But unlike those hosts who treated their workaways like medieval serfs, Keith focused on the cultural exchange. He was probably the only host in the world who had read the Workaway webpage very carefully because, hidden deep in the Workaway rules and regulations, he found a note that stipulated that the host should provide a meaningful cultural experience for the guest workers. And so, focus on the cultural interchange he did. As a result, his workaways did light housework, like pulling out wild agaves, pruning oleander bushes, or painting random walls around his cottage. While his workaways spent time pottering around the house and garden, Keith busied himself devising plans for their cultural enrichment. UNESCO would have been proud of Keith's day trips.

In their free time, Keith's workaways were driven up and down across Andalusia from Sevilla to Cordoba, Granada to Jaén, exploring world heritage sites, ancient theatres, Moorish mosques, gothic cathedrals, and Renaissance palaces. They could be spotted eating churros with hot chocolate on the top of Sierra Nevada one day and grilling sardines on a Marbella beach the next. No expense was spared, and no trip was too long or too time-consuming. I suspected that the reason Keith spent so much time with these complete strangers was his loneliness.

Keith and Delia had moved to Spain to escape the haunting memories of their son's death. Freddie's cold body was discovered in his council flat in London. He died of a heroin overdose just before his twenty-fifth birthday. Shortly after, Keith and Delia left the UK and spent a year living in a caravan in different expat communities on the coast before they decided to settle inland away from the crowds. They had sold everything that they owned in the UK and moved to Spain to start a new life in the sun.

In hindsight, I feel that their relocation was Delia's idea. In response to the family tragedy, she had transformed her life. She became a raw vegan and engaged in a regime of yoga that would have made any Indian ashram proud. In fact, it was her intention to start a yoga retreat in the charming rural cottage that they had purchased.

While Keith supported his inconsolable wife on this journey of reinvention and self-discovery, he ended up spending most of his retirement alone, in the middle of nowhere, with no one to talk to and no money to move his own life plans forward.

The reason for his solitude was that soon after the honeymoon period of moving to sunny Andalusia was over, Keith and Delia realised that they did not have enough money to start a yoga retreat business. Delia, in the act of selfless sacrifice, offered to drive up and down to the UK to do odd consultancy jobs to keep their finances afloat. But, as the years went on, her trips became longer and more frequent. Most of the time, she sojourned in London in her daughter's tiny apartment. One might think, unkindly, but not unfoundedly, that Delia preferred the bustling of the capital city to the cold mountain air of Al-Ándalus. Keith would spend his time looking for workaways to come and keep him company under the guise of doing odd jobs and preparing the yoga retreat to open.

Anyone who has ever worked for free or in exchange for food and shelter, as is the case with workaways, will attest that such arrangement breeds nothing but contempt towards the host. Were I to engage myself as a free labourer, I'd have the worst attitude.

'I suppose you couldn't have swept up these leaves scattered all over your patio *yourself*? You had to invite *me* all the way to Spain to pick them up for you,' I imagined myself huffing and puffing in the Andalusian sun.

'Oh, how difficult it would have been for YOU to remove these weeds. You just could not do it yourself!' I would give my host a dirty look behind his back.

That would have been me. But most of Keith's workaways seemed amicable and happy-go-lucky. I would often invite him and his workaways over to my place to give him some respite from having to continually entertain them.

As soon as the apartment and the pool were ready for my motorbiking guests, I set up some tapas on the patio table with some wine, water, bread, and our own olive oil. As soon as I placed the wine glasses for everyone, Keith and his workaways, Jodie and Kent, drove up to the house. We sat down and chatted about their adventures. They were a couple of teachers in their late twenties who had decided to take time off their jobs and travel the world using the Workaway scheme. They used the air miles accumulated on their credit cards to travel from one country to another. Career workaways like Jodie and Kent are often an excellent addition to any social gathering. They always have stories to tell about the ghastly places where they had been accommodated and the weird hosts that they had worked for.

This time was no different. Jodie regaled us with a particularly gruesome story of a recent experience. She and Kent had been given a room in a dilapidated cottage in the Alpujarra mountains. The room had wallpaper peeling off the walls and live electric cables sticking out of holes where electric sockets were once installed. At night, she could hear packs of wolves howling in the distance. The menacing sound seemed closer and closer to the cottage as the hours passed slowly at night.

During the day, she and Kent were supposed to renovate an old swimming pool with nothing at their disposal but a few sponges, a hammer, and a broken screwdriver. Because their progress was slow, the host kept on threatening not to provide them with any more food. It was thus a blessing when Jodie saw Keith's workaway post asking for help around the house. Jodie and Kent kept their plans secret from their exploitative host, and on their day off, they packed their bags and disappeared on a municipal bus leaving the outraged slave master far behind.

I could sense the feeling of relief in her voice as she praised Keith's hospitality. Keith's accommodation was first class. In their never-ending efforts to start a yoga retreat, he and Delia had renovated three bedrooms adjacent to their living room. The rooms were equipped with brand-new Ikea furniture and had *en suite* bathrooms. If you are not British, you may find it difficult to understand the Brits' devotion to this Scandinavian brand. It trumps political allegiances, religious belonging, and ethnic backgrounds. To paraphrase Karl Marx: " IKEA is the opium of the Brits".

Even the nature-loving and tree-hugging Delia couldn't resist the allure of IKEA. Whenever she came back for a brief visit 'home', the following day, she and Keith would be off to Malaga to that dreadful warehouse-of-a-shop. On their return, their medium-sized sedan would be filled to the brim with brown boxes: chests of drawers, shelves, kitchen cabinets, night tables, candlestick holders, salad bowls, lanterns, and cushions. Their pilgrimages to IKEA were always an expedition, with roof racks attached to the car and a pile of yellow-and-blue shopping bags resting on the back seat of their right-hand-drive Rover.

We asked them once if we could join them on one of their IKEA expeditions — for a simple day out — but our suggestion was met with stony silence. I reckon the trips must have been a private ritual where Keith was allowed to eat meatballs, and Delia filled the void in her life with things that promised a fresh start; a tidy and organised home where there was a place for everything and everything in its place. It must have been the aspirational furniture displays of snug living room sofas, bookcases filled with knick-knacks, and decorative curtains in the windows that drew them into the shop. They promised an instant home — a home that Keith and Delia had lost without warning.

The power of products and brands is that they fill your heart and soul with warmth and happiness for a short while. They fill the emptiness for a minute. Once Delia and Keith brought the flat-packed boxes to their new house, the feeling of displacement and powerlessness would come creeping back. They'd leave the furniture that they had bought unpacked for future workaways to assemble. Feeling restless, Delia would go online and book herself more jobs in the UK. A few more days would pass, and she'd be saying her goodbyes.

'I'm sorry we didn't get to meet this time. Hope I can stay longer next time. Send my best to Robert,' she'd send me a message an hour or so before setting off on her long drive across Spain and France. She never stayed for more than a couple of weeks in her Spanish house. Most of her time was spent alone in the car somewhere between Spain and the UK, forever going back and forth searching for a home — a modern-day Persephone trapped between the Underworld and Arcadia.

As Jodie was informing me how nice Keith's bedrooms were and what a convivial host he was, I heard a motorbike in the distance. Since hardly any vehicles passed on the road outside our house, I knew these were my guests. I tied Bobby up to the table so that he would not chase the bike, excused myself, and went to the top of the driveway to welcome my American guests.

FIFTEEN

HOLIDAY BRAIN

J onathan and Susanne arrived in style on a brand-new Ducati touring motorbike, wearing expensive helmets, jackets, gloves, and boots. The wife hopped off the bike and removed her helmet. As soon as she opened her mouth, I knew that she was from California. It's not only the accent, which is soft and easy on the ear, combined with a sporty physique, but also the general demeanour of Californians that makes them very easy to spot abroad. The woman oozed confidence and familiarity. She started right off without any perfunctory introduction. She greeted me as if we were good friends and began to talk as if we had been in conversation for the last hour or so.

'Oh my God! It was so hot! The highway was the worst. From Valencia to Granada, we hardly ever stopped. The road from Granada was terrible too, then we got lost. We were at the *tanatorio* in Montefrio — do you know it? — but then I told Jonathan that it can't be your place, and so we asked in a restaurant, but they didn't know where you live,' she chattered away without a break while stripping off her motorcycle gear.

'Oh, hi there!' she waved at Keith and co. as she sat down at the table and grabbed a glass of water. As she made herself at home, Jonathan joined us. I offered him a drink since he seemed to be shattered. They were both in their late fifties, both a picture-perfect stereotype of the jet-set Californian with well-defined muscles, little or no fat on them, faces gently kissed by the sun but not burnt, golden hair, and piercing blue eyes. However, it was clear from their dazed expressions and vacuous smiles that sitting on a Ducati Multistrada for hours on end had taken its toll on them.

They must have been exhausted from holding on for dear life for hours all the way from Valencia because they didn't even ask to see their accommodation. Like sailors disembarking after weeks at sea, they extricated themselves from the Ducati with wobbly legs and blessed the solid ground underneath their feet. On seeing the patio, they immediately plonked themselves down, and holding a glass of wine in one hand and eating olives with the other, they told us all about their adventures.

An hour or so later, they were ready to check in. After taking their luggage to the apartment and making themselves at home, they remerged in civilian clothes — gone were the leather trousers and boots. Fashionably clad in jeans and T-shirts, they were ready to look for a pizza in Montefrio. Now that their personal belongings were safe in the apartment, there was space on their bike to purchase some groceries for their stay. I gave them some simple instructions on where to shop and told them to ask the shopkeeper about a pizzeria. The thought of buying a takeaway pizza in Montefrio had never occurred to me personally, but one never knew. So off they went in search of a pizza takeaway.

The thing about Montefrio and the area where we live is that, at the time, there were no fast-food takeaways. The concept of buying hot food to take home in order to eat alone in front of a TV was still quite alien. And why would anyone eat alone if they could sit in a lively restaurant in a park or in the middle of a town square? For less than ten euros, you could have a three-course meal, called *menú del día*. In Spain, going out to eat at a restaurant does not require a special occasion. At lunchtime, you find most restaurants filled to capacity with working men and women enjoying their main meal of the day. This is in stark contrast to many northern European cities where, at lunchtime, office workers buy an overpriced cup of coffee and a dry sandwich and sit in front of their laptops staring at YouTube or other social media.

While the Americans were out exploring, I said goodbye to Keith and his workaways and went inside. It had been a very long day. I was ready to go to bed when I heard the sound of the water pump humming behind the house. I looked at the kitchen sink, but the tap was off. I checked the bathrooms, but there were no apparent leaks. I peeked outside, but the Ducati was not there, which meant the guests were still searching for their elusive takeout. To eliminate all the possible culprits, I first checked the uninhabited apartment but did not find any burst pipes or leaks anywhere. What was left was to inspect the bathroom where the Americans were staying. I hated to do it, as I worried that I may come across as a snoopy landlady. But water is precious, and I could not listen to it being chucked away.

I grabbed the spare key to the guest accommodation and went upstairs to their terrace to open the sliding door. Of course, as luck would have it, just as I was about to insert the key into the lock, I heard the unmistakable sound of the V-twin Ducati. I briefly weighed my choices: I could run downstairs like lightning in the hope that they had not seen me trying to enter their room, or I could stay where I was and wait for them. Even though the latter option was awkward for me, I felt it was a safer and saner choice. So, I waited for them outside their apartment. I felt like a Victorian schoolmistress waiting for naughty kids to show up so that I could tell them off.

They noticed me as soon as they started to climb the stairs. In a manner that I was getting used to, Susanne began to talk as if we were already in the middle of a conversation.

'There are so many people on the street at night. It's very noisy. We had a good table at the pizzeria, so we ate there. The waitress didn't speak any English, but we managed with my high-school Spanish. They really speak so fast here,' Susanne would have happily continued her monologue. Still, as Jonathan started to unlock their door, I felt it necessary to explain my presence outside it.

'Sorry to bother you,' I apologised. 'I was about to check on your bathroom. Could you do me a favour and see if there's any water leaking there. It's that the water pump is running, and I don't know why.'

'No problem,' Jonathan went inside and came back a few seconds later, looking abashed. 'I'm so sorry. We left the faucet on. It's my fault. I washed my hands before we left, and I must have left it on. At home, our faucet turns itself off automatically. I didn't notice that the water was running. It's all fixed now.'

My heart sank. I was wondering how much water had been wasted when ever-so-helpful Susanne interjected.

'You know what you should do,' her voice was slowly beginning to grate on me now, but I smiled and encouraged her to continue. 'You should put a sign in the bathroom, next to the faucet. Like 'Please make sure to turn off the faucet!', or something like that, so it doesn't happen again.'

'That's a great idea,' I thanked her for her insight. I bid them goodnight and marched off to check the water tank behind the house. As soon as I turned the corner where they couldn't see me, I started to fume.

Yeah, sure, lady, I thought to myself on my way to the water tank. *I'm going to put a sign next to everything that guests use.*

As any hotelier will attest, most holidaymakers lose their ability to do basic things without causing self-harm, damage, or injury. My fellow hotelier, Emma, calls it *holiday brain*. Because of holiday brain syndrome, I would have to put signs everywhere in the guest accommodation.

Patrons would be welcomed at the door with a sign telling them how to open and close the said door. I might also add a note on how to use a key and next to it stick a sign on the glass door:

'Please don't lean against the glass door as it may fall down and kill you. Have a nice day.'

Once the guests have managed to enter their accommodation without maiming themselves, they'd need a few signs in the living room and the bedroom primarily for their own health and safety: 'don't touch the fireplace when the fire is burning', 'don't start electric fires', and 'don't use your own air-conditioning units'.

The kitchen would need to be wholly plastered in passive-aggressive notes and 'friendly reminders':

'Please refrain from frying pizza in the frying pan. Burnt cheese is impossible to clean, and we'll have to throw away the frying pan. Have a great day!'

'If you'd be so kind as not to put hot pots and pans directly onto the wooden surface of our kitchen counter, that would be great. Enjoy your stay!'

'To avoid the smell of burnt plastic, don't turn on the kettle if there is no water inside it. BTW please don't put tea bags directly into the water kettle. Have a fantastic stay!'

'If you wouldn't mind, please don't use the wooden countertop to cut, chop or slice your food. There are at least three cutting boards in your kitchen. Don't hesitate to let us know if you need more.'

These were just some issues that bothered me as they usually required costly repairs or replacements. Other issues, like using cushions to conceal chocolate stains on the sofa, rearranging armchairs to cover up a coffee spill on the carpet, stashing broken glassware under a cupboard, and covering the whole place in sunflower seed shells were part and parcel of the holiday rental business. They were also the main topic of conversation whenever we met Emma and Stefan. Like a group of professional poker players, we'd sit down, get drinks and keep our cards close to the chest until it was our turn to reveal them.

'That's terrible,' I'd summarise Emma's story of a sofa bed that failed in its impromptu role as a trampoline for a pair of adolescent guests. I would then start on my own tale of abuse and destruction.

'Do you know the spare blankets in the bedroom? For the winter? So, this girl took the expensive fluffy white blanket from the wardrobe and put it on the ground by the pool to lie on,' I would vent indignantly while Emma and Stefan would nod as if they were all too familiar with this situation.

'Well, you think that's bad,' Stefan would interject. 'One French woman had her children draw with crayons on the walls inside the house.'

'What!' I was livid.

'Yes. I went to check the apartment after they had left, and there were dozens of colourful drawings on the white wall in the living room. I contacted her, and she admitted that her children had drawn on the wall. She paid for the paint.'

We were all mortified at the behaviour.

'That's nothing,' Stefan would continue. 'Last year, we had to replace a set of doors because a guest punched holes in them. First, he denied doing it and claimed there were holes in the door when he checked in, but eventually, he paid for it.'

We could spend hours drinking cava and venting our frustrations. The best stories soon became canon and were often reiterated several times over, which allowed us to vent our frustrations. But that's precisely where such therapeutic tales belong — as private points of conversation between hoteliers. Posting a warning sign each time you are wronged by a customer would only lead to madness.

'Yeah, I'm gonna put up a sign,' I was mumbling sarcastically to myself in my fake Yankee accent as I opened the lid of the water tank.

It was already dark outside, so I brought my mobile phone to use as a torch. I shone the light inside the tank and saw that there were maybe five hundred litres of water left in the three-thousand-litre tank. It would be enough for tonight, but it wouldn't last until the end of their stay. I closed the lid, switched off the torch on my phone, and went back inside. I didn't sleep that night. I tossed and turned, trying to figure out how to get more water into the tank without driving the 4x4 with the trailer. I hoped a solution would present itself if I stopped worrying about it.

SIXTEEN

THE SHERRIFF OF BERRUGUILLA

S ince I couldn't sleep, I got up early and took Bobby for a walk. As we walked past Rafa's house, I saw him working on one of his mystery projects outside. I called them 'mystery projects' because I had never seen the end results of his tinkering. The outbuildings were filled with tools, machines, and half-finished projects that occupied his retirement years. Rafa was both a retired electrician and a retired farmer. It's common for olive farmers in our area to have two jobs. Some have small businesses or shops in the village; others work as builders, carpenters, plumbers, or electricians. They put these jobs on hold during the olive season or have family members tend to the shop while they work on the olive trees. Those who can't be substituted by family members, like teachers, vets, and accountants, hire seasonal labourers to work their land.

Rafa was now retired from picking olives, so his younger relatives tended to his trees. He, in turn, spent his days making improvements to his cottage, refurbishing an old barn, and even installing a modern bathroom and kitchen in his house. Some of these renovations might have been triggered by watching our house reform that lasted over a year. Since he was a frequent observer on our building site, it must have whetted his appetite for construction. He would often stop by to ask Robert to use one of his carpentry saws to cut bits of scrap wood into the desired shape or to borrow a nail gun to build a little shelf. Once he came by and asked if we could lend him a roller to paint the new kitchen. It was just before lunchtime, so the village shops were closing.

Curious about what Rafa and Loli were up to, Robert grabbed an assortment of rollers from our garage and followed Rafa to his cottage. He came back two hours later.

'What happened?' I was keen to find out what he had been doing there for so long.

'I painted their ceilings,' Robert answered nonchalantly while washing his hands covered in spots of white paint.

'Why were *you* painting *their* ceilings?'

'Because Loli was getting on and off a chair with a tiny roller. It would have taken her days to paint the ceiling.'

If there was one thing that I knew infuriated my husband a lot, it was people using tiny tools to do a big job. In the past, I've seen him get agitated at the sight of a friend chopping carrots with a small paring knife. So, I could only imagine his frustration when he saw petite Loli jumping on and off a chair to paint a fraction of the kitchen ceiling at a time.

'She could have broken her leg on that wobbly chair,' he explained his reason for taking over from her.

'I hope you were polite?' I checked as I knew he had a tendency to be quite short when he was in his 'helpful' mood.

'Yes, of course,' he sounded indignant at the suggestion. 'I had a bigger roller than hers, so I showed her how quickly I could do it. The ceiling there is so low, I didn't need a chair or a ladder.'

I was all ears, vetting this interaction.

'She was very pleased,' he continued. 'I did the kitchen, and they did the bathroom — they're putting new tiles there next week, so they wanted to paint the ceilings before they put in the tiles. Then I had a small glass of brandy with Rafa. Or maybe two.'

I was confident that having a six-foot-four *robotnik* paint one's ceilings must have put Rafa and Loli in a good mood, and so I let Robert off the hook.

It was now a year later. Even though it was still before breakfast, Rafa had an assortment of bits and pieces set up on a wooden bench by the tractor. As it often happens to many of us in old age, Rafa was loath to throw anything away that might one day become handy for one of his projects. As a result of his hoarder's mentality, scattered around the house, one can find a hotchpotch of things that should have been discarded long ago: old aluminium window frames, an odd bathtub, a pile of old ceramic tiles, old lampshades, a broken chair or two, some metal bedframes, and bits and pieces of asbestos roof covering. Many of these items came from our own reform project, and I felt guilty towards Loli for us allowing Rafa to take these scraps whenever he visited our construction site.

'¡*Hola*!' Rafa shouted when he noticed me on the road and gestured to summon me over.

I was bombarded with questions. 'It's very hot! How are you doing? When is Robert coming back? Does the dog miss him?'

'I'm fine, thank you. I have some American guests from California.'

'How nice!'

'I need some help with water,' I cut to the chase. 'Could you drive our car with the trailer from Jaime's water tank to our house? I'm not good at driving with a trailer.'

That was an understatement of the year. Thus far, I had driven with the trailer twice in my life. And that was on a flat asphalt road. I never had to reverse it up a hill or transport a one-thousand-litre water tank on it. I was sure that I'd damage the car and the trailer if I attempted to drive it up and down the hills around our house.

'Yes, of course. I'll come at four o'clock.'

The sense of relief was overwhelming. I went home, skipping all the way to my gate.

You can't buy this type of neighbour, I thought to myself. Rafa didn't make me feel like I was imposing or inconveniencing him. In fact, he made it sound like I was doing him a big favour with my request.

It wasn't the first time that Rafa had come through with his kindness and generosity and saved the day. Two years earlier, when we moved in and started our renovations, he insisted that we buy a trailer and a portable water tank. We trusted his advice and did as we were told. In hindsight, that trailer has been one of the best purchases we made after moving to Spain and has saved us a lot of money. Soon after we got it, we used it to bring water to the construction site and to bring building materials to the house.

The trailer had also become indispensable for collecting firewood from our neighbours' fields after the olive trees had been pruned. Because many of the landowners around us prefer life in a cosy apartment in Montefrio, Priego, or Alcalá to the cold, stone cottages that their ancestors inhabited, they don't need much firewood for the winter. Every spring, as soon as the trees are pruned, they ask us if we want to collect the thick branches from the fields. It's a win-win arrangement, they get rid of the unwanted wood, and we get free firewood. Not every farmer will allow others to collect firewood for free. Some store it over the summer and sell it in November in anticipation of the freezing winter months.

As I contemplated how wonderful my neighbours were, I looked at my house with renewed optimism. It was good to feel that I was not alone and that there was someone a few hundred metres down the road who was willing to help. I took a deep breath and was about to walk up the driveway home when I saw Bobby running towards me with an unidentified object in his mouth. As he approached me, I realised in horror that he had dug up all the rubbish that I had so sloppily buried the day before and was now scattering it all around the field.

'That will be a nice surprise for the guests. Thanks, Bob,' my sarcasm was lost on him as he was busy re-burying the more precious pieces of trash.

Being of the terrier family, his canine nature is to search for things hidden underground and to dig them out from narrow crevices. He couldn't believe his luck. He buried the aluminium foil that he had dug up a few minutes earlier and went back to the rubbish pit to continue his labour. With his terrier genes activated, he was not going to stop until everything was dug up and re-buried in various secret locations. To his great disappointment, I put his lead on and dragged him home. Once Bobby was locked inside, I went to the garage to get the shovel.

I was about to return to the garden when I heard Susanne's cheerful voice on the terrace behind me. She was standing by the wooden balustrade with a cup of coffee in hand, admiring the views. We exchanged pleasantries, and I asked her if she had slept well and whether she needed anything in her apartment. I hoped that this would end the chitchat, but she was eager to get involved in my life and started a barrage of questions about the house, the area, and the olive trees. It went on and on, but as a courteous host, it wasn't for me to end the conversation.

'Are you working in your garden? Do you need help?' she pointed at my shovel.

'Oh, no. I'm fine,' I assured her in horror. All I needed was for her to go down to the field and see how all my household rubbish had been spread all over the place by Bobby. That would make for an interesting review.

'We'll stay by the pool today and relax,' she informed me.

'That's awesome,' I assured her. 'Have a great day!'

If she were Dutch or English, simpler adjectives, like 'nice' or 'good', would have sufficed, but being American, I was sure that she would not settle for anything less than 'awesome' or 'great'.

I went back to the field and dug a proper hole. I collected the rubbish that Bobby had so carefully hidden around and about and re-buried it. As a precaution, I put some good-sized rocks on top of the 'grave' to prevent Bobby from digging it up again.

After siesta, Rafa arrived, and I went with him as a passenger to collect the water for the tank. When we arrived at Jaime's tank, I connected the pipe and opened the tap. Once the cube was filled, Rafa drove it up the hill behind our house to fill our water tank. Robert and I had a regular gardening hose positioned there, and instead of a water pump, for which we had no money, we used gravity to move the water from the trailer on the hill to the house tank below. I explained to Rafa that it would take about fifty minutes to empty the cube.

'That's fine,' he said. 'Will you need another cube?'

'Yes, please.'

We sat down under an olive tree, expecting a long wait.

'Have you been to other parts of Spain?' he asked. This was a reasonably manageable topic of conversation in a foreign language, but still, I needed a second to gather my thoughts.

'We visited Madrid. It's very beautiful. Very big. The parks are very beautiful. I love the Prado Museum,' I elaborated in my low-intermediate Spanish, using the wrong past tenses and over-enunciating my words while he listened carefully. 'We went to Torremolinos. I like the sea and the beach.' I didn't mention Granada or Cordoba, as these two cities are very close to where we live, and it was implied that we had already been there.

'If you like the sea, you must go to Almeria,' he interjected. 'The sea there is very warm even in October. The beach is very beautiful too, and there aren't many tourists in September.'

'That's a good idea,' I said to keep my free Spanish lesson going. 'Last year, we visited Calahonda in the middle of September. The prices are low, and there are not many people in the hotel or on the beach.'

I could see from his expressions that he did not know where Calahonda was — in all fairness, it is a nondescript fishing village near Motril, which we chose to visit the year before because of a special end-of-summer hotel deal.

'It's a small fishing village,' I explained.

'Have you been to Mini Hollywood?'

'Hollywood? No, but our guests are from California.'

'No,' his puzzled expression told me that we were not on the same page. He reached for this wallet and took out a photo. In the picture, dressed in a sheriff's costume and pointing a pistol at the camera, was Rafa. He showed me another picture of his wife, Loli, dressed as an Indian chief, and another one of a posse of cowboys shooting at each other in the middle of a Western town.

'Where is this?' I asked.

'It's in Almeria,' Rafa took the photos from me and put them away in his wallet. 'They filmed a lot of Westerns there.'

As we waited for the water to drain from the tank on the trailer, Rafa told me about the Westerns and the theme park, but I wasn't sure I understood it all very well. The photos and the stories piqued my interest, and later I read more about Mini Hollywood in English.

Indeed, some American filmmakers shot hundreds of Westerns in Almeria. Many actors and stuntmen were Spaniards and Italians, hence the term *Spaghetti Western*. Their dialogues were dubbed into English before the films were released in the movie theatres in the US. Once the popularity of Westerns started to wane, some of the film sets were purchased by the local actors and stuntmen, who then turned the film sets into tourist attractions or theme parks. I made a mental note to visit Mini Hollywood next time we had a little time and money to spare.

Rafa and I made two more trips together that September to fill the water tank. He lent me a hose with a larger diameter, which we connected from the cube to the house tank. It shortened the time it took to transfer the water significantly. Two weeks later, Robert returned, and we set the wheels in motion to build a tank to store our well water, which was abundant in the spring, to use in the summer.

SEVENTEEN
A LITTLE HELP FROM DOWN UNDER

I t took Robert two weeks to finalise the specifications for our water tank and get a quote.

'A hundred thousand litres — that should be enough for the whole summer,' Robert estimated our water consumption during the dry months. 'I did about twenty trips just last August.'

Robert was sitting on the patio with a drawing and a calculator in hand.

'We could make the tank taller,' he proposed after some more calculations. 'If we make it one metre taller, we will get about a hundred and forty thousand litres.'

'Yes, but the tank will be sticking out behind the house. It will look ugly,' I argued for the aesthetics over practicality. 'Also, how are we going to put it together if it's five metres high?'

I brought forth Robert's fear of heights and my deep dislike for working on tall scaffolding — an aversion developed after the first year of renovating the house when we spent many unhappy hours on top of the roof. We settled on four metres, or thirteen feet, a height which sounded challenging enough.

We asked Jaime to place the final order on our behalf to ensure there were no misunderstandings about what we wanted and needed. The tank was custom-made from galvanised steel sheets by the same local company that Jaime had used for his water tank. While we waited for the tank's sheets to be pressed, we found space behind the house where we would place the tank. This meant levelling the area set for the foundation, putting in steel reinforcements, and pouring thirty centimetres, or twelve inches, of concrete. Because the excavator or the cement truck couldn't access the area where we wanted to build the platform from the front of the house, I had to call our neighbour's son Pepe and ask his permission to drive the excavator and the truck across his wheat field to access the back of our house.

'What did he say?' Robert asked me when I came back to the patio table from under the oak tree — the only spot around the house with reliable mobile network coverage.

'He said that we can do it before it rains,' I communicated Pepe's message to Robert. 'But not after the rains because it will compact the soil.'

'Ok,' Robert understood Pepe's concerns that driving across a wet field would create deep ruts that would remain when the clay dried. 'When is the next rain?'

I looked online at the weather forecast and noted that heavy rain was predicted for the following weekend. This meant that we had about eight days to finish the platform. That afternoon, Robert rushed to Montefrio to order the steel and book the cement trucks.

'Ángel will deliver the steel on Wednesday,' he reported on his return. 'He said he's swamped because everyone wants to complete their projects before the rain. And the cement trucks will be here on Friday afternoon.'

'But we have guests here until Saturday,' I wasn't sure how we were going to manage the construction of the foundation and provide hospitality.

'Well, it's the only time they can come. Friday afternoon or Monday, but we won't have the steel on Monday,' Robert explained.

It was not ideal, but building the foundation for the water tank was a priority to ensure our future water supply. And since we were planning to use the new water tank to collect the rainwater over the winter months, it all had to be done before the heavy rains came. Otherwise, we would miss the rainy season and would have to spend another summer driving up and down, bringing water to the house one cube at a time. Serendipitously, we were almost fully booked that October, which was great for our finances but terrible for any construction work.

'Most of the work is behind the house, so we should be OK,' I resigned myself to the proposition. 'Let's just keep it all quiet and tidy.'

As it often happens when juggling several things at once, it's impossible to plan everything, and all you can do is hope for the best. To level out the area for the foundation, Jaime agreed to come over with his faithful excavator. I knew it would not take him a long time, an hour or less, to prepare the ground, but I wasn't too excited about our Dutch guests having to look at a big yellow excavator parked outside their kitchen window. To make sure that they were spared the view of the excavator, I needed to get them out of the house for the morning. Unfortunately, it was the end of their long holiday in Spain, and they had already been to the Alhambra in Granada and the Mezquita in Córdoba. I informed them about a few other attractions, but they were familiar with those too. The only thing left was to send them on a bicycle trip around Montefrio.

It took me a couple of days to plant the idea of a bicycle ride in their minds, but it wasn't difficult. Most Dutch are avid cyclists and keen explorers, so the evening before the excavator was to arrive, Stefan dropped off their bikes and helmets at our house. I encouraged them to set off as early as possible to avoid cycling during the hottest time of the day but also to keep them unaware of the upcoming construction project that was to begin behind the house. I drew them a map of a route from our house to Montefrio and back and told them to call Stefan if they had any trouble getting back. Stefan had already told us that collecting exhausted bicyclists from the side of the road and bringing them home by car was the bread and butter of his bike rental business. I didn't expect to see my guests for several hours.

I was thus quite stunned when I saw them zigzagging between the olive trees behind our house just two hours later. Jaime was still busy digging the soil with his excavator and didn't need our immediate assistance, so I walked over to the fence where they'd stopped to look at the excavator in action.

'Oh! You're building another house,' the tall blond man asked with innocence in his blue eyes. They were both in their mid-twenties, and I had to forgive their naivety. Then again, it is possible that a six-by-six-metre foundation might be deemed spacious enough for a small house in Rotterdam.

I explained to them that we were building a foundation for a water tank — it all seemed to go over their heads, and they didn't have any more questions.

'So how come you've managed to cycle to Montefrio and back so quickly,' I changed the topic. 'You must be very fit.'

'Oh, no!' the blue-eyed girl with the body of an Olympic athlete explained. 'I saw the first hill, and we decided to cycle in the opposite direction. I hate hills. We went to Lojilla and found a restaurant.'

'*Gallope*?' I asked, even though it is the one and only restaurant outside the village of Lojilla.

'I think so,' the girl said. 'They didn't speak any English, but we had some coffee, and then we cycled back. If you don't mind, you can call Stefan to collect the bikes. We'll sit by the pool now.'

Even though it was October, it was almost thirty degrees Celsius, or eight-six Fahrenheit, outside. The water in the pool was about twenty degrees Celsius or sixty-eight Fahrenheit. These were perfect summer conditions for anyone used to spending summers by the Dutch North Sea coast. I wasn't surprised when I heard them jump into the pool with a big splash.

'I hope they don't mention this construction work in the review,' I said as I reported back to Robert.

Half an hour later, Jaime was done and drove away in his excavator at a snail's pace while we tidied up the area and installed some shuttering for the concrete that was to arrive the following Friday. By the end of the week, our young Dutch couple had left, and we were hosting an Australian couple on their grand tour of Europe — I was very excited about our Aussie guests.

It's difficult to explain my enthusiasm for hosting guests from Australia. It may be that for us, it's a completely unknown place and so distant that, in my mind's eye, I saw them disembarking a huge sailing vessel after weeks at sea; as if they were visitors from another planet or undercover ambassadors for their country and its culture. It's the appeal of the foreign and undiscovered that draws me in — I imagined myself sitting by the fire and listening to their tales.

Tell me more about this wonderful land, I pictured myself saying, as if they were modern explorers, and I was but a simple peasant whom they had encountered by chance.

At the time, the most exotic guests we had hosted was a pregnant couple from Israel. Like with the Australians, I was overenthusiastic in anticipation of their arrival. Being naturally nosy, ten minutes after they checked in, I found out that they both had ancestors from Cracow in Poland who had fled to Israel after the war. This established a secret bond, and I listened with bewilderment to their stories of growing up in Israel, serving in the Israeli army and their lives in Tel Aviv. One man's mundane is another's treasure.

I soon found out that the Israelis' sightseeing schedule was impossibly over-optimistic. On the same day that they'd landed in Malaga, they visited the Picasso Museum *and* went to Granada to explore the Alhambra before coming to stay with us for the night.

'What are you going to do tomorrow?' I inquired.

'Tomorrow we must see the Mezquita in Córdoba, then we go to Sevilla, and then we sleep in Cadiz,' short and skinny Shira, who was the driver and the planner, explained to me while her ballooning, pregnant spouse looked at me in horror. Miriam was six months pregnant, and her calves and ankles had tripled in size from the air travel and the hours spent in the car.

'That's not a good idea,' I gave Shira my honest opinion. 'It's impossible to find parking in Sevilla's old town. You'll have to walk for hours.'

'Perhaps we could visit Córdoba and then drive to Cadiz,' Miriam suggested to her wife.

The following day, they abandoned their ambitious sightseeing plans entirely and asked me whether they could stay by the pool until late afternoon, when they would drive directly to their hotel in Cádiz. I congratulated them on the idea, and they spent a quiet day by the pool, perhaps regretting that they had made impossible travel arrangements that could not be changed at the last minute.

Now that we were expecting our first guests from Down Under, I became overzealous again. I looked at their Airbnb profile and saw that they, too, were hosts.

'They're from the Kimberley,' I informed Robert in a nonchalant tone that implied that 'the Kimberley' was a place that I was exceedingly familiar with — it wasn't.

'Which part of Australia is that?'

'I have no idea,' I had to admit.

While many Australian cities and regions sound strangely familiar to me — most likely due to my hours of binge-watching season after season of *Australian MasterChef* — I would definitely make a fool of myself if I were placed in front of a map and asked to point out where they actually were located. Perth, Brisbane, Sydney, Melbourne, Alice Springs — I recognised all these names, but which one was in Victoria and which one was in Queensland or another territory was a complete mystery to me. I consoled myself that it's generally tricky to grasp the geography of a country one has never been to and decided to drop the subject.

Megan and Gill arrived in the early afternoon. It was still sunny and unseasonably hot. They complimented me on the beautiful views that they had taken in on their journey to our house. I thanked them; thus, smugly implying that I had a hand in the final design of the snowy caps of the Sierra Nevada and the endless olive groves. I soon found out that they were country-hopping from one European city to another. It was their life-long dream. So far, they'd visited London, Paris, and Barcelona and were heading to Lisbon after a stopover in

Andalusia. Once they told me about their travels, I decided to seize the moment and forewarned them about the cement trucks arriving the next day. I apologised and explained why we had to rush with the cement when Gill interrupted me.

'I'd love to help,' he said, but I wasn't sure if I understood him correctly. It must have been the cheerful singsong quality of the Aussie accent that made me doubt what I had heard him say.

Is he being sarcastic? I wondered. But his sincere expression did not show any evidence that he was. On seeing my confusion, he explained:

'I'm sick and tired of doing nothing every day. It's nice to see the castles and so on, but I'd like to do some physical work.'

This could not have been better news because we needed an extra pair of hands to help spread the concrete once it was poured from the trucks. I appraised his physique — he was in his late fifties, short, and brawny. His greying ponytail suggested a free spirit.

'That's wonderful. Thank you,' I told him. 'The cement trucks will be here tomorrow around five p.m.'

'Great!' he confirmed with enthusiasm. 'I'll need a pair of Wellingtons, though.'

'I'll find you a pair. No problem,' I assured him.

I wished him and his wife a great afternoon and bid them goodbye. When I told Robert that his Australian guest would help him and Jaime spread the concrete, he was delighted.

The next day, Gill was ready to work well before the trucks arrived. I gave him a pair of wellington boots and work gloves, and he and Robert went behind the house to inspect the job at hand. A few minutes later, Jaime arrived with a young man from Puerto Lopez who brought a machine to vibrate the cement. Soon, I heard the concrete trucks on the road.

I locked Bobby inside the house since he has a terrible habit of chasing cars. The two cats sat on the terrace and watched us run back and forth. Once the first concrete truck was behind the house, the driver set up a funnel to pour the cement onto the new foundation, and the work began. It took us about three hours of pouring, spreading, and vibrating the concrete mixture. As soon as the job was finished, I set up a table with some cold beers and tapas to thank Gill, Jaime, and the young man for helping us.

In his usual manic way, Jaime declined the offer of a cold beer and rushed off to do another project. Even though it was already past eight in the evening, I was sure he wanted to squeeze in a couple more hours of work into his day. On many a warm evening, we'd be sitting on the patio late at night enjoying wine and entertainment while our industrious neighbour would be on top of the hill clearing the rocks from underneath his wife's olive trees or doing some weeding. Knowing that he was not in the habit of stopping for just a second to take a well-deserved break, I did not take it personally when he declined my offer of cold beer and tapas and, instead, wandered off to his cottage. The young man from Puerto Lopez left too.

Gill, on the other hand, was thrilled to join us for a cold beer and a selection of *jamón* and cheese. He went to his apartment to shower and came back twenty minutes later. It seemed that the hard physical labour had rejuvenated him.

'I needed that,' he said as he took a swig at a cold Alhambra beer.

I assumed that he meant the cold beverage, but I was wrong.

'I was getting really tired of doing nothing,' he explained.

As it transpired during our evening conversation, Gill was, in fact, a professional concrete layer. He had spent many years working in the opal mines in Australia, where he was responsible for laying concrete. On hearing that, we bombarded him with questions about his life in Coober Pedy and the underground houses that can be found there. We spent a lovely evening — chatting about Australia and imagining life working in the opal mines. The sky was covered by the clouds, and there was no moonlight, so I set out dozens of lanterns with tealights which provided our little gathering with a lovely warm ambience. I kept on refilling the tapa dishes with goat and sheep cheese from Montefrio and my neighbour's homemade dry sausage. In return, our helper ate with gusto while entertaining us with stories from his homeland. Around midnight, he decided to go back to his apartment. As he was leaving, he said:

'I think this has been the best time I've had during this trip.'

I gave him a puzzled look.

'Doing some work, sitting down with locals, eating simple food. It's been perfect. Thank you.'

He and his wife left two days later and journeyed to Lisbon. Because it started to rain heavily and continued to rain throughout November, Robert couldn't build the water tank.

'Why don't we put off this job until my sister and Michal come for Christmas?' I suggested. 'In the meantime, we can renovate the old bedroom and turn it into a library, then we'll have a decent place to eat our Christmas dinner when they come here next month.'

Robert agreed, and we spent November and the first half of December building a library and a mudroom on the first floor of our cottage. The mudroom, or a small entrance for shoes and other winter clothing, would help keep the floors of our humble abode reasonably clean during the long winter months when kilograms of soil get dragged on the soles of our boots into the house whenever it rains.

EIGHTEEN
SAINT NICHOLAS COMES TO BERRUGUILLA

W hile we put the finishing touches on the new library-cum-dining room and the new mudroom, the one issue that I didn't know how to solve was the Christmas tree. As I scratched my head, wondering where to get a Christmas tree from, I remembered distinctly throwing the old artificial tree away before we moved to Spain. It was a small plastic affair that I got at the Carrefour supermarket in Al Ain at a time when Robert was at a nearby hospital with a broken leg. Had he been able to walk around freely and not attached to several IV tubes, he would have never agreed to the purchase of such an abomination as a plastic tree. I had to sneak behind his back because my mother was visiting us that Christmas in the Emirates, and it would have been difficult to explain to her why we did not have any Christmas ornaments.

If she were to see us via a video call, I might have lied and said that we were in a Muslim country and thus could not get our hands on any Christmas adornments. But since she was about to land in Dubai, she would see for herself that not many nations love Christmas festivities and decorations as much as the Gulf Arabs do. It's a perfect holiday for them — the extravaganza of excessive buying, giving, eating, and decorating. Never in my life had I seen such beautiful, tall, and luminous Christmas trees as I did in the United Arab Emirates.

'I won't need this again,' I remember saying to myself when I tossed the plastic tree into the bins outside our compound in Al Ain in June of 2014, a few weeks before the shipping container was scheduled to arrive.

But now, three years later, I deeply regretted that decision. My nephew, who was three years old, and my niece, who was two, were coming to spend their first Christmas with their auntie and uncle. I feared they might be awfully disappointed by the austere character of our celebrations. My sceptics' guide to religious holidays was going to fall on deaf ears. Auntie and uncle would appear joyless and somewhat Calvinist instead of 'cool' and 'enlightened'. I could see us etched in the kids' memory as a copy of *American Gothic* — my pale face devoid of any Christmas cheer and holding a muddy spade instead of tinsel and jingle bells. I didn't want us to be that couple, but I wasn't sure how to get hold of a Christmas tree in sunny Andalusia. For weeks before my family's arrival, I looked around for clues as to where Andalusians might get their Christmas trees from.

The only sign of forthcoming Christmas in the nearby villages was the small illuminated figures of Santa climbing up balconies and terraces. With a burlap sack over his shoulder and his thin doll-like arms holding the balustrade for dear life, it made him look like a robber, a rogue Santa, who was set on taking away your presents instead of delivering them. Besides the balconies that were adorned with the sneaky Santa who looked like he was trying to break into people's houses, the only other place that seemed to embrace the joy of

Christmas decorations was the Chinese shop in Alcalá. There, expats longing for a slice of home could obtain the prerequisite plastic tree with all the glittery trimmings and tinsel that the heart desired. I knew that I would never convince Robert to buy a plastic tree from China, so I looked at other options.

One alternative was presented to me by Blanca, our old Spanish teacher whom we met by chance at a Tuesday market in Alcalá.

'*Belén*,' she said. 'It's customary to have *belén* in your house for Christmas.'

As usual, when lost in translation, I pretended that I knew what she was talking about, but I was perplexed.

'What's *belén*?' I asked Robert as soon as Blanca moved off into the crowded market.

'Bethlehem?' he informed me. Once again, my husband's knowledge of rare and obscure Spanish words surprised me. The same person who wasn't sure how to spell his own address in Spanish knew the Spanish name for a small town in modern-day Palestine. Between us, we figured out that *belén* meant a nativity scene.

As it often is with language, once I had learned this word, I saw nativity scenes everywhere. They were in shop window displays, supermarkets, patios, and even inside the Chinese shop. Although I had not seen a nativity scene since I had left Poland fifteen or so years earlier, I was very familiar with the characters and the general setup. But I had doubts whether my niece and nephew, both brought up as atheists, would appreciate it. Unless I made it out of Lego, I didn't see what use it would be for them.

'Who is the baby?' my baby niece, who had a soft spot for other babies, would inadvertently ask.

'It's the Son of God.' I'd explain.

'Is he the God?' she'd ask, pointing at Joseph.

'No, he's just a carpenter from Bethlehem.'

'Why is he looking after the baby?'

'He's helping his mum.'

'I like that they have a donkey and a horse in their house,' Kosma, who loves all animals, would say.

'It's not a house. It's a barn. They had to escape from an evil king who wanted to kill baby Jesus.'

'This king?' Kosma would point at one of the kings bearing gifts.

'No, another king.'

'No, they didn't,' my sister would bossily start arguing with me over minor details. 'They were travelling to Bethlehem when Jesus was born. Then King Herod ordered his troops to kill all the babies because he had heard that one of the newborns was the King of the World.'

On hearing about the baby massacre, Kosma would walk away to cry a little bit in private, while Zoja, who has a more scientific mind than her artistically-oriented brother, would drill us on the topic.

'But where is the baby's daddy?' she would ask again. She hated loose ends.

'In Heaven,' I'd inform her.

'With Santa and the reindeers?' Kosma would come back hoping for a happy ending to the horror story.

'No, but wait till you hear what happens to the baby at Easter.'

Whilst I considered explaining to the children the difference between heaven and sky and dragging myself into a new cycle of Christian-inspired hell, I decided that it was time to invent our own Christmas traditions. Ones that were not burdened by centuries of religious psychosis and decades of our own family's disappointment. We'd make a Christmas tree from olive branches. Like conifers, olives are evergreens, and the leaves have a slightly musty, oily scent.

The great thing about small children is that they are still discovering the world and will thus unequivocally believe anything that an adult tells them. Following the well-established tradition of telling children ridiculous stories at Christmas, a few days after their arrival, I told them that we would cut some olive branches to make a Christmas tree — they didn't even raise an eyebrow.

I grabbed a branch cutter from the garage, and off we galumphed into the field to cut some branches for a Christmas tree. It's customary to prune the olive trees in the winter, so removing a few branches wouldn't harm the trees. Once inside the house, I arranged them in a wide-mouthed vase and set it on the floor near the fireplace. The decorating of the impromptu tree took a considerable amount of time, as it usually does with small children who get easily distracted by tinsel and Christmas baubles.

Most of the colourful tinsel made its way around Zoja and Kosma's necks, while their teenage stepsister, Amelia, was determined to finish the job as artistically as possible. Once covered with glittery ornaments and lights, it was impossible to tell what kind of tree we had used to imitate the traditional conifer.

I really outdid myself that year as far as inventing new Christmas traditions. On the morning of Christmas Eve — the most important day of Christmas for Polish people — instead of terrorising the whole family with cleaning and cooking, we went for a long walk to explore the nearby ruins.

It was a gorgeous sunny day. But because it was December, my sister refused to believe that she could walk around in just a light jumper. Instead, she dressed her whole family in their heavy winter jackets, scarves, and hats. About twenty minutes after leaving the house, we had to make an emergency stop by the cherry orchard to undress. The jackets were stashed away into the backpack that my brother-in-law, Michal, carried everywhere they went in those days. The rucksack that once accompanied him and my sister on adventure holidays of rock-climbing and bungee-jumping off abandoned bridges was now filled with wet wipes, baby sunscreen, an assortment of juices, and gummy bears. As soon as Kosma caught a glimpse of the Haribo packet inside his father's rucksack, he and his sister started to moan and beg pitifully.

'Ok, ok,' my sister negotiated with them while stashing her own jacket into the backpack. 'But you must promise me that you will walk by yourself without crying. OK?'

She took out the packet of sweets and held it in front of their faces. Both kids were now exhibiting levels of concentration I had never suspected they possessed. Their eyes were firmly fixed on the colourful packet, and their minds were willing to do anything to be awarded their treat. The resemblance to dog training was uncanny, but I decided not to point this out. I have learned the hard way that most parents hate it when you compare their precious offspring to canines

— no matter how accurate the observation might be. It was a shame because had my sister followed Cesar Millan's way, she would have known that the treat should be handed out *after* the dog has performed its task and not before. But prudence and an unwillingness to engage in my sister's combative side prevented me from interfering.

On seeing the kids 'Sit!' in front of my sister, Bobby joined them, curious about what goodies were being distributed and why. While he himself deserved a reward for staying with the pack and constantly herding the kids — a self-appointed job — I wasn't sure what Kosma and Zoja were being praised for at that moment. Nevertheless, a lovely peaceful silence fell upon us while their mouths were glued shut by the gelatinous sweets. I now understood my sister's eagerness to hand out Haribo. As we strolled along in peace and quiet on the dirt track between the olive hills, Amelia spotted a lonely kaki tree.

'Are these mandarins?' she asked me, pointing at the small orange fruit in the distance.

'No, it's kaki or persimmon,' I explained.

Seeing this exotic fruit in its natural environment caused a lot of excitement. We all approached the tree, and everyone helped themselves; everyone except me. By December, I'd had as much kaki as any one person could eat in a lifetime. I wasn't worried that my neighbour would mind if they helped themselves from the tree. I knew from experience that most kaki trees yielded more fruit than any typical family could consume. It was customary in late October and throughout November to gift and regift whole bags of the kaki fruit that abound in the area. After a month of eating kaki, most Andalusians will start packing the fruit into old shopping bags and gift it to friends and neighbours in the towns and cities. They'd often suggest keeping it inside a closed container with a little bit of brandy or whiskey to eliminate the bitter taste that the unripe fruit has.

There are few things that Andalusians hate more than waste, and so having a bunch of *guiris*, a Spanish word for ill-mannered foreign tourists, happily picking fruit from a tree and preventing it from falling to the ground and going to waste is a dream come true. I was sure that if the owners of the tree were to see us, they would not believe their luck. I assured everyone that no one would mind if we took some fruit. They all filled their pockets with the fruit and vowed to come back the next day.

There are several ruined *cortijos* in the vicinity of our house. Most are very small and narrow and entirely unsuitable for a modern family. There is even an abandoned *hacienda* where we like to visit and discuss together what we'd do with it if it were ours. While the *hacienda* house is really magical and could easily be converted into a small boutique country hotel, it was the ruined property on the hill opposite from it that always caught our imagination. To start with, it had a dominating view of the charming *hacienda*. However, having had a taste of being a hotelier, I wasn't wholly convinced whether my heart was still in it as much as it initially was. Did I want to devote the rest of my life to cleaning dozens of rooms, making beds, scrubbing patios, filtering pool water, arranging pot plants, keeping common areas spick and span, and responding to clients' requests?

After careful deliberation, both Robert and I decided that life on a *hacienda* wasn't for us. I can't explain why we were hiking across the countryside and debating which property we'd buy and renovate if we won the lottery or some such. One might have thought that the horrors of renovating a house once would be enough to keep us disenchanted with the idea of reviving an old *cortijo*, but as a daydreaming project, we have never abandoned this topic. I need to emphasise that these conversations were utterly theoretical because, as the careful reader will recall, our bank balance was minimal, and we had a bigger fish to fry in the form of supplying our existing cottage with water. Nevertheless, I thought my family would like to inspect some old *cortijos* and imagine life in a bygone era.

The specific *cortijo* that Robert and I liked to fantasise about bringing back to its former glory was a beautiful old farmhouse where the main house and all the outbuildings were surrounded by a continuous white wall about eight feet in height. The only things that a passer-by could see from the track outside the house were the green crowns of two ancient date trees almost four metres, or thirteen feet, in height. The entrance to the walled courtyard was guarded by a pair of imposing matching wooden doors decorated with wrought iron strips and nails.

Over decades of neglect and exposure to the sun, various layers of paint had become visible on the doors' surface. Pink, blue, and green stain had been used in the past to coat the doors, and now this historical veneer formed a nostalgic remnant of days gone by. The two-metre-tall doors were usually left ajar. As we stepped inside over the imposing threshold, we could see the incredibly tall trunks of the date trees right in the middle of an ancient stone patio. The stone floor was partially covered by lush ivy.

Behind the date trees, we found the old façade of the main house decorated with a set of traditional painted tiles depicting the Virgin Mary — a favourite ornamental motif for Andalusian farmhouses. The front entrance was densely overgrown with thorny rose bushes that had spread wild and rendered the old building inaccessible. Even though it was impossible to peek inside the old house, I enjoyed visiting the patio and absorbing the atmosphere, entertaining wistful thoughts.

Our Western romantic obsession with ruins is not new; there have always been periods in European history when we have drawn, painted, and written about them, sometimes to excess. Some art historians may argue that ruins prompt us to contemplate death, decay, and our own mortality, but I disagree. They make me think of the fact that life does go on after we die — the ivy keeps on growing, the roses blossom every spring, and the trees bear fruit even when there is no one around to prune and water them. The footsteps have disappeared. The kids' laughter on the patio has dissipated into nothingness. The friendly chatter of neighbours outside the walls is long gone. But life continues.

I was happy to see that my family was as enchanted by the old farmhouse as Robert and I were. We walked around the perimeter and discussed different options for refurbishing it. We took several photos of the old green door and the patio. Once outside the courtyard walls, we admired the sprawling olive hills and the old *hacienda* in the distance.

'When is Robert leaving for Oman?' my sister asked as we started descending the hill towards home.

'A week after you leave,' I told her.

At the end of November, Samira had contacted Robert again to ask him if he'd be interested in being the headmaster of the school that he had just helped her open two months earlier. After he'd left, it turned out that work had started to pile up for her, and she had not been able to manage the whole school by herself. It didn't take us particularly long to decide that he would take on the job. We agreed that he'd go there alone, and I'd stay in Spain and mind the house and the dog and run the *casa rural* in the spring. It was an excellent opportunity for us to save some money and to continue our renovations and house improvements.

'But how will you get to the shops?' my sister asked.

It was a valid question and one that I myself wondered about in the weeks before Robert's departure. I had managed with Keith's help for a month in September, but now he and Delia had gone to the UK for the winter to enjoy the central heating of their daughter's rental apartment in London. They wouldn't be back until March.

'I'm looking for workaways to stay with me,' I replied.

Because my sister and Michal were not familiar with the concept of 'workaways', we spent most of our walk home with me explaining what it was all about and telling them funny stories about Keith's workaways — the only workaways I had met at that point in my life.

'I've posted an advert on the Workaway site that I need a couple — I prefer a couple because they can entertain themselves in their free time,' I explained. 'I specified that they need to have a car because one of their jobs will be to drive me around.'

I could see the concern and bepuzzlement on my sister and Michal's faces, but they were too polite to tell me how idiotic the whole idea was. If I had stopped for a minute to think it through, I might have found a better solution and saved myself the months of misery and frustration that the workaways were to subsequently impose on me. Unfortunately, Kosma interrupted us, and I never got back to rationally evaluating the workaway idea.

'Bad dog! Bad dog! Stop! Bad dog!' he was yelling in a panicked voice.

I was surprised to hear him shout like this at our dog because my nephew has a very kind heart and loves all animals dearly. As I turned around, I saw that the 'bad dog' was, in fact, his sister Zoja. Kosma had attached Bobby's lead through the belt loop on her jeans. When I last saw the two of them, they were playing nicely and taking turns 'walking the dog'.

It seemed that one of the 'dogs' had got bored with walking to heel and was now running down the hill at full speed, with the 'master unable to let go of the lead. Soon the 'bad dog' and Kosma overtook us. Kosma's screaming and shouting only attracted Bobby, who had been investigating rabbit holes but now decided to join the duo in their break-neck descent. Bobby's barking at Zoja only encouraged her madness as she accelerated downhill, screaming that her legs wouldn't stop.

Soon, she was going to trip on a stone, fall down, hurt herself, and ruin Christmas, and so I ran down after them to stop them. It was fortunate that Kosma was wearing a hoodie which made him easy to grab onto. Once he was pulled back, he let go of the lead and soon after, his sister decided that running loose with no one attached to her was no fun at all. We all took a deep breath, and after a round of Haribos, the kids marched home.

When we arrived at our gate, Amelia asked me about the yellow fruit that grew on a tree right next to the entrance of our house.

'It's quince,' I said.

I picked an exceptionally healthy specimen from the tree and told her to smell it. The scent of ripe quince is something that I distinctively associate with late autumn in Andalusia. It's zesty, citrusy, and rosy. My neighbours use quince fruit to make the Andalusian speciality, *dulce de membrillo*; *membrillo* being the Spanish word for 'quince'. It can be boiled down into a very thick paste or jam that is traditionally spread on cheese and served for dessert.

While it goes well with cheese, the amount of sugar needed to make *dulce de membrillo* is such that it gives me an instant sugar rush and a persistent headache. The thing with quince is that until it's boiled down, it's completely inedible — the raw flesh is like yellowy wood. To enjoy it as a dessert, you have to peel it, core it, and boil it with some sugar and vanilla until it's soft. As I was explaining this to Amelia, we decided that we could use it like apples and make a quince pie instead of the traditional Polish apple pie.

Once in the kitchen, we were all-hands-on-deck. We spent the afternoon together preparing a variety of Polish dishes with Spanish ingredients and English touches to satisfy everyone's Christmas expectations. While the food is usually at the centre of any Christmas celebration, we were also going to bring Santa, or Saint Nicholas as he's known in Poland, to Berruguilla.

Christmas is a holiday for children, and the whole production of tinsel, decorations, and lights are just smoke and mirrors to draw their attention away from whoever delivers them the presents. In Poland, it's customary for Santa to appear in person on Christmas Eve, and after a brief interrogation of the children, he hands out the gifts to the delighted kids. The job of Santa is traditionally delegated to an uncle or another supplementary male because having your own dad disappear from the dinner table just minutes before the long-awaited Santa arrives would be too suspicious.

As generations of Polish uncles will attest, pulling off a Santa trick in a regular city apartment requires some cunning. It entails the clandestine collaboration of all the adults involved, a chain of secrets and plausible excuses, and understanding the connections between different doors, windows, elevators or lifts, staircases, and balconies. But in a rural *cortijo*, it was simplicity itself. All Robert had to do was pretend to go to the bathroom, walk past the kitchen, and away from the dining room. Then he'd change into his Santa outfit that my sister had surreptitiously brought from Poland.

He'd then quietly leave the house through the patio door in the living room, which you could not see from the dining room, and he would reappear, knocking on the mudroom door adjacent to the dining room where we were all sitting and distracting the kids with comestibles. The timing was of the essence here. As we finished our Christmas Eve dinner of *pierogis* with bacon, baked cod with vegetables, and a Mediterranean dish of mussels steamed in white wine that my vegetarian sister insisted on preparing and eating that Christmas, the frequency with which Kosma was asking us about Santa was increasing exponentially. I was about to suggest that we taste

Amelia's quince pie when we heard a terrible racket right outside the dining room window.

This incarnation of Santa, it seemed, had taken a great deal of creative license and had created a character of his own. Forget the gentle jingle of bells or a friendly *Ho! Ho! Ho!*. Our Santa sounded more like a homicidal maniac trying to break into the house by smashing all the windows with a stout cudgel. In an instant, all hell broke loose.

Bobby started to bark incessantly, drawing on all his *bodeguero* courage to protect us. The kids began to scream, undecided whether to cry in fear or rejoice in happiness. A set of decorative tealights got knocked down from the piano, and hot wax spilt all over the floor. I didn't know if I should start cleaning the floor while the wax was still hot or hold on to the wine glasses that were in danger of falling victim to Santa's madness. This Santa knew how to make an entrance! Few things in life are as heart-warming to observe as the look of sheer delight and bliss appears on a child's face when they're about to open their Christmas gifts. For me, it made the whole Christmas production: the decorations, tree, lights, and cooking, well worth it.

The suspense leading to this moment was intoxicating for my niece and nephew. They didn't have to work for the reward. They didn't have to do anything after receiving the gift. All the moment announced to the world was that *because we all love you so much, we have made a whole charade of our lives to keep you entertained for weeks until this very moment.* And now that you have what you wanted, you can go and do exactly what you'd do if you were the king of the world — eat sweets and play with your long-awaited toy. And that's what they did.

That year, Kosma and Zoja made our Christmas magical, not because they were exceptionally well-behaved or amusing to be with, but because they brightened up the room with their childish innocence and simplicity. There are not enough baubles and angel hair that one can put around a house to replicate this feeling if there are no children around. The Christmas production without its main actors is like a suspense novel where nothing ever happens.

In years to come, Kosma often reminisced about his first Christmas in Berruguilla. He was three years old that year and was just starting to form memories, so I felt decidedly pleased that I had managed to plant some good memories of his visits to Spain. Zoja, being only two, had only vague recollections, which were mainly distorted by competing versions from different family members. The next time my family came to spend Christmas with us, two years later, I hoped we could replicate some of these experiences, but by then, my sister and her partner were constantly bickering with each other and on the verge of separating. Instead of cheerfulness, their behaviour left only bitter memories and divided our family for years to come. But in December 2017, that particular future disappointment was unimaginable.

NINETEEN
EPIPHANY

E leven days after Christmas Eve, it was time for my family to fly back home. They were leaving early in the morning before the Three Kings Day, one of the most festive occasions in the Spanish calendar but one that neither Robert nor I had celebrated before. To avoid the potentially upsetting transition from living in a house full of festive cheer to returning to the deathly-quiet tomb that we usually reside in, I decided that, after dropping my family at the airport, Robert and I would go to Ronda for a night to explore the famous city for the first time.

It never ceases to surprise me how much the passenger-driver dynamic depends on the nature of the car journey. When we collect our loved ones from the airport and drive with them through the mountains to our remote cottage, the atmosphere in the car is usually electric. We make plans for the immediate future: 'We should buy some mussels and fresh prawns for supper. Good idea. Let's stop at Mercadona in Huétor-Tájar.'

We exchange gossip about family members and friends: 'Did you hear that Aga is getting a divorce? After fifteen years! What a shame.'

We tell each other what has been going on in our lives: 'We've just renovated the library. Wait till you see it.'

The conversation on the way from the airport is always light; it flows with no strings attached and no commitments made. It's the opposite of the journey to the airport when the atmosphere is sombre, and topics are hard to find. It's too early to reminisce about the stay — I save this topic for the next time we pick them up from the airport. 'Do you remember last time, when we…?' we will say in the future. But not now. You can't go down memory lane to revisit things that have just happened; memories need time to establish themselves. Instead, we pepper our conversation with perfunctory *thank-yous*. That trip to the airport was no different.

'Thank you for coming.'

'Thank you for having us.'

'Thanks for helping us build the water tank. We would not have managed without your help.'

'Thank you for driving us around. It's so much more relaxing not having to drive around here.'

'Thanks for the Christmas presents and the Polish sausages.'

'No problem. Thanks for…' it went on for a while until we changed the theme and started making plans for the future.

This was a difficult topic to address because the only time we could take holidays together was during the winter. My sister's tattoo and piercing studio was in a resort town by the Baltic Sea, and summer was her busiest time of the year. The same applied to our small holiday rental business. We just couldn't travel when ordinary people went on holiday. This left winter as the only time we could all meet.

'You should spend Christmas in Poland next year,' my sister suggested, and an uncomfortable silence filled the car.

I was reticent about visiting Poland between October and March because it's the greyest and the most soul-destroying time of year in my home country. After years of living on the outskirts of the Empty Quarter (the desert that encompasses most of the Arabian Peninsula), I consider any temperature below twenty-two degrees Celsius, or seventy-one Fahrenheit, to be 'freezing cold'. I was loath to be rude to my sister by declining to visit them the following Christmas when most of the roads would be covered by a metre of snow, so I decided to change the subject.

'I have found two Polish chefs who will stay with me when Robert goes to Oman,' I told them.

'Two Polish chefs,' Michal echoed, and I couldn't blame him. It did sound like characters from *The Muppet Show*. Unlike Michal, I was very excited about my find.

'You won't believe the number of weirdos who contacted me from the Workaway site,' I got everyone's attention. 'A woman wrote to me from the Netherlands and said that she could stay and walk Bobby, but she could only do light work. She's seventy-five.'

We all laughed at the prospect, not because we were unkind but because we knew how much backbreaking work there was to do around our cottage. Heavy lifting had to be done daily just to keep the place warm and clean. After each 'holiday' at our Andalusian retreat, Beata and Michal returned home with back pain, strained muscles, and twisted joints.

I imagined an elegant, if not fastidious, elderly lady in her impeccably tidy Dutch apartment. I was sure that she would be shocked if I were to hand her an old cement basket and ask her to fill it with logs bigger than her thighs and then tell her to carry it from the woodpile to the house every morning. She would have to do that at the start of each day if she wanted to be warm while drinking her morning coffee. We all agreed that she would not have had a good time at my place.

The topic of workaways seemed to cheer the adults in the car up while the kids kept busy colouring in their Disney picture books. I continued to recount the different 'misfits' who had written to me, offering to help to chauffeur me around and do some household chores. There was a sampling of human experiences, from some being born to hardship and seeking a new life in Europe to those born to privilege and in pursuit of an alternative lifestyle.

Colombians and Venezuelans asking if I could provide them with work visas, digital nomads with kids in tow travelling around the world, single white men who apparently had nothing else to do, Polish women demanding that I pay them for the work that they would do if they came to Spain, gap-year students from Italy and France, and a whole plethora of blue-eyed, tree-hugging, and world-loving souls who I knew would just get on my nerves. I shared each of their stories as if it was a comedy routine and kept the show going all the way to Malaga. I don't know why I mocked them and their lives. Even worse, why I made other people snigger at them. It was not the first time in my life that I have laughed in the face of distress.

The last time I was overcome with involuntary chuckling was at my grandmother's funeral. Confronted with the open casket and a crowd of wailing old ladies, I had to move to the pew in the back to try and get myself under control. Soon my cousin joined me, and together we sat smirking uncontrollably at the gaudy plastic wreath, the worn-out old ladies' rosaries, and the tattered holy saints fixed to the walls. Here we were, my beloved grandmother's favourite grandchildren sitting isolated from the rest of the mourners, having a good old laugh. Many rites of passage have distinct odours. A Catholic funeral has the suffocating smell of frankincense and rose water. It's mainly rose water, the perfume of choice of my grandmother's generation, that I associate with her departure.

In retrospect, I should have gone with the seventy-five-year-old Dutch lady. She might not have been able to plough the field, strim the grass, or carry the heavy water pump, but she would not have annoyed me as much as the two chefs did, and she might have had some good stories to share. I will never know.

That night we all slept in Malaga because my sister's flight was in the middle of the night. The following day, Robert and I took the car, now five people lighter, to explore the historical city of Ronda, which is about halfway between Malaga and Montefrio. Apart from seeing Ronda on TV a few times before, my only experience with the place was a social media feud that I had dragged myself into with a pair of Keith's workaways.

They were a British couple who, after retiring from the military, had decided to devote the rest of their lives to cycling around the world and blogging about it. They were interesting enough, and so I followed their globetrotting expedition on social media with some regularity. All until they posted a series of photos from a bullfight in Ronda. They provided captions under the pictures that provided a 'cultural' excuse for attending this cruel spectacle.

Ronda is famous for its Plaza del Toros, or bullring, which was built from stone three hundred years ago. If I had read their post on the bullfight during the daytime while eating lunch or taking a break from building, I would have ranted about it to Robert and then forgotten about it by nighttime. Unfortunately, I saw it late at night after I had already consumed my evening dose of red wine. I was worked up about the whole thing, especially by the fact that bullfighting is still legal in several European countries and remains a tourist attraction.

Powered by three or four glasses of *Crianza* — I might have lost count — I decided that it was high time I took a strong stance against the cruel practice and appointed myself as 'defender of the bulls'. Strong words were exchanged on social media as I poured scorn upon the blogging couple for participating in the torture and killing of innocent animals for entertainment. Soon, other social media vigilantes joined in, and sides were taken. Needless to say, I had to leave the thread since it was now midnight, and the notifications of new comments were coming faster than I could read them.

It was pretty apparent that there were many other people in the world who had nothing better to do in the middle of the night than to fight for justice by insulting complete strangers on social media. On observing the enraged Hydra that I had brought to life, I unfriended the couple, unfollowed their blog, blocked further notifications on the post, and went to bed. As an excuse, I can only say that there is very little to do in and around Cortijo Berruguilla at night. I don't know what other people's reasons are, but I'm sure they're just as valid.

I was just finishing telling Robert about this bullfighting incident in my social media history when we entered the city of Ronda. When I booked our B&B, I ensured that one of the search criteria was 'free parking on premises'. I was confident that there would be no parking in the old part of the city. And so I was very surprised when the GPS directed us towards a very narrow, one-way street. Once we were halfway down the road, the GPS informed us that we had arrived at our destination.

'It's here,' Robert, who is much more observant than me, pointed to a puny B&B sign over an imposing wooden door.

'But where are we supposed to park?' I asked the obvious.

We were now stopped in the middle of the road with stone townhouses to either side, leaving about half a metre of free space on each side of the vehicle. Soon, I heard a bread van behind us hooting frantically, as they usually do to let people know that they're coming down the road. While the bread van stopped behind us and waited for his customers to come down to the street to get their fresh bread, I knew that I didn't have much time before the vendor would want to continue on with his journey. I jumped out, careful not to scratch the door against the wall of the house we had stopped next to and told Robert I would ask the receptionist of our B&B where the parking was. I took my phone, in case he had to move the car.

I grabbed the giant bronze door knocker, which was decorated in the form of a head of some disfigured medieval creature, and gave the door several resounding thuds. Soon, a small, smartly dressed woman appeared. Her resolute body language suggested that she was in charge of the business.

'Hola! We have a reservation for tonight, but where can we park,' I explained the situation briefly and pointed to Robert sitting in our 4X4 two metres or so from her front door.

'You can park outside here,' she gestured vaguely around the B&B entrance.

I knew that this would not work. In the best-case scenario, our Nissan Patrol would block the road for any vehicle broader than a Fiat

500, and in the worst, it would get scratched to bits if we parked there overnight. I didn't even bother presenting Robert with this alternative.

'Is there anywhere else where we could park?'

She seemed to understand my concern without having to ask.

'You can drive to the end of the road,' she pointed in the direction. 'Then, on the left-hand side, there's public parking. I'm sure they have free spots today. But if you can't park there, come around again and park in this street,' she pointed to an even narrower street that we had just passed on the way. 'There is never any traffic there.'

I went back just as the van driver behind us was getting into his vehicle and repeated the instructions that I was given. We found the public parking without any problems.

'Twenty-five euros per day!' Robert was indignant when he saw the sign at the entrance.

That was a third of what we were paying for the room. I agreed that the price was extortionate, especially in light of the fact that I had booked us accommodation with 'free parking on premises'. We decided to give the side street a try and re-entered the system of narrow, one-way roads until, once again, we arrived at the beginning of the street where the B&B was located. Just before our GPS announced that our destination was on the left, we turned a sharp left into a very tight, steep roadway. As we halted to ponder what to do next, our B&B owner appeared in the doorway of the back door of her establishment.

'You can park here,' she motioned toward the stone wall on the side of the road. 'These cars are not going anywhere today because it's the Epiphany.'

We looked to where she was gesturing, and indeed, there was a string of cars parked closely along the medieval wall.

'I don't think anyone will be driving a truck through this road,' I said, implying that we might as well give this parking solution a try.

'OK,' Robert agreed, not wanting to drive between the thirteenth-century ramparts anymore. 'I will go back to the cross-street and reverse up here, so when we want to go home, we won't have to drive up this road.' He pointed in the direction of the steep street that became narrower and narrower the higher it went.

It was a valid point because it would not have been the first time that we had got stuck in a tight corner. I went out, and with the assistance of the B&B owner, we helped Robert reverse back onto the street so that he could turn the car around and reverse it up the alleyway. Seeing that we knew what we were doing, the B&B proprietor left us, and we spent another five minutes reverse parking up the hill and squeezing the car into the snuggest of parking spots.

'We're not going anywhere else in the car today,' Robert announced as he took the keys out of the ignition.

'Tell me about it,' I thought to myself while I scrambled to the back of the car and passed him our luggage from the boot to the front of the vehicle. There was not an inch left behind our car to open the back door.

'We'll explore it on foot,' I assured him that I had no intention of watching him drive around anymore. Because Ronda developed into its splendour during the Moorish rule, I was sure that most points of interest would be within walking distance of each other.

Our room was neat and tidy, but it was decorated in gold leaf, which is not to my taste. However, the room's decor suited the aspirational, regal ambience of the town and the coincidence that it was the holiday of the Three Kings. Our room had a minute balcony, which overlooked its twin in the house on the other side of the road. This immediately captured my imagination.

With my mind's eye, I could see the medieval dwellers of the street walking past the stone buildings shouting greetings to the residents; vendors pushing their rickety wagons and advertising their fresh produce or other goods for the benefit of housekeepers and cooks. I wished I could sit on the balcony for a few hours reimagining the past (or an idealised version of the past), but there was no time. As a tourist, one has many obligations, and soon we were back on the medieval streets searching for Ronda's famous monuments on foot.

The town centre was not very far from our B&B, and so we spent a couple of hours strolling the ancient passages, standing on bridges, and admiring the famous gorge. It did not take long before I started daydreaming again. I fancied myself a modern-day Lord Byron roaming the Roman fortifications in search of a muse. But even a romantic soul needs sustenance, and after a few hours of walking around and taking selfies in front of ancient and some not-so-ancient monuments, we spotted an Argentinian grill. It was only eight in the evening, so most restaurants were still empty. We decided to take advantage of the situation and ordered a feast of grilled meats washed down with wine and beer. We finished our mighty repast with a complimentary dessert.

By nine o'clock, we were still the only guests in the restaurant, and the waiter took it upon himself to entertain us with a tasting session of seasonal liqueurs or *digestivos*. If other patrons had been present, we might not have received numerous samplings of *vodka caramel*, *resoli*, and *mistela* — all equally delicious, sweet, and heart-warming. After he poured us each drink, the waiter stayed by the table, awaiting our verdict. We showered him with compliments for the ambrosia and congratulated him on the food, the drinks, the region, the country, the people, and the entirety of Spanish culture.

We then proceeded to compare and contrast the liqueurs, which required that we consume a few more shots each to better understand the depth of flavour that they offered. In this jovial atmosphere, our bellies filled with perfectly grilled meats and worries dispelled by heavy consumption of *digestivos*, I did not think that we could have ended the Christmas holidays on a higher note, but I was wrong.

Glancing out of the panoramic restaurant window, we observed groups of people rushing down the alley, all in the same direction. Robert asked the waiter where everyone was going, and he explained that the Three Kings' parade had just started. I understood now why the restaurant was empty, even though all the tables were set with white linen, wine glasses, and cutlery. Obviously, the majority of the locals were going to eat out after the parade, at around ten or eleven at night.

'If you leave now and go to the end of this road, you will catch it,' he encouraged us not to miss it.

And that's what we did. The main road was lined on both sides by crowds of people laughing and cheering in joy. Colourful floats, with music and lights, passed us by. At first, I didn't realise what it was that the characters on the floats were throwing at the people. I thought it was rice or colourful confetti, but soon I looked around and saw groups of children and tweens running between the crowd and collecting the wrapped candy that had fallen to the ground into plastic bags that they had brought for this purpose.

On each float, someone was responsible for hurling handfuls of sweets over the residents' heads. It was every child's dream come true — a torrent of candy from the heavens. Even though delicious treats were falling from the sky, no one was pushing anyone or jostling for position. We looked at each other — we really could not have congratulated the Spaniards more on their ability to celebrate in style.

But a week later, the mirth and the festivities of Ronda were all but a distant memory. Once again, I was alone. Many long, dark, and lonely evenings lay ahead, including the night when I nearly accidentally killed myself.

TWENTY

TWO CHEFS

The thing that put me off Vito — the male chef — was that he had an incredibly annoying habit of leaving tiny piles of food on his plate at the end of a meal. He would then play with these scraps with his fork. The way he slowly chewed each mouthful of food and took unreasonably long breaks between each serving did not help either. Both his girlfriend, Jana and I would be finished with our plates long before him. Because of this annoying habit, I acquired a growing dislike of him. I first observed his disconcerting eating habits on the second day after their arrival. Early in the morning, the two chefs had dropped Robert off at the Malaga airport, and when they returned, they offered to cook for me.

I was invited over to 'their place', which was one of our guest apartments, for six p.m., which is a strange time to eat in Spain, as it's neither lunchtime nor dinner time. Still, I accepted their invitation gracefully and said that I was looking forward to some homemade gnocchi and pork chops. The menu was explained to me with the unnecessary detail that is more characteristic of amateur chefs, not the professionals they had presented themselves to be. This might have been my first clue to the fact that whatever they had written in their Workaway profile about being travelling chefs did not match exactly with reality. Tasty nuggets of truth were served to me in small amounts over the next two months.

At six p.m., I closed down my laptop. That winter, I had been commissioned to write a series of English exams for university students in Saudi Arabia and had strict deadlines every week. I opened the fridge and found a bottle of cava. With a gift in hand, Bobby and I went outside and round the corner to the rental apartment. I had allocated them the east-facing apartment because it enjoys direct sunlight for most of the day, which, during the winter months, makes a significant difference to the ambient temperature inside. The west-facing apartment needs to have the fireplace going all day to keep it warm in January.

As I knocked on the glass terrace door, I saw both of them busy in the open-plan kitchen. The food was nowhere near ready, and they both looked hot and bothered from the steaming pots and pans and from kneading dough. It was my worst nightmare — watching people cook in real-time. As a devoted fan of *MasterChef*, I'll drop whatever I'm doing in an instant upon hearing Gordon Ramsay shouting at his apprentices on TV. However, watching amateurs cook at their own pace, without the drama created by professional writers and editors who know how to make a story out of boiling an egg, is excruciating.

As I waited on the other side of the sliding glass door for my chefs to notice my presence, I could see knives and forks being dropped to the floor, spatulas flying, and a multitude of ingredients being tossed about. Tins and jars were being constantly lifted by one 'chef' or the other, and the labels were scrutinised over and over again with obvious doubt and bepuzzlement.

I could empathise with their situation. It's always a challenge to cook with ingredients that you are not familiar with and come from packages that have labels in a foreign language. When we first arrived in Andalusia, our weekly grocery shopping trip in Mercadona used to take forever. Everything seemed to be in the wrong place. On one of our first trips there, it took us a good twenty minutes to locate the eggs. We started our hunt with a degree of optimism as we foolishly assumed that we would find the eggs on our own. I left the trolley by the ice cream section. It was forty degrees Celsius, or one hundred and four Fahrenheit, outside, and the ice cream freezers provided a pleasant microclimate. Robert was assigned to search the left side of the shop, and I would scour the right-hand side aisles. We reunited after ten minutes with nothing to show for our efforts.

'How do you say 'eggs' in Spanish?' Robert decided to go and ask one of the friendly attendees.

When I say 'friendly attendees', I mean it. As I found out years later, Mercadona is a family-owned supermarket chain with a very firm sense of loyalty to small towns and their local employees. Most of the staff whom we met in our first year in Andalusia still work there: Bea with her lush curly hair, a somewhat clueless but always smiling Ignacio, bright-eyed Merce, and others. Some workers come and go, but there is definitely something in Mercadona's business model that puts a human face back into a big supermarket chain.

I took out my pocket dictionary — my phone was very basic in those days and didn't have a translation app — and searched for 'egg'.

'Huevo,' Robert read from the page stressing the *h* and skipping *u*. I had a vague feeling that it was not the correct pronunciation.

'I don't think you should pronounce the *h*,' I suggested, but my advice was ignored.

Undeterred, Robert approached a shop assistant who was artfully arranging watermelons in the fresh produce aisle. He returned a minute or so later, looking cross.

'I don't understand these people,' he was fuming. 'Why can't they make an effort to understand me! I said *HEVOS!*'

I didn't want to argue. As a non-native speaker of English, I'd been in situations where my listeners refused to understand what I was talking about just because I had changed one phoneme in a word. I walked over to the same shop assistant and showed her the word written in my dictionary.

'Ahhh! *Uevos!*' she exclaimed as it all started to make sense to her. She motioned me to follow her to the frozen fish section, where the eggs were stacked between two freezers and a shelf of *paté ibérico* and ketchup.

I would have never put it here, I thought to myself as I thanked the assistant, grabbed a packet of eggs, and marched back to the trolley.

We went through the same charade again on the same day, looking all over the shop for cooking cream. I expected to find it with other dairy products, but it was hidden in the fresh fruit section. Pickled cucumbers — a staple of any self-respecting Polish woman — should have been next to pickled peas, pickled artichokes, and roasted bell peppers, but no. After numerous visits and months of searching, I found pickled cucumbers next to the olives, peanuts, and almonds. They were obviously considered to be *aperitifs* or snack food. And if you really want to have a fun day in Mercadona, you can ask for something exotic — like rice vinegar or wasabi, which are essential to making sushi.

'Where is the rice vinegar?' I once asked an attendant in Spanish.

I wasn't being outrageous. I was planning to make sushi rolls for a party. I got the idea after I spotted sushi rice and Nori sheets on a shelf and assumed that the rest of the ingredients would be available in the same supermarket. I placed the rice and the seaweed in the trolley and went off in search of the other components of the dish.

'Vinegar?' amiable Ignacio reiterated and took me to the vinegar and rice section where I'd just come from.

The shelf with vinegar was in the rice and pasta aisle for some reason. I looked at the greying middle-aged man and shook my head.

'Not rice and vinegar. Rice vinegar,' I tried to explain, but he looked at me as if I had just invented a new type of food. 'It's rice vinegar to make sushi.'

I picked up the small bag of sushi rice from my trolley to show him the photo on the label, but he gave me a blank stare. It did not seem to click. I let him go and went around the supermarket a few more times, trying to think of all the possible combinations with which rice vinegar and wasabi might be sold, but to no avail. I wasn't very surprised — to say that sushi is not very popular among local people in Alcalá or Montefrio would be an understatement. Only the bravest and most eccentric of our local residents pride themselves on liking foreign foods such as sushi or curry. Perhaps it makes them appear sophisticated and cosmopolitan. As it was, the only successful foreign food restaurants in Alcalá were family-run pizzerias and kebab joints.

Defeated and confused why a shop would sell only half of the ingredients that you need to make sushi, I paid for my sushi rice and Nori and went off to Lidl — a German chain of supermarkets that British expats particularly cherish. Lidl is also famous for its random selection of foods from all over the world. There, you will find Polish *pumpernickel*, Swedish Wasa *knäckebröd*, Greek *halloumi* cheese, Italian *mascarpone*, German gingerbread, and Korean *kimchi*, all next to a selection of Bulgarian wines and Portuguese beer. It is the United Colours of Benetton of grocery stores, and it didn't disappoint. There, between the English brown sauce and the Mexican *jalapeno* sauce, I found rice vinegar and wasabi, but no rice or Nori sheets.

Watching the two chefs fumble through the assortment of products that they had purchased brought back memories of many food misadventures that I had experienced, but it was getting cold, so I knocked on the glass again. Jana finally saw me and stumbled across the living room, trying to avoid the bags and suitcases that they had spread out all across the floor.

'I'm sorry about the mess,' she said as she ushered Bobby and me inside. 'We're still unpacking.' She closed their suitcases that were spilling out in the middle of the living room and dragged them out of sight into the adjacent bedroom.

I gave her the wine and sat down on the armchair. I braced myself for being forced to watch them cook and entertain at the same time. Keeping a lively and engaging conversation while cooking is a skill that only a few professional chefs possess. Ramsay or Oliver may be fun to watch while they simultaneously chop carrots and regale their audience with anecdotes. But most ordinary people can only do one thing at a time. They either focus on the cooking and ignore the guests or try to amuse the audience and therefore start chopping off their fingers and throwing food on the floor.

The two chefs in front of me decided to engage in some sort of entertainment relay. Jana, who was more forthcoming and eager to please, started to explain why most of their life's belongings were stored in the reusable Lidl and Mercadona bags that were scattered in front of me across the floor. The supermarket bags were filled with socks, pants, T-shirts, and towels mixed in with a blender, random cooking pots, a cutting board, an electronic tablet, headphones, and other bits and pieces that make up our lives.

'We got the Volvo last summer,' she started her tale in the middle. 'It was only five hundred euros.'

I could see why their car was so cheap. It was almost twenty years old and heavily rusted. It was on Polish number plates. I speculated whether it was even legal to drive in Spain, but I decided not to get involved in their problems and listened to them take turns as they chronicled their tribulations.

'We came to Spain to look for work in a restaurant on the coast but didn't realise that there would be no jobs for us in August, so we worked in a burger café on the beach in Benidorm and slept in the car.'

A litany of misfortunes followed: from having to leave Costa Blanca at the end of the summer season, to having their car broken into and their passports and other documents stolen, grafting away in a tourist restaurant in Pamplona, to cleaning a rural B&B in Navarra for food and board. It seemed that everywhere the poor couple went, they were bullied, pushed around, and generally abused. The stories were quite engaging, if not amusing. As I pondered each debacle, I noticed that the bottle of cava that I had brought with me was on the table near the fireplace, still unopened. This bothered me somewhat.

Shall I tell her to put it in the fridge? I deliberated.

I didn't want to reveal how petty I was so soon into our acquaintance, but I could see the wine was getting warmer by the minute. I was now so focused on this small detail that I stopped listening to their tales of woe and nodded my head automatically, lost in my own thoughts.

Why don't they offer me a glass of wine? I've been listening to their stories for thirty minutes now, and they haven't offered me anything to drink, I thought to myself while they were recounting the time when they had to share a flat on Costa de Sol with seasonal workers from Morocco. *I gave them a perfectly chilled bottle of wine. Why don't they just open it already?*

'The Moroccans didn't like our dog,' I caught a fragment of her story.

'Your dog?' I was surprised to hear they had a dog.

'Yes, we have a dog, Dolores,' Jana explained. 'She's been travelling with us all that time, but we've decided to leave her at the B&B in Navarra. We told the owners we will collect her when we have full-time jobs on the coast.'

That's never going to happen, I thought to myself. The jobs in hospitality are usually seasonal. Many restaurants, hotels, and bars on Costa del Sol are closed from October until April. The few restaurants that remain open have their local staff and wouldn't be interested in hiring transient workers. But I didn't want to break their spirits, and so I refrained from exploring the topic further.

'You may get lucky,' I assured them instead and decided to enquire about Dolores. 'So, you will drive for nine hours from Malaga to Navarra to fetch your dog?' I asked and saw uncertain expressions on their faces.

'It's nothing,' Jana said wistfully as she knelt down by the fireplace to scratch Bobby's belly.

As far as ingratiating techniques go, playing with someone's pet is at the top, but it did nothing for me. In fact, it made me feel sad for her because it was so misguided.

'He's going to bite you,' I informed her tersely and looked at the unopened bottle of wine. She pulled her hand away, stood up, and went back to stirring the tomato sauce.

I decided to take charge, so I grabbed the wine glasses from the shelf and opened the bottle of cava. I poured a drink for everyone and put the bottle in the fridge. Now, comfortably set with glass in hand and the fire roaring by my side, I explained:

'He's a rescue. We think that he was badly abused as a puppy because he hates people cuddling him. So, it's best if you just leave him alone, let him be.'

On hearing this, Jana told me the story of their dog, and another half an hour passed before the food was served. While we ate, Vito tried to amuse me with a very long, tedious story of how his father's work partner swindled his family out of money. It sounded like a plot of an action film, but I stopped listening when I saw that he had left a minute portion of gnocchi on the side of his plate. Vito began moving the two gnocchi pieces in random zig-zags across the plate. This took up all my attention for the rest of the meal. When we finished, I'd had enough of the live cooking show. I told them that they could start the 'work' part of their 'Workaway experience' the next day by weeding around the house.

'Let's meet outside at ten o'clock,' I suggested. In January, the difference in temperatures between night and day is drastic. During the day, you may find yourself walking outside in a T-shirt and taking in the sun at lunchtime because it can be twenty degrees Celsius or sixty-eight Fahrenheit at that time of the day. But at night, the warm air suddenly becomes freezing cold, and the thermometer drops to below zero. You rarely see olive farmers out before nine a.m. in the winter because the fields are usually covered in hoarfrost. So, to be kind, I suggested that we start work at ten o'clock when the frost would have thawed.

By ten in the morning, I had already taken Bobby for a long walk, read the news, drank coffee, and answered several work emails from my editor. A few minutes past ten, I saw Jana walk past my library window to the patio. I went outside to greet her. Instead of waiting for Vito, who was fiddling with his shoelaces, I took her to the garage and showed her the gardening tools. As soon as her boyfriend's head appeared in the garage door, we all went down to the areas that needed weeding. Satisfied that productive labour was going to be performed by my new minions, I went back to the library to work on my texts.

Not ten minutes had passed when I saw Jana outside the library window motioning for me to come outside.

'We are not which ones are weeds,' she explained.

I followed her to the area where they had been directed to work and saw Vito sitting on a stone by the flower bed.

'Look,' I started pointing at plants. 'This is rosemary, don't pull it out. This is an anemone flower, so leave it. That one is lavender — it needs trimming. This one is a sage bush, it can stay as it is, and that one is jasmine. Everything else is grass or weeds. If we don't pull the weeds out now, they will spread terribly in spring.'

They nodded their heads in seeming comprehension. So, with no further questions, I left them to do the work. No sooner had I sat down and re-read my last two sentences before I was interrupted again. This time, it was Vito silently gesticulating through the window.

'There's one plant we're not sure about.'

Once again, I followed him to the garden. This time Jana was sitting on the stone with a blade of grass in her hand.

'Is this a vegetable?'

It occurred to me that the two chefs had no idea what they were doing in the garden, but I had a deadline that day and didn't really have time to invent another job for them, so I explained that the thing in her hand was, in fact, common wheat, the seeds of which blow over from my neighbour's field and spread in my garden.

The work — both mine and theirs — went very slowly that day. I was called in to consult with them at regular intervals. On one of the 'inspections', Vito suggested that there must be something that I could put down to stop the weeds and long grass from growing between the flowers and herbs.

'We'll look on Amazon tonight,' Jana promised, hoping to find some magical solution to what had obviously become hard labour for them.

Her idea cheered Vito up, who mansplained to us that there are special plants that stop weeds from growing near them. On that note, I left them discussing a world without weeds and prayed for a quiet half-an-hour or so to get some of my own work done.

The next day, I decided that since weeding wasn't their *forte*, I'd let them choose between cleaning the garage or upcycling some old furniture that I wanted to reuse in the rental apartments. They decided to restore an old mirror and a wooden bench first. Then they cleaned and organised the garage. After a week with the two chefs, I felt confident that the two could manage on their own, and so I decided to take up an offer that I had just received from Cambridge to attend a teachers' conference in Dubai in March. I would first fly to Oman and spend a month in Sur with Robert. Afterwards, I'd fly to nearby Dubai for the conference. My old friend and cubicle neighbour, Claudia, would give me a ride from the teachers' conference, which she was also attending, to Abu Dhabi where I'd stay with Elena, another close friend from our days in Al Ain. I'd have a week in Abu Dhabi to catch up with my old friends and colleagues from the university.

Once I had hatched this plan, it was impossible to change my mind. February is a positively unpleasant month in the mountains of Andalusia. The memory of freezing west winds and horizontal torrential rain was still vivid in my mind from the year before. The idea that I could swap carrying baskets of firewood in the rain for swimming in the Indian Ocean was compelling. I thought about it for a day and convinced myself that going away to the Middle East was the only logical thing to do. The cats and Bobby would be looked after by the workaways, who would also do some light house maintenance. It all worked out perfectly in my head. In hindsight, I must have felt really lonely and miserable to decide to leave all my earthly possessions in the hands of two vagabonds.

I spent another week preparing the chefs for my departure by showing them how everything in the house worked and whom to call in case of an emergency. On the second day of February, they drove me to Malaga airport, from where I flew to Berlin. It was at Berlin airport that I had my first-ever panic attack. It started with a terrible premonition that came over me as soon as I disembarked the plane. Soon, my chest started to get tight, and I realised that I couldn't take in a deep breath. I had to sit down on the stairs by a café. With my hands trembling and feeling slightly dizzy, I felt an overwhelming sense of dread. I couldn't understand it. I'd flown hundreds of times before. I'd travelled across Europe many times on various forms of transport. It couldn't have been the journey.

With trembling hands, I took out my phone from the laptop bag and turned it on to see what time it was. I had to calm down before my connecting flight to Muscat. As soon as I heard the phone start, I looked at the screen and couldn't believe my eyes. There were three missed calls from Merce — my neighbour opposite the road. I felt sick to my stomach. Merce had never called me before. We had exchanged numbers a year or so earlier, but if I needed anything or if she wanted anything, she would always come over instead of calling or sending a message.

Really dark thoughts came over me now.

Have they burnt the house down? I wondered. *So quickly?* I'd only been away for six hours.

I had to call her back, or I would not be able to continue the next leg of my journey.

'Is everything OK?' she asked in Spanish when she heard my voice.

That's what *I* wanted to know. Why was she asking me? I was alone, far away from home, and on the brink of a nervous breakdown, and it was 'riddle-me-this'.

'I haven't seen you or Robert in a while,' she explained.

As she said that, I realised that the last time she saw me was before Epiphany when my sister was still in Spain. I never had a chance to tell her that Robert was going away again or that I was going to fly out for the winter. She must have had a shock when she came almost a month later to see an old rusty Volvo on our driveway and two thirty-something-year-old foreigners running the show.

Perhaps she thought that we had been kidnapped and held hostage by some con-artists. I didn't know why the word 'con-artist' came to my mind. It must have been my subconscious thoughts coming up to the surface.

The 'travelling chefs' were not exactly what they presented themselves to be on their Workaway profile; 'cooking bums' would have been a more accurate tagline for their profile page. They lived out of their car and carried their belongings around in supermarket bags. Now that I was thousands of kilometres away from home, the realisation that I had left everything that I owned and my beloved pets with complete strangers hit me.

Have they stolen everything and driven off? I wondered while awaiting some explanation for the unexpected phone call, but none was forthcoming.

'I'm in Berlin now,' I said to Merce. 'I'm going to Oman to stay with Robert. I will be back on the 17th of March.'

'*Vale*,' she sighed in relief. *Vale* is one of those filler words which means hundreds of things depending on the situation. On this occasion, it meant *Good to hear it!*

'There are two Polish people in the house,' I went on in case she called the Guardia Civil to have them arrested. 'They are looking after Bobby and the cats.'

Another *vale* was offered up, which told me that it was a good idea that I had explained the presence of strangers in my house. I asked her to send me a message if there was any trouble at home, and after a few more pleasantries, we disconnected. Talking to Merce seemed to calm my nerves. I still had a few hours to kill before my next flight, so I got up off the stairs, dusted down my jacket, and went in search of a quiet place where I could work until my flight was called to the departure gate.

TWENTY-ONE
IN THE EMPTY QUARTER

Apart from New York itself, few places on Earth will make you feel as if you were on the set of *Sex and the City* as much as Dubai. It was a breezy March morning as I marched down Shaikh Zayed Road with my *grande latte* in hand. As I passed a cosmopolitan crowd of pretty Indian and Arab girls all clad in Gucci and other designer brands, I couldn't help but feel an inner glow. The pizazz of the city was clearly rubbing off on me. But more than that, I felt at home. The people, the streets, and the landscape were all very familiar.

In many ways, the Emirates was the place where I became an adult. When I first came to Dubai at the age of twenty-seven, I had no career, few prospects, no opinions, and had not seen much of the world outside of Europe. I was thinking about how much my life had changed during the last twelve years while heading towards the Ritz-Carlton Hotel — the teachers' conference venue — to say goodbye and thank the organisers and my boss for bringing me there. I had a horrible hangover from the farewell party I had been invited to the night before, hence the oversized coffee in hand.

After the conference, I was going to hitch a ride with my friend Claudia to Abu Dhabi to see some old friends. By now, I'd been away from Berruguilla for five weeks, and my life in Andalusia seemed very foreign and distant. When I spoke to others about my life in Spain, it felt like I was reporting on someone else's life. The night before, as I sat in a fancy restaurant at the Rotana Hotel, I struggled to explain to my colleagues from Cambridge Middle East what exactly it was that I did in my cottage in the mountains day in and day out. From listening to their conversation, it appeared that they were all high flyers — one day in Cyprus, the next in Istanbul, Riyad, Jeddah, Cairo, and then back to Dubai for a fun weekend in their luxury apartments on the umpteenth floor overlooking the Gulf.

In contrast, my week consisted of days that were more or less the same; get up, take Bobby for a long walk to the asparagus field, read the news and drink coffee, write, potter about, write, walk with Bobby up the hill in front of the house, cook supper, watch TV, drink wine, read, and sleep. The next day, repeat in the same order. The days when my routine differed usually involved some sort of household disaster or chore, like attending to a water leak, fixing a broken water pump, chopping firewood, or spending an hour on the phone with the electricity company begging them to come and re-attach the electric cables that had fallen down in the wind. While a congenial Filipino waiter kept my wine glass topped up, I looked around the table at the shiny, happy people who were dining with me and realised how shabby my regular life was in comparison. But I wasn't jealous. It wasn't for me anymore.

Despite all the sparkle of Dubai, I wasn't interested in surrendering my freedom again. I watched the evening's proceedings with eyes wide open, like a tourist on a fascinating safari. It was fun to watch the

Dubai lifestyle from a distance, but I had no interest in joining in again. It was all too alien and strange. In my dull life, I was a free agent. I did as I pleased and when I pleased. It must have been the realization that I had escaped this mental prison that made me smile throughout my stay in the Middle East.

'You really are glowing,' my boss, James, said on seeing me enter the Ritz-Carton lobby on that last day of the conference in Dubai.

'Thank you,' I beamed. I didn't tell anyone how content I was to see that what I had left behind over two years earlier hadn't changed much. The last few days in Dubai reassured me that we had made the right choice to leave when we did. This was not a place where I could thrive. I said goodbye to my Cambridge colleagues and went in search of my friend, Claudia, and her Blueberry.

'Blueberry' was the name that our students in Abu Dhabi had given Claudia's microscopic, blueberry-coloured vehicle. In a land where no car is too big for the road and no expense too small to spend on four wheels, the Kia Picanto is an eccentric's choice. Seeing it parked outside the hotel between a white Land Cruiser and a bright yellow FJ Cruiser, I had to admire its compact nature and puritan style.

'I left my suitcase in the hotel lobby,' I told Claudia, who was sitting sideways in the driver's seat, shelling pistachios. The packet had the name of the hotel where Claudia and Ingrid had shared a room during the conference. In the back passenger seat, I saw Ingrid's platinum blond head, barely visible from behind the front seat headrests. The back seats were filled to the roof with freebies from the teacher's conference; I could see the logos of different publishers on various glossy paper bags, posters, and presents still in their wrapping paper.

'That's a good bounty,' I nodded at the loot in the back seat as I went around the car and took the seat next to Claudia. I turned back and greeted tiny Ingrid, lost between the gift bags and EFL posters. Ingrid was in her seventies, and Claudia was not much younger, but they both refused to retire and return home to New York State. They laughed at my comment. Claudia hitched up her long hippy skirt, and I noticed that she wasn't wearing her sandals. She closed the driver's door, and off we went. Soon, we joined the seven lanes of Shaikh Zayed Road to collect my luggage.

The 'Blue Bug' — another name that was coined for Claudia's car — weaved in and out between giant 4X4 trucks, but for most of the time, we stayed close to the right-hand lane to be ready to take the exit to my hotel. We didn't want to miss the turn-off as it would have involved a half-an-hour detour in tracing our way back. But no matter how much I strained my eyes to see ahead and how much Ingrid, from the confines of the back seat, tried to anticipate what turn-off was coming, exiting Shaikh Zayed Road at the correct place on the first attempt was truly impossible. When I spotted the metro station that I remembered was near my hotel— it was already too late. We should have got off the busy highway five minutes earlier.

'That's my hotel,' I informed Claudia as we passed it on our right-hand side.

A hundred kilometres an hour, or roughly sixty miles an hour, may be a bone-rattling speed in the little Blue Bug, but we were still the slowest vehicle on the road. I felt guilty about missing the turn. From my past life in the UAE, I knew that the next turn-off where we could make a U-turn was about fifteen minutes ahead. At that point, we'd enter the tremendous spaghetti junction outside the Mall of the Emirates. I wasn't sure how we would be able to get back onto Shaikh Zayed Road without getting lost — I was beginning to wonder whether I really needed my suitcase and the clothes that were in it.

But Claudia seemed to have a better idea than to continue driving on Zayed Road. She took us off the highway down an unpaved, narrow service road, and we negotiated a maze of narrow streets between the skyscrapers until we were spat out onto Jumeirah Beach facing the Burj Al Arab Hotel — the famous landmark shaped like a sail. Claudia seemed very pleased with herself.

'I used to know all these roads like the back of my hand,' she referred to her over a decade-long tenure at a government university in Dubai.

While she drove us through the back alleys of Dubai, I admired the humongous air-conditioning units of the five-star hotels and the parking lots. Here, behind the front entrances of the hotels, concealed among the overflowing bins, broken sun-loungers, and rusty service trolleys, lies the heart of the metropolis. A group of Filipino waitresses, all wearing the same uniform, were sitting on a low wall between a car park and the back entrance of a fancy hotel. There was no chitchat, just eyes glued to their phones and fingers scrolling.

Behind them, a gaunt Bangladeshi gardener in a yellowing Panjabi was watering a few strands of desiccated grass and some sickly-looking date trees — there was little life left in his posture and demeanour. When he was a little baby in the crib, freshly brought home from the hospital, rosy-cheeked and clear-eyed, did his mother hope that one day that he would travel across the Indian Ocean and water the desert for a living in order to send a few takas home every month to help her make ends meet?

A sweaty Syrian valet — a lit cigarette in one hand and a packet of red Marlboros and a lighter in the other — walked quickly from the car park back to his post at the front of the hotel. His mandatory white shirt, wet and stuck to his armpits after hours of outdoor work, was antithetical to the image that it was supposed to project.

Everyone was displaced and away from their homes and families. A thin miasma of humid Gulf air covered their faces and did little to hide the sweat and tears on which this glamorous city was built; lives lost, time wasted, hopes forgotten. Soon, the Blue Bug was back in the simulacra of a cosmopolitan city, and we were once again overlooked by the gilded façades of the world's best hotels. The misery of the foreign workers who serviced these hotels was comfortably hidden away from our view.

Claudia took charge of our expedition and located my hotel quite easily. After rearranging some of the luggage in the minuscule boot, we were back on Zayed Road, heading towards Abu Dhabi. It's not a very long drive, and most of it is through the vast desert which covers most of the Emirates. I was going to sleep over at Elena's. Elena was a long-time friend from Al Ain, but she had now moved to Abu Dhabi and lived in the Al Baniyas suburb on the outskirts of the capital.

When Robert and I first moved to the UAE, Al Baniyas used to be a traditional desert village with modest one-storey houses for local residents and a row of old-fashioned shops run by Egyptians and

Indians. But now, as Claudia entered the suburb, it was unrecognizable. Since we'd left, Al Baniyas had transformed from a small village into a commuter town — from a distance, I could see the lights of a brand-new shopping mall which I assumed was the centre of this new development. Large parts of the area consisted of gated communities and hundreds of apartment blocks with manicured gardens and perfectly maintained pavements for the residents to walk to the mall and back.

Since there were hardly any street names signposted, Elena fed me directions on the phone which I passed on to Claudia. We spent half an hour or so looking for her apartment block, which was not easy since every street and building looked exactly the same. Finally, I saw Elena's slight figure balancing on the kerb of a car park on the highest pair of stilettos invented by man. It was six p.m., and the sun was setting. With the desert temperatures changing at night, a sudden gust of wind blew Elena's abaya open, and we were greeted by a glimpse of Elena's shapely legs.

It's not mandatory for Western women to wear an abaya in public in the UAE. Most wear regular clothes, but some may wear the black cloak on the way to the gym to cover tight-fitting yoga pants or to hide any other attire that may be deemed inappropriate by pious eyes. It was evident that Elena had put on her abaya to cover up the fact that she was wearing very skimpy shorts. This subversion of the purpose of abaya is not exclusive to Western women in the Middle East, however.

A decade earlier, when I worked on a female-only campus in Al Ain, I witnessed my share of abaya insurrections by my Emirati students. These small acts of resistance always made me smile. 'In your face, patriarchy!' I'd think to myself at the start of a morning lecture when I saw pyjama pants sticking out from underneath an abaya. I had to smile again on seeing this Southern Belle billowing in the breeze in her stilettos and her bare legs exposed in the middle of a Muslim neighbourhood.

'Y'all so late. I've been waiting for hours,' I heard her gently rebuke me in her Texan drawl as I exited the car to greet her.

I'm not sure if it's a Southern thing, but no matter whether you'd last seen her two minutes, two days, or two years earlier, Elena likes to start a conversation in the middle and then work her way forward from there. Following this principle, she proceeded without greeting or perfunctory introduction to tell me, Claudia, and Ingrid all about her day at a plant nursery and the heated argument that she had got into with the Pakistani seller of bougainvillaeas. Most of the story did not make any sense to us because we were given no points of reference or background information about the brouhaha. Still, one thing was crystal clear to the listeners: Elena had been drinking for most of the day.

I gave Claudia a wink and retrieved my luggage from the boot of the car. I told her that I'd see her the next day since I planned to stop by the university to say hello to my old colleagues. We were also going together to Lucia's house for drinks the next day. I waved Claudia and Ingrid goodbye and followed Elena to her block of flats, accompanied by the echoing clank of the suitcase's wheels and the sharp click of her stilettoes.

The entrance lobby of the building was neat and clean but also quite soulless. The Egyptian-looking doorman in a dingy brown suit leered shamelessly at my inebriated friend. I was sure he'd seen his fair share of her antics coming in and out of the flat. Once we got to her floor, I saw with horror children's toys, scooters, and bicycles scattered all along the corridor. I had seen this before in apartments in the Emirates. Parents of large families have the habit of sending their kids out to play in the passage right outside the neighbouring flats. Their screaming and shouting would reverberate across the marble corridors and disturb everyone living in the apartments, but no one would say anything. There is an unwritten law in the Middle East that little boys can do whatever they want, and if you disagree, you risk facing the fury of their indignant mothers.

'Why do you hate children?' a Pakistani neighbour once asked me when I confronted her about the noise made by her brood right outside my house in a compound in Al Ain.

It's a good question, I thought to myself as I observed her ten-year-old whacking the heads of the lilies that grew on a patch of grass in the centre of the compound with a cricket bat.

Once we were inside Elena's apartment, I extracted a bottle of champagne from my suitcase. But instead of opening it, I decided to put it in the fridge for later.

'Why don't we go and get something to eat?' I suggested to Elena, who was now talking incessantly about a gay friend of hers who had visited her the night before and insisted on making Korean food. The story was well-rehearsed and had its ups and downs designed to keep the listener at the edge of their seat.

'Do you like Lebanese food or Indian. There's also a Vietnamese restaurant,' being an insecure hostess, she started listing all the restaurants at the mall.

'Lebanese is fine,' I said. I was hoping that getting some food into her might clear her head.

After growing up in an affluent neighbourhood in Dallas, my friend had serious food issues, which oscillated between not eating at all for days or binge eating cookie dough. It was a miracle that she still had any hair left on her head since most of her nutrition came in the form of wine or brandy and an occasional hamburger — which she insisted on having served raw — during the weekends at the hotel club.

As soon as Elena had ditched the abaya and changed into a pair of jeans and a T-shirt, we went to the mall.

'My brother wrote to me and said that my ex-husband is getting another divorce,' she said as we were crossing the road.

'Which ex-husband?'

'The American one — the one who married our Mexican housekeeper,' she reminded me of the story of her first marriage. 'He's marrying her eighteen-year-old daughter now.' There was a definite tone of revenge in her voice.

Once we sat down at the Lebanese restaurant, Elena started to order food as if we were catering for a small wedding. I was confident that she hadn't eaten in a while. Soon the Lebanese classics started to appear on the table: varieties of hummus, stuffed grape leaves, *tabbouleh*, *fattoush*, *kibbeh*, and *kofta*. The mezze must have brought back memories.

'My mother-in-law used to make delicious *kibbeh*.'

I understood that she was talking about her second husband's family.

'We had a gorgeous little villa among the olive groves,' she told me. 'Just like your place in Spain — a real paradise with figs, dates, oranges. So beautiful.'

'Was it in Beirut?' I couldn't remember all the details of her second marriage to a Lebanese businessman.

'It was on the outskirts. One day, his mom asked us to go and get some sweets from a bakery. There was going to be a family celebration or something. Tariq, my husband, placed the order at the bakery, and while I waited for the cakes, he went out to buy cigarettes in a nearby shop. Suddenly, a group of men came into the shop shouting in Arabic and waving guns and rifles in the air. I couldn't understand what they were saying, so I ran away from the shop. I thought they were going to rob the bakery or kill someone. They had these Yasser Arafat scarves – you know?' I nodded.

'I was hiding somewhere in the park when Tariq called me on my mobile. He was furious. *Where the 'f' was I? What the 'f' was I thinking?* I embarrassed him. We'd only been together for a couple of months, so I'd never seen him angry like that. I got scared, but I had nowhere to go — I only had my phone with me, and my cat, Tiki, was still in the house. I told him where I was, and he picked me up from the park.

What the 'f'? he said.

I thought they were going to kill me, I told him.

They were hunters — they came to get food for a hunting party. They were going to the mountains.

I was silent for a minute — how was I supposed to know?

I tried to explain when he grabbed the back of my head and smashed my face against the dashboard. My nose was bleeding, you know ... there was blood everywhere.'

The waiter leaned over and put down a platter of grilled meats in front of us.

'Is everything OK?' he asked.

'It's great.'

I gave him a phoney smile as I tried to process the horrific story my friend was telling me. Elena was not dissuaded by the interruption.

'But he couldn't stop. He punched me again so hard that my head hit the passenger window and cracked it. He drove home. When he parked outside the house, I was hysterical. He called his mom, who lived next door, to come and get me. They snuck me into the house, past the family members who were chatting in the living room and locked me in a spare bedroom upstairs. I went inside the house because he said he was going to choke Tiki.'

I'd never heard this part of the story before. I looked down at all the Lebanese food in front of us, but we had both lost our appetite.

'They wouldn't let me out for weeks. The mother told the other family members that I was ill. She took my phone but forgot to take my passport.'

'What?'

I was aghast. This was a type of story that you hear on *Banged up Abroad*, and not from your friend.

'After a couple of weeks, his mother let me out of the room to walk around the house. They wouldn't let me on the street, though. She said I was an alcoholic and would only get whiskey. I obliged her for a few days until she gave me back my phone. I went to my room and called my brother in Texas. I told him what had happened and begged him to buy me and Tiki tickets back home. I couldn't use Tariq's credit card. A few hours later, my brother sent me a text message with the booking number and date. He also contacted the embassy and gave me a number to a person who was to escort me to the airport.'

The rest of Elena's story was straight from a spy thriller. On the day of her flight back to the US, a car appeared outside her husband's house. Fortunately, Tariq was away on business in Saudi, which meant that Elena could drag her suitcase and the cat carrier downstairs to the garden, from where she was swiftly taken into the embassy car and driven away to the airport. Tariq's mother never saw a thing, and even if any of the neighbours saw the American wife disappear in an unknown car, they kept her secret. A few weeks later, she received the divorce papers from her husband's lawyer.

After hearing this story, I needed a drink. We asked the friendly waiter to pack up the leftovers so that we could take them home.

'Did I tell you I'm seeing someone?' Elena said as we were crossing the road back to her flat.

'No.'

'It's this cute Egyptian doctor,' she beamed with pleasure. 'His name's Mohammed. I met him six months ago when I fell down in the kitchen and fractured my shoulder.'

'What? I didn't know about that.'

'I was mopping the floor in my high-heels when I slipped and fell flat on my face onto the floor.'

I thought with horror of the hard tiled floor in her kitchen and Elena's fondness for high heels.

'I didn't think much about it until I woke up on the sofa in the morning. Half of my face was black and blue, and I couldn't move my arm.'

I wondered how much detail she left out from her story, but I didn't say anything. Why was she mopping floors in the middle of the night in high heels? Why did she sleep on the sofa? There was really only one answer to these questions. I felt quite sad about it all.

'Are you sure you want to get involved with another Arab man?' I asked instead.

'All the Western men are either with their wives or gay, and I can't be alone forever.'

It was true. I've heard this from other single female colleagues in the Emirates.

'Just don't get married to him, please,' I begged her as we entered her flat.

'No, he's just a friend.'

As I opened a bottle of champagne, I knew very well that she would get involved with 'Dr Mohammed' and that it would end in tears. What do you tell a person who only makes terrible choices? I grabbed our glasses and walked in the direction of the terrace when I noticed a small black-and-white photo on the wall of the opulent living room. The picture was somewhat lost among the enormous sofa, hundreds of decorative pillows, chandeliers, pink and purple flowers, and a silver candelabra.

'That's a lovely photo,' I commented as I peered forward. It showed a teenage Elena with a short bob and freckles on her nose. She was sitting on the back of a pick-up truck with her arm around the shoulders of a ten-year-old boy.

'It's my brother, Greg. He died when he was sixteen,' she said as a matter of fact.

'What happened?'

'He fell off his bike and hit his head on the sidewalk. My parents thought he was OK, so no one took him to the hospital to check his head. He fell asleep that night and never woke up. He bled into his brain — there was nothing they could do.'

Oh my God, I thought. I was speechless. We'd been friends for years, and it was the first time I'd heard this story. 'I'm so sorry.'

I looked at the photo again — I was surprised to see that Elena had freckles. She looked really pretty, albeit vulnerable, without the heavy make-up and botox treatments that she now subjected her face to.

'My parents divorced a year later,' she said.

'How old were you?'

'I was six years older than Greg. When he died, I was already married. He was my favourite brother, you know,' she said as we sat down.

I looked up to the night sky, but even though we were practically in the middle of the Empty Quarter, I couldn't see a single star because of the light pollution from the apartments, the mall, and the busy highway nearby. We could smell the sand and the dry air of the *Rub al Khali*, as it's called in Arabic. Once one of the most inhospitable environments on the planet, it was now home to millions of people from almost every country in the world.

'Why don't you move somewhere else,' I asked Elena.

'I can't move. This is my home now,' she was adamant. 'Where could I go? I don't want to go back to the States. There are no jobs for me in Europe, and I don't like Asia very much. I can't just pack up and go like you did. And do what? Start my own business? It's not easy,' she started to rant.

I spent the rest of the night convincing her that there were other places in the world where she could thrive, where she could start her own business and be her own boss. But between her visits to the kitchen for a surreptitious shot of vodka hidden in the cupboard behind the breakfast cereal, I knew it was a losing battle. It was a conversation that we'd had many times before, but it never ended in the way I hoped it would. Even though she was unhappy, she could not leave the plush comfort of the gilded cage.

TWENTY-TWO
DOWN MEMORY LANE

The next evening, I was sitting on Lucia's terrace in the centre of Abu Dhabi. Lucia was a seasoned English teacher from New England who used the teaching job to travel the world. We were not very close friends, but, so far, she and her husband were the only people from Abu Dhabi who had visited us in Spain. They didn't come to see us specifically but made sure to stop by Montefrio during their tour of Europe. They came when Robert and I were still in the middle of renovations, so they didn't see the end product of our labour, but at least she could share her impressions with my other colleagues and friends.

On hearing about my short stay, Lucia organised a potluck supper.

She had made an oversized jug of *mojito*, and we were well set up to reminisce about the past. I knew everyone who was gathered at the house except for an older, well-dressed lady who turned out to be Lucia's ninety-year-old mother, visiting from Boston. I liked the fact that she was introduced to everyone as 'Mother' — it set a certain tone and made me feel that I was in a stage production from the 1960s, somewhere between *Who's Afraid of Virginia Woolf* and *A Streetcar Named Desire*.

Mother was very friendly and eager to listen to our stories, even though some of the references to people who were not present at the gathering must have been confusing for her. By then, my friend Christine had gone off to Fiji, Jeff had got a job at a university in Iowa, and Claire was back in Toronto looking for a job. There were many other friends and colleagues who had left the Middle East, and we briefly went over what they were up to.

To let us girls talk and catch up, Mother decided to serve the food that was in the kitchen. As she returned from the kitchen, the expression on her face told me that she saw something revolting. She put down the quiche and samosas and went back to the kitchen to get other dishes. I surreptitiously investigated the source of her revulsion. During her years in Abu Dhabi, Lucia had adopted two giant dogs: an Afghan hound, Bobby, and a spindly Saluki, a desert hunting hound called Zarafa. While the Afghan was quietly sitting near the table waiting for possible scraps, the Saluki was deep into Claudia's toes. She must have taken off her sandals when we sat down, and the poor animal was licking between her toes and all over her feet as if they were made of Kentucky Fried Chicken.

'Claudia, that's disgusting,' I stated the fact without thinking. At that moment, Mother returned with another platter of snacks and thanked me with her eyes.

If Claudia were a stranger, I would have left the room and excused myself from the party to avoid seeing the nausea-inducing display. But, since we were good friends, she didn't seem to take offence and, instead, put her sandals back on and shooed the dog away. The conversation didn't stop for even a second. I've always considered it a sign of solid friendship if you can tell someone when they've crossed a line or when they're being gross. You'd never hesitate to inform your brother or sister when something hideous has attached itself to their face. In life, it's only the people who love us the most who dare tell us when our wardrobe sucks, remind us that it's time to dye our hair or point to a piece of ham fat hanging from our chin after lunch.

If you can't trust your best friend to tell you that going shopping in mismatched flip-flops is one step from a loony bin, who else can you rely on? If your friends don't tell you that using a cotton handkerchief that hails from the presidency of Ronald Regan is sickening to everyone, your enemies will only smirk and laugh behind your back. The lucky among us have a loving spouse or a close family member who will inform us of the general impression we make on the public. But if you're single and reside in a foreign country, you need a gentle nudge in the right direction from your friends now and again.

For the rest of the night, we sat on the terrace, drinking *mojitos* and reminiscing over funny stories from the time when we all worked together. My favourite stories evolved around the cheapskates, like the head of the linguistics department, 'Jean-Luc Picard' — as I called him for his clean-shaven head and French-Canadian origin — who for years slept on a yoga mat in a vast bedroom in his luxurious but empty villa in Al Ain and used aluminium foil for curtains.

Or a maths teacher called Jack who would bring empty Tupperware containers to the university each time there was a function with a buffet and proceeded to fill them with food minutes before the event started. You have to understand that he didn't want people's grubby fingers all over *his* food. Once his week's supply of ready meals was safely stashed in the cool box conveniently located under his desk, he would join the party.

But the king of the penny-pinchers, and the hero of many stories, was my nemesis, Desmond, or 'Des'. He was a rotund Chinese-Californian man in his late sixties who will go down in my private history as the man who stole food from the Bangladeshi cleaners.

Desmond and I were never great fans of each other, but it was the day when he brought a cat in a box to his office that made me despise him. Desmond was a very lonely man who needed a companion. However, being incredibly stingy — he also brought empty

Tupperware containers to university events — he didn't want to pay for a cat from a rescue centre. Instead, he went on a cat hunt by the bins outside his apartment in Khalifa City — a then-new, low rent suburb almost an hour's drive away from the university.

Somehow, he had caught a semi-feral cat that usually spent its days scavenging in the municipal bins and fighting for its territory with other strays. Desmond plucked it straight from the street and placed it in his living room, expecting his domestic bliss to be complete. Did he really think that a feral cat was going to sit by his feet and gently purr as Desmond drank whiskey and read the news on his tablet in the evening? Did he expect the poor creature to patiently wait for him by the window whenever he returned home from work?

I can only speculate what Desmond's plans were towards the poor creature, but instead of Mr Fluffy, he got himself a real Don Riff-Raff. I imagined that when Desmond was at work, Riff-Raff ran his criminal syndicate from the apartment, making phone calls to his soldiers to collect 'taxes' from the other strays and running a numbers game. Being trapped in Desmond's apartment must have been a big setback to Riff-Raff's felonious ventures.

'I'll get out soon,' he'd explain in a raspy voice to his capo on the phone. 'As soon as the door is left ajar, I'm outta here. In the meantime, don't lose us any clients. *Capisce?* I gotta go now, see ya!' Riff-Raff would hang up on hearing Desmond's car being parked outside. Before the door opened, he'd jump on top of the bookshelf, where he would hide away from Desmond for the rest of the evening, quietly plotting the little man's demise.

'He jumped off the bookshelf on top of me and scratched my head. I almost lost an eye. This cat is crazy,' I overheard Desmond explain why he had brought the cat in the box to the office. 'I need to get rid of it.'

'What are you going to do with it?' my colleague Hilda asked. She and Desmond were talking just outside the teachers' cubicles.

'I'll leave it by the bin near the park. He'll be fine.'

'Has he been sterilised and vaccinated,' Hilda was not having any of Desmond's excuses.

'Not yet. I was going to wait until he settles down.'

I suspected that Desmond had brought the cat to the university and had shown it to poor Hilda because he knew that she would not let it be thrown out onto the street. Our German-Canadian colleague, Hilda, was dubbed the queen of crazy cat ladies of Abu Dhabi, a moniker which spoke volumes about her commitment to her feline friends.

Like most Middle Eastern cities and towns, Abu Dhabi overflowed with stray and feral cats. Whole colonies lived in municipal bins, parks, and gardens. Even inside Al Ain Zoo, there were several feline families living on the scraps left by the cleaners and café owners. At the university, we had several resident cats who were fed with dry cat food that was donated to the university janitors by students and teachers. Most *al fresco* restaurants had a gang of cats that prowled under the tables and demanded to be fed as soon as the main course was served.

Sooner or later, any expat with a dash of empathy ended up homing, fostering, rescuing, and feeding the cats. At one point in time, I had two cats inside my house, a family of five in the garden, and four in foster homes that I had arranged. Looking for homes, catching, sterilizing and releasing, rescuing kittens from the street, and driving to and from the vet with sick or injured cats was my regular pastime, as it was for many other expat and local women.

But Hilda took her mission to another level — she was the Oskar Schindler of the feline world. She'd always find room for one more cat. Sleepless nights were spent thinking of solutions to rehome cats, constantly posting the details and pictures of homeless kittens on her Facebook page and raising funds for sick animals. It was obvious she wouldn't let Des abandon his cat.

'Give it to me,' she ordered Desmond, true to her German roots. I could hear in her voice that she was slightly miffed at having one more protégé to look after, but saving cats was her life's calling, and she could not look away.

Relieved, Des handed over the box to the already overwhelmed cat lady and went off to get himself a free cup of coffee from the teacher's lunchroom.

'I'll need this box back,' he had the audacity to tell her as he sauntered off to the kitchen.

As I listened to Desmond from my cubicle, my blood started to boil. But revenge — in the name of poor Riff-Raff — was best served cold. He might have been a rascal, but he didn't ask to be taken away from the comfort of his bins and transported all over Abu Dhabi for no reason. The next morning, I was in the staff kitchen making myself a cup of coffee. Because of the long commute from Al Ain, I used to leave home early to avoid the eight-a.m. rush-hour and kilometres-long traffic jams when every family in Abu Dhabi tried to drop off their children at school and get to work all at the same time.

I was waiting for the kettle to boil when I spotted Desmond's favourite cereal bowl next to the coffee mugs. It wasn't really a cereal bowl, but an instant noodle bowl — as suggested by some Chinese symbols printed on its black surface — which he got for free from Lulu hypermarket when he bought a supersaver bag of fifty packets of instant noodles. Desmond would never eat his breakfast at home. To save water, milk, and electricity, he prepared his breakfast in the staff kitchen between his morning classes.

As I heard the kettle button trip, a thought occurred to me. I grabbed Desmond's favourite breakfast bowl, opened a bottom cupboard and hid it deep in the corner behind the supplies of sugar, coffee, and spare mugs left behind by previous employees. I hoped to cause him just a little bit of bother to avenge the poor cat that he mistreated.

Sometimes karma needs a little help, I thought to myself as I saw Desmond in the corridor, flushed after climbing the staircase to the first floor.

I drank my coffee and went on with my day. Because our cubicles were in different parts of the building, I had no idea whether Desmond had noticed the disappearance of his cereal bowl until I sat down for lunch.

'Desmond's furious today,' my friend Chris said.

'Oh, why?' I assumed my poker face as I set the clock on the microwave.

'Someone stole his cereal bowl,' she said. 'I was making a cup of tea earlier, and he was searching the kitchen like a man possessed. He was opening and closing all the cupboards and got quite aggravated. Apparently, someone stole his bowl.'

While the idea of Desmond searching all the cupboards frantically in vain put a smile on my face, I realised I had to confess to someone since I didn't fancy being accused of stealing an old chipped noodle bowl. Chris laughed off my confession, and we decided to leave the bowl where it was.

'I'm sure he'll find it sooner or later,' I said. 'It's not such a big kitchen.'

It was a few days later when I came across Desmond in the staff kitchen. He was heating up some sort of concoction made of spring rolls, a slice of quiche, and some cheese tarts that he had purloined from a recent bioengineering conference. Because he had just set the clock on the microwave, he could leave the kitchen, but, for some reason, he felt obliged to chit-chat.

Soon, he was telling me all about the grand larceny that had occurred in the staff kitchen — his cereal bowl had been stolen. He was shaking his head, not able to compute why someone would commit this heinous crime. I was obviously not going to fess up, but as Desmond was mourning his loss, I saw Kiran, our service staff, arranging teacups and refilling sugar bowls. Our eyes locked, and I knew that he knew where the bowl was. I had put it right next to the sugar and coffee bags, so Kiren must have seen it. I found it hard not to grin and decided it was time for me to leave the kitchen.

'I'm sure you'll find it soon,' I said and left.

The breakfast bowl miraculously reappeared on the kitchen counter by the teacher's mugs a few weeks later — just as Desmond had acquired another supersaver bag of instant noodles and was gifted another free bowl from Lulu.

Desmond's antics and thriftiness were a regular source of entertainment for everyone. Even our Bangladeshi cleaners must have exchanged stories of this wealthy American wandering around the campus with his Tupperware containers all ready to save a couple of dollars. But it was during my final month at the university that he outdid himself.

A few weeks before I was due to leave for Spain, I decided to organise a farewell lunch for my work colleagues whom I liked and whose company I found enjoyable. Needless to say, Desmond was not invited. It was a low-key event, but because I had ordered food from an Indian restaurant, there was a lot of food leftover.

At one o'clock, we all had to go back to our teaching and other duties, so we wrapped the food up in the original aluminium containers, covered it, and put it in the fridge in the kitchen that was used by the service staff. I then told the cleaners that this food was for them. There were several containers of butter chicken curry, biryani rice with meat, and half a cake that my friend Julie made for the party. An hour or so later, I was walking back to my office from class when Kiran approached me and told me that Mr Desmond had taken the cleaners' food from their fridge.

'Where is he?' I asked Kiran.

'He's locked himself in the teacher's kitchen.'

I closed my eyes for a second in disbelief.

'I was trying to get in to make coffee for Mr Jim, but the door was locked.'

There were two kitchens on our floor, one for the service staff and one for the teachers. Kiren used the staff kitchen to eat his meals and take breaks with his colleagues, but he made tea and coffee to order in the teachers' kitchen.

'I'm sorry about that. I'm going to look into it,' I told Kiran and went to the teacher's kitchen.

As Kiran reported, the door was locked, which was very unusual. I knocked on the door, but there was no answer.

You little rat, I thought to myself.

An hour later, on my way back from another class, I noticed that the teachers' kitchen was open. I stopped by Desmond's office. There he was. I looked at his shiny bald head and his pointed rabbit teeth. A year earlier, his two front teeth had fallen out because of his age or because of some unattended gum disease. Instead of seeing a prosthodontist right away, he glued his incisors to his gums with chewing gum and spent a year lobbying our HR department to include dental insurance in our employment package.

The memory of him pulling out his front teeth during lunchtime with bits of gum at the end was still vivid in my mind. He'd eat his food and place them back in front. It was a pathetic display from a man in his early sixties who was well-travelled and was a senior lecturer at a university in one of the wealthiest countries in the world. I didn't know what to say.

'You need to return the food to the cleaners or reimburse them for what you have taken from them,' I told him and walked away, ignoring his denials.

I enjoyed hearing these old stories again. These were our classics. A few hours later, as I sat alone in a taxi on the way to Elena's apartment, I felt sad about leaving my friends behind once again. I also realised that I didn't have close friends in the place where I now called home. Admittedly, our neighbours were always helpful and cordial, and we knew some people from our Spanish class. But I didn't have a circle of good friends with whom I could sit down, share gossip, and talk about nothing and everything.

I need to make friends. I resolved somewhere on the Abu Dhabi highway on the way to Baniyas.

TWENTY-THREE
A MADWOMAN DOWNSTAIRS

I returned to Spain in the middle of March. Because my plane landed at midnight, I booked a room at an airport hotel and asked Vito and Jana to collect me the following day. They insisted that it would not be a problem to come and fetch me from the airport immediately after I had landed. Still, I was not keen on being driven along the narrow and winding mountain roads in the pitch-black with a Michael Schumacher wanna-be behind the steering wheel. At least in broad daylight, other drivers would be able to see him and swerve into the nearest ditch to avoid a head-on collision.

Before I had left, Vito had driven me to the shops in Alcalá la Real a few times. After each expedition, I felt grateful to get out of the rusty death box alive. The thirty-minute drive to Mercadona with Vito was a life-changing experience — a blur of olive trees, a smudge of Nevada mountains in the background, and a hazy shape of an occasional pensioner walking by the side of the road, unaware of how close they had come that day to meet their Maker. When I saw Jana and Vito the morning after my arrival in Malaga, I was so relieved to find out that it was her who was going to drive me back home from the airport. It turned out that Vito didn't have a driving licence on him — it was either stolen or lost or something else; the stories didn't add up.

'So, what's new?' Jana asked in a cheerful voice once we left Malaga and were cruising on the highway in the direction of Huétor-Tájar. 'Tell us everything.'

I looked at this strange woman. The tight ponytail accentuated her round face. Every few minutes, she'd take one hand off the steering wheel to pull down her T-shirt, which was at least one size, if not two, too small and revealed the inevitable ageing of her midriff. The skinny low-cut jeans did not help either. While she looked like a teen who had swapped bodies with her middle-aged mother, Vito took on the appearance of an after-hours porter. For some reason, he was wearing a formal long-sleeved shirt with a collar that used to be white but was now yellowish.

I didn't understand these people. Their world did not make any sense to me. I didn't want to talk to them about my friends and my life. I felt that if I did, I would let them in, and they might stay. Each time they opened their mouth, they turned the knife a little — the clichéd observations, the worn-out jokes, the pointless minutiae. I couldn't let them in, but the silence was getting uncomfortable, and there was another hour's drive before we would reach home. My mind went blank. I looked to my right at the green almond trees on the Alpujarra mountains — they were in full blossom when I had left, I thought.

'I had a very nice buffet breakfast in Dubai,' I finally said to everyone's relief.

It was a topic that we all could relate to. What good would it have been for me to drone on about Robert's friends in Sur, Samara and her son, Elham, Moona, Fahima, Wael and Abdel, or their new idea to start a resort spa on their father's land outside Sur, or my colleagues from Exeter who I met at the conference, or dinner with Christine and Mark who had come to Dubai all the way from Sudan, or my old friends and colleagues Julie, Claudia, Lucia, or my old boss Jim who was planning a new life in the Dominican Republic? They all had interesting stories, but I didn't want to share them with these two strangers who had ended up on my doorstep by chance and who were soon to disappear anyway. So instead, we talked about waffles and omelettes and the ins and outs of buffet breakfasts.

'We looked at getting chef's jobs in Dubai,' Jana told me. 'I didn't know there were so many hotels in the UAE.'

This was a perfect topic of conversation because several years earlier, Robert and I used to socialise with two professional chefs from New Zealand who worked at the Burj Al Arab — then the only seven-star hotel in the world. They used to entertain us with hilarious stories from the kitchen and the misdemeanours of the *nouveau riche* Muscovites who dominated the dining rooms. I related some of these stories, and, in return, Jana and Vito told me some of their stories of 'customers from hell' from the various restaurants that they had worked for.

It was a pleasant ride home as we all had a common enemy ('unruly customers') to feel indignant about. Unfortunately, it was the last affable conversation that we had together that spring. Soon I'd arrive home and see the extent of Jana and Vito's neglect of my property and their pure laziness; there weren't enough funny restaurant stories in the world to keep me calm.

It started as soon as we parked outside the gate, and Vito jumped out to open it by hand.

'The remote doesn't work?' I asked.

'Ehhh... it does,' Jana hesitated. 'But it's faster this way.'

As we waited for Vito to push the electric gate open, I noticed something on the ground by the well house. As soon as we drove past, I realised that it was the water pump from the well.

'Why is the water pump on the ground outside the well?'

'The electrician left it there,' Vito told me, excusing himself.

Electrician? I thought to myself. I had called in our electrician, Rafa, from Oman in February because of a report that the pump wasn't working.

Are you saying it's been lying outside for over a month now? I wanted to say but decided not to confront him.

'Stop the car,' I said and got out to put the pump back inside the well house where it would be protected from the elements and thieves.

Vito followed me like a diligent apprentice ready to learn.

'The pump costs five hundred euros,' I told him, hoping to make him understand my irritation.

'The electrician left it there,' he reiterated. 'We couldn't use it anyway because the well is dry.'

'I know, but you tidy up after the electrician, or you ask him to tidy up. Did he tell you what the problem was with the pump?'

'I didn't see him. They came one morning, I saw the car by the gate, but by the time I came down, they were gone.'

Are you telling me that strange men showed up at the gate, went into the well house, pulled up a pump from the bottom of the well and fiddled with it and that you didn't even check who they were? I wanted to ask.

'And you didn't notice the water pump on the ground for a month,' it was a statement and not a question.

I opened the steel lid to the well and lowered the pump back down to where it belonged. A quick look into the abyss confirmed that, indeed, the well was almost dry. There was maybe a metre of water left at the bottom. It must have been why the pump was not working. By that time, we'd had suffered two years of drought and would need heavy rain for the groundwater level to come back up to what it had been before. I closed the door to the well house and walked up to the house. At first, I could not figure out what was bothering me about the field and the garden, but soon I understood why they looked odd. There was dog poo everywhere I looked.

'Did you take Bobby out for walks twice a day?' I asked Jana as I got to the house. She was opening the boot of the car to retrieve my luggage.

'Yes, of course,' she lied.

It was glaringly obvious from the amount of dog poo around the house and in the field that they had simply opened the front door and left him outside to do his business. I decided to let the topic of dog excrement go. By now, Vito, instead of going to his apartment to relax after driving up and down to Malaga, was now putting on a pair of gardening gloves.

I didn't want to talk to him anymore because everywhere I looked, I was confronted by disappointment. These were two able-bodied, thirty-year-olds. For six weeks, they had a few simple tasks to perform: maintain the house, do some gardening, feed the cats, and walk Bobby. I opened the front door to my house to see an obviously obese Bobby jump out in excitement.

'What happened to Bobby?' I asked as I greeted my overjoyed pet, who was now jumping half a metre up into the air and barking incessantly with happiness.

'What do you mean?'

'Why is he so fat? Did he eat his dog food?'

'No, he ate with us.'

I had enough of this, but there was still more to come. I understood now what lay behind my anxiety attack at the Berlin airport as I was leaving Europe. I must have subconsciously known that this Workaway experiment was not going to work. I was now putting the pieces back together. As I walked into the library, I was confronted by the scent of wood. Because it was the first time that I had been away from home for so long since we rebuilt the cottage, I had never noticed that our house smelled like an old Siberian cottage — it was the smell of the pine cladding on the ceiling mixed with the smoke from the fireplace.

I took in another deep breath and put down my suitcase. I was home. It felt good, but I also wished I were alone. Instead, I looked out of the window to the left and saw the two muppets doing impromptu gardening in the flower bed that now had metre-long weeds growing out of it.

Upstairs, in my bedroom, I saw Twiggy and Whitey, sleeping under the blankets on the bed. It took me a minute to assess the damage. The place was filthy. It hadn't been cleaned since I had left, and there was a two-centimetre layer of dust everywhere. It also smelled of old cat litter, which evidently had not been changed in a while. I looked at the cat feeders — there was neither water nor dry cat food in them. I had left ample money for pet food, but I now had a strong suspicion that it had been used for something else. The cats themselves did not seem too bothered. On hearing me, Whitey got up, jumped off the bed and started to stretch as if I had never left the house.

'I told you she would be back,' he meowed to his housemate, Twiggy, as he licked his hind leg. 'She can't find a better job than this one.'

'Thank God!' Twiggy replied, purring under the blanket. 'The new staff are terrible!'

'Girl! Tell me about it. It's been over a month, and they still can't get my order right. I told them time and time again that the wet food is for you, but they keep on mixing it up. How difficult is it to remember one simple order?'

'I know. And the filth. It's incredible. Have you seen the dust under the bed? There are dust balls the size of my head.'

'Don't even start me! I'm going out. Tell the old girl to tidy up, please. See you later. *Ciao bacalao*!'

Whitey stood by the terrace doors like an Egyptian pharaoh expecting his servants to open them for him. I swung the doors wide and went downstairs to get water and food for the cats. I bumped into Jana, who was now coming up with a bottle of water. She had clearly just remembered about the cats. I didn't want to shout at her, especially since I was clearly outnumbered and in the middle of nowhere.

'They must have just finished their water,' she anticipated my question.

I felt like a disappointed mother of teenagers who had arrived home after a holiday. As I walked about the house, the kids were frantically fixing things, tidying up, and covering up their neglect. I had to remind myself that these two were only a few years younger than me.

This must be a different generation? Are these the 'Millennials' that I've been hearing about? I wondered. I didn't like being the old, grumpy woman on the scene.

Have I become Mrs Bucket? I looked in the mirror by the main entrance. *Maybe you are being unreasonable?*

In this Bizarro World, I found it hard to tell right from wrong. Before I had time to self-interrogate my whole sense of identity, Bobby ran into the house with a raw, rotting chicken leg in his mouth. The meat had been hidden underground for some time because it was covered in fresh soil. I was glad to see that he wasn't attempting to eat it and just wanted to show me his treasure. As soon as I tried to take it away from him, he growled at me and ran back to the garden to re-bury it.

By then, I was lost for words and went to the pantry to get the vacuum cleaner because the layer of dust on the bedroom carpet would have caused me to choke at night. I didn't see Jana or Vito for the rest of the day. They were sensible enough to avoid my company for the next few days. I'd give them instructions in the morning on what had to be done and would go back inside the house to work on my projects since I still had a few deadlines to meet that spring. As I went back to my writing routine, my life came to resemble that of an old spinster circa eighteen hundred, plus the laptop and the internet, of course. To keep the creeping loneliness at bay, I developed a list of jobs that needed to be done in a particular order every day.

Job one, take Bobby for a walk. Job two, drink coffee and read the news. Job three, tell the workaways what to do. Job four, write. Job five, have lunch. Job six, potter around the house, pretend to work and search the internet for answers to random things that are stuck in my head. Job seven, go for a walk with Bobby. Job eight, write until eight p.m. Job nine, open a bottle of wine and cook dinner, and job ten, watch *Call the Midwife* on Netflix.

It must have been the heart-warming nostalgia of the show that made me tune in for more every evening. The friendly group of midwives and nuns who fixed the world with their kindness and the sweet tones of Vanessa Redgrave definitely filled a void in my own life. The borough of Poplar, the part of East London where *Call the Midwife* takes place, became a magical kingdom where babies born to syphilitic prostitutes were healthy, older gay men with Alzheimer's found love, and a teenager with Down's syndrome — one of the main characters — was well-loved and respected by everyone in this working-class district circa the 1950s. Evil and cruel men entered this place occasionally, but they were soon eliminated by a random factory explosion, a fire at the docks, or by incidentally falling into the river Thames.

Once I developed my daily routine, it soon became written in stone. While I fancied myself some sort of modern-day Emily Dickinson — wandering from chamber to chamber of my haunted house in the middle of nowhere, others might have seen it differently. One day, as I was busy doing random jobs around the house, I heard a knock on the mudroom door. It was Jana. She was holding a pot which she proceeded to hand over to me.

'Here's some soup for you. I hope you like soups. I made a lot.'

I let her inside so that I could transfer the soup into a Tupperware container so that I could later flush it down the toilet. I was already annoyed that she was disturbing my daily routine and possibly delaying the rest of my day's 'busy' schedule. The soup was some sort of bone broth, and while I don't mind soups, I am usually suspicious of soups made by strangers. I reassured Jana that I'd be delighted to eat it later. While I was busy in the corner of the living room that constituted our downstairs kitchen, Jana made herself comfortable on the tiny sofa next to Bobby. With my back to her, I suddenly saw my place through her eyes.

Most of the furniture that occupied the space that Robert and I referred to as the living room-cum-kitchen was original and came with the house. In the middle of the ceiling, there was a hideous chandelier that was home to a family of spiders who wove their web freely across our walls and gave our abode a slightly gothic appearance. Some of the walls still had yellowish watermarks from when we lived without a roof and were regularly flooded. Despite several coats of paint, the stains would inevitably come back like some demonic entity haunting us with a reminder of our first year in Andalusia.

The floor itself was an abomination to good taste and logic. It was a 'modern' black and white checkerboard design that would have been perfect in the Mad Hatter's house, but in a rustic cottage in the middle of the olive groves, it was completely out of place — I felt. What I referred to as 'the kitchen' consisted of a fridge, a gas cooker, a cupboard for pots and pans, a sink, and a dish-drying cupboard above the sink. The fittings were in the 1970s brown and beige, which was for the best since these tones camouflaged a lot of grime.

While I could blame the previous owners for the mismatched decor and lack of refinement, the filth that covered most of the surfaces was my own personal touch. Even though I had given the place a good clean on my arrival several days earlier, my cleaning tends to be very superficial, and the gunk was deeply embedded into various nooks and crannies, especially in the Indian hand-carved cupboard that we had bought in Dubai many years earlier. It was the only piece of furniture in the living room that was pleasant to look at.

I turned around and saw what she could see in plain sight: the combination of cheap and expensive, nice and horrible, and among it all, an opinionated thirty-nine-year-old who was just so full of herself that all she could see were the splinters in other people's eyes. I imagined Jana going back to the apartment.

'What's the old lunatic doing now?' Vito would ask her.

'She was sewing up a curtain or something. I'm not sure. There was some fabric on the table in the living room.'

'What does she do there all day?'

'I have no idea. The place is gross.'

'I know. Have you been in the pantry behind that kitchen?'

'I know. The walls there are black with mould.'

'Yikes!'

'That's not all. There are mice, spiders, ants, and all sorts of creatures crawling in that so-called 'pantry'. And it's filled with boxes, floor to ceiling. It's a horror show. I saw some snorkelling equipment, a motorbike helmet, fishing rods, tennis rackets, and more.'

'Jeez! She does live like a crazy hermit. Do we need to call someone to help her? She might be a hoarder or mentally ill.'

'She could be. I saw her once talking to Bobby.'

'Can you please call that woman in Marbella again and ask her when we can start work there?' Jana would plead with Vito.

'She said the first week of April but told me to wait until she confirms.'

'In the meantime, make sure we lock this door at night and close all the shutters. Do you think she's watching us?'

'Could be. She is a psycho. I was just trying to make conversation, and I told her that if she likes sewing, she could post things on Etsy and sell them online. I was just trying to help her, and she looked at me as if I had just served her some dog poo and called it a cake.'

A few days later, Jana came to see me again, interrupting my solitude.

'Would you like a glass of wine?' I offered insincerely.

Jana was a slow drinker and tended to sip on a glass of wine for hours. I was worried that if she accepted, she'd delay Job ten on my schedule — a nostalgic trip to 1950s London. She must have sensed my reluctance and declined.

'Vito and I will be moving on.'

'Aha,' this was music to my ears.

'We got jobs in a hotel in Puerto Banus. They open for the season next month and want us to start a bit earlier to do some training in the kitchen.'

As I'm unfamiliar with all the suburbs and towns on Cosa del Sol, I asked, 'Where is that?'

'It's a very luxurious neighbourhood in Marbella…' she droned on for a while about how posh and fancy the hotel where they'd work was.

'Congratulations!' I said when she finished telling me all about the hotel in Puerto Banus as if it was her first-born child. I was genuinely happy for them — we all need a break in our lives, but mostly for myself to not have to endure them much longer.

When she left, I turned around and walked to my kitchen corner. There on the fridge was a to-do list.

Plough the field
Spray herbicide
Plant potatoes
Get firewood
Build a shed behind a house
Plaster the utility room
Install lights outside

It was time for me to take charge of my own life.

'I'll just have to sort it all out myself,' I told Bobby, who was in a deep sleep on the armchair by the fire.

I went to the library and got a pencil. I wrote at the bottom of the list on the fridge:

Get a Spanish driving licence
Find a driver
Find a builder

And in my mind, I added one more item that was long overdue:

Make some friends

TWENTY-FOUR
A HOOPOE MAKES HIMSELF AT HOME

A week after the workaways had left, I decided to face the biggest obstacle to my independence and drive our 4X4 with the manual gearbox. My sudden determination to drive the car came from the fact that my rubbish bags were starting to pile up, and I couldn't wait another three months for Robert to take them to the bins. Neither could I ask Trish to put them in her car.

Trish was an English woman who had responded to my looking-for-a-driver ad in a local social media group. She lived in the next village and agreed to drive me once a week to Alcalá and back so that I could run my errands. But, as it was with Keith the previous

September, I did not want to ask her whether I could fill her car boot with my smelly rubbish bags.

Since I had decided to take control over my life once again, I was juggling several things simultaneously, and no day was the same. There was no more room for routine, which was perhaps for the best since I had been diving deep into an obsessive state of mind. After a brief search, I accepted a quote from a local builder from Montefrio, Paco, to plaster the utility room next to the living room and build a shed behind the house to protect the gas heaters and the small water tank. He kept me occupied for several days by sending me photos of the materials he wanted to use. I then had to Skype with Robert and check that he, too, was satisfied, and then go back to Paco to confirm. As it was Robert's second stay in Oman, we had figured out how to use a VPN to make video calls even though Skype was still banned there.

I originally wanted to hire Dani, the builder who helped us reform our cottage when we first arrived. However, because it was only the first week of April, Dani was still busy with his olives. Even though he had finished picking the fruit in March, there was still a ton of work to do, such as pruning, clearing the weeds, and adding fertiliser at the bottom of each tree, before he could sit down and relax for the summer — or, in his case, hire himself out as an *albañil*, which translates to a *builder*, but includes everything from laying bricks, building walls, plastering, tiling, installing windows and doors, building swimming pools, putting on roofs, and more.

I explained to Paco that all the construction I had asked for had to be done before the twentieth of April when I planned to open our holiday rentals for the season. It was a bit late in the spring, but because I was on my own and still had a few writing deadlines from Cambridge, I needed more time to get the place ready for paying guests. I went over everything that had to be done while sitting at the big dining table in the recently constructed library. I loved that room.

After almost two years of working at the kitchen table and jostling with builders for workspace for my laptop, I had a perfect writing room. The dark and heavy wooden beams, which were there for purely aesthetic reasons, gave the room a slightly medieval feel. And the contrast of dark wood and white cottage walls was particularly pleasing to look at.

Instead of buying bookshelves, Robert had built the library shelves from bricks and cement in a way that they became part of the room. As a result, when seated in the middle of the room, I was surrounded by books from floor to ceiling. I wanted the edges of these bookshelves to have a line of decorative tiles. However, because we had a limited budget, I was allowed to select only twenty tiles with different Moorish patterns, which we then placed in strategic spots in the vertical sections of the bookcases.

The tiles resemble beautiful hand-painted bookmarks. To finish the library, I insisted on a low-hanging Moroccan lamp in the middle of the room, which has subsequently led to many emotional outbursts from Robert since he tends to bang his head on this charming decoration when he leans over the table in the centre of the room. Each time this happens, he threatens to throw it away.

One might think it strange to build a library, even though neither of us had purchased a paperback since we moved to Spain from Abu Dhabi. In the beginning, we used to buy second-hand books from *The Little Britain* shop in Alcalá — most bookshops in our area don't have English titles on sale. While it was nice to have something to read, I found it frustrating not being able to get the titles that I wanted.

That's when we discovered Kindle and the ability to buy any book or magazine in any language with just a single click. I ordered two Kindle readers through Amazon and collected them from the Repsol station in Montefrio — the couriers refuse to bring our parcels to the campo. For two book hoarders, the excitement of figuring out how an e-reader works and the realisation that we could now get any book at any time was overwhelming.

In our past life, we used to spend Saturdays going from one second-hand bookshop to another looking for titles; it was thus somewhat incomprehensible how easy it was to buy e-books. I remember how thrilled I was the first time I finished an e-book on my new Kindle, and without leaving my bed, I clicked on the next title in the series that I was engrossed in at that time.

The convenience of e-books means that many of us — namely

book hoarders — are deprived of the comforting feeling of being surrounded by piles of books. Japanese, which comes in handy in describing emotions and experiences that Indo-European languages fail to name, calls this feeling *tsundoku*. It is often explained as the feeling one has when one piles up books to read at a later stage. I wasn't planning to read or re-read any of the paperbacks that surrounded me since, with age, I've become unable to read the tiny print on the yellowing paper that many of the Penguin classics and similar publications are printed on. Looking at the neatly shelved books all around me made me feel very calm and happy. I felt *tsundoku*.

Considering the amount of daydreaming I engaged in, one might have been fooled into thinking that I had nothing else to do. In fact, I had an imminent deadline that evening and should have been writing feverishly. The liquescent Dali clock hanging by the door was ticking loudly. *Tock — tick — tock — tick — tock — tock — tock*. It reminded me of our first trip to Spain. I saw the melting clock in a window of a souvenir shop on one of the narrow streets in Madrid. It was Sunday, and the shop was closed when we first saw it. But we were both so determined to get the Dali clock that we made an effort to remember where the shop was and came back first thing on Monday morning, worried that they might have sold it to someone else.

I had been sitting in front of the laptop for two hours and hadn't written anything. I looked at the text on the screen and changed a word in one of the sentences. Time was melting in my mind. The red geraniums on the windowsill outside caught my eye. They reminded me of my grandmother, whose balcony was filled with red geraniums. For many decades, they were her pride and glory. Everything else in her life might have fallen apart, but keeping her flowers a healthy red and the foliage a lush green was one thing that she could control.

Behind the geraniums, I could see the ancient bay leaf tree that seemed to double in size each year and another evergreen tree with long, deep verdant leaves that thrived despite our neglect and inability to identify it. It became apparent that I was experiencing an acute case of procrastination. I started tapping my foot on the floor and looking around the room for inspiration. It was time to do something else.

'Let's take the rubbish out,' I told Bobby, who was sleeping on the carpet under the table. In a second, he was on full alert.

I hadn't driven our 4X4 since the last autumn when Robert attempted to teach me how to tow the trailer up the hill loaded with a tonne of water. Since he had left, I would run the car for ten minutes once a week to make sure the battery hadn't died, but other than that, the car was parked in the same spot under the oak tree where he had left it in January. I tied Bobby's lead to the passenger seat's headrest and loaded up the boot with my rubbish bags.

What's the worst thing that can happen? I thought to myself. *I might stall the engine and get stuck. I might meet a tractor on the road and have to reverse uphill to let it pass. I'll just ask for help.*

I reassured myself by recalling a story my friend Julie had told me about her attempt to drive a manual car. It had been some decades earlier in Vancouver. She was visiting relatives when one of them said that she could take their car back home to her parents' house instead of taking the bus. Not wanting to appear silly, she agreed to take the car even though she had hardly ever driven a manual car. After half an hour of driving on the highway with other vehicles hooting behind her and drivers gesturing in anger, her nerves gave in. She managed to pull over in an emergency bay, got out, and lit a cigarette to calm her nerves. As she stood by the car, a good Samaritan pulled over to help.

Again, instead of admitting the truth that she had little idea how to drive a manual car, she told the stranger that she had a heart condition and was experiencing a mild episode. *Would he mind driving her car to her parents' house,* she asked, dropping her cigarette butt into a puddle. And so, he did. He took her to her parents' house, from where her dad had to ferry him back to the spot on the highway where he had left his own car. All this to save the women's rights movement from embarrassment. Feigning a heart attack to get a stranger to drive me back home would be my last resort. Thus, with a clear plan in mind, I set off.

The municipal bins are about a nine-minute drive away from the house. It was all going very smoothly until I arrived at my destination and, with a false sense of confidence, decided to be fancy and reverse uphill to park right by the containers. There was no need to do this. I could have parked on the side of the road and walked ten metres to the bins. Once I had offloaded the rubbish bags, I could have driven to the bottom of the hill and turned around on a flat surface. Instead, I chose the less travelled path and decided to practise a series of complex manoeuvres on a narrow mountain slope.

Starting a manual car parked uphill or downhill is my Achilles' heel and the main reason why I am loath to drive around in a manual car in hilly Andalusia. After years of operating an automatic car, I upgraded my licence to include a manual vehicle only a month before moving to Spain. However, I had to retake the driving test to change my driving permit from an automatic to a manual car.

By then, I had well over two hundred thousand kilometres, or a hundred twenty-five thousand miles, of driving under my belt, but it was all on straight, flat desert highways. I had used the handbrake once or twice in all those years since I just put the car in 'park'. As a result, my manual driver's exam was all plain sailing until I was asked to stop the vehicle on the hill and start it again without rolling back all the way to the bottom of the ramp — moving backwards would have been an immediate 'fail' on the test. I tried the first time and immediately stalled.

'You can try two more times,' the chatty examiner reassured me.

On hearing this, I got so nervous that I stalled again. As we sat there, parked uphill with my foot firmly on the brake, not wanting to roll down backwards, and holding on to the handbrake, I knew that I was not going to make it.

'I think you'll have to take a few more lessons and redo the test,' the examiner saw how stressed I was.

'I'm moving to Spain next month. I won't be able to come back to repeat the exam,' I explained.

I was now very agitated because I was sure I would never pass the driving test in Spanish and on unfamiliar roads — at least not very soon.

'It's not common in Spain to drive automatic cars, so I want to have this licence in case of an emergency. If my neighbour needs to go to a hospital, or if there is an accident. I live on a farm.' The examiner listened.

'My wife lives on a farm in Karela,' he said. 'Let's try one more time.'

And as I struggled to engage the engine with the clutch while letting go of the handbrake, I felt a sudden jerk, and the engine decided to cooperate. Off we went up the ramp. It wasn't me who had suddenly figured out how to make the clutch and the handbrake work together. It was the examiner who depressed the accelerator pedal on the instructor's side of the car. I was in shock at what had just happened but didn't have time to dwell on it because he was now giving me further instructions.

'Put it in second now. Don't race the engine.'

I did just that, and I drove down the slope and past the other students and driving instructors who were busy chatting among themselves and seemed unaware of what had happened. I thanked him, mainly with my eyes as I didn't want to betray his trust, and went inside the building to collect my manual driving licence. Now, two years later, with no one to tell me what to do and no pressure of failing an exam, I was going to teach myself how to drive a manual car.

'You can do it,' I assured myself after I had stalled the engine for the third time.

I was now parked across the country road blocking any traffic that might happen to come along. I hoped no one would see the spectacle I was making of myself, but then on the horizon at the bottom of the hill, I saw a van coming towards me. It was old Pablo. He would ask a lot of questions if he saw me blocking the road, and worst of all, I knew he would tattle on me to Robert the next time he saw him. I had less than a minute to sort myself out. I didn't need more encouragement than that. Now, with renewed concentration, I listened to the engine and finally felt it engage with the clutch. People had told me before that to start a car on an incline, I had to 'feel the clutch', but unless you're alone in a car on a quiet country hill and have your pride at stake, it's difficult to understand what they are talking about.

I was so relieved when I got it right. I parked the car on the side of the road leaving enough space for Pablo to pass, and took the rubbish bags out. I waved at him as he went past. He stopped for a few seconds to say hi and ask when Robert was coming back, and then he went his way. On my way home, I saw my other neighbour, José, in my rear-view mirror. He was in his ancient Land Rover Defender — one of the most popular cars in the countryside.

Another big mouth, I thought to myself.

I looked ahead, praying not to screw up. I stopped by the postboxes, not that I was expecting any mail, but because I wanted José to overtake me and go home without witnessing any possible mishap on my part. As I got out of the car and opened the postbox, he stopped his car.

'I didn't know you have a driving licence,' he chirped.

He wasn't accusing me of anything but rather made a natural assumption based on the fact that for the first two years as his neighbour, he had never seen me drive a car.

'Yes, I do, but I don't like driving a manual car. I prefer an automatic gearbox,' I told him.

We went on for a few minutes, comparing notes on the advantages and disadvantages of manual cars versus automatic. Once I exhausted my assortment of *A mí me gusta* and *A mí no me gusta*, or '*I like*' and '*I don't like*' sentences, he asked me whether Robert was OK and then drove off.

I drove slowly to the house on the dirt track, hoping not to meet anyone coming the other way as that would require careful manoeuvring up and down the hill next to a very deep ditch, and by that time, my nerves were shattered. As I approached our gate, I saw a splash of colour hopping on the ground. It was an exotic-looking bird, one I had not seen before.

Even though I'm not a bird aficionado, I had to congratulate this little fellow on his appearance. I assumed it was a male because of his flamboyant look. It was an extravagant combination of colours and patterns — a bright orange chest contrasted with the black and white stripes on his wings. The long thin beak accentuated the magnificent orange crown, which was tipped with black and white beads. The outfit was definitely more suited for the catwalks of Paris than a rural country road in Andalusia. Presented at the Paris Fashion Week, the ensemble would have been welcomed by loud applause and hurrahs. But if I decided to walk the streets of Montefrio dressed in a silky orange blouse, zebra-patterned pants, and a massive orange headdress with black and white beads jingling in front of my face, my neighbours would worry about me.

The little bird looked up at me, spread its zebra wings and flew away in the direction of the oak forest at the top of the hill. I was so impressed by its bold demeanour that as soon as I got home, I went straight on the internet and conducted my first ever bird search.

What type of bird has an orange chest, black and white wings, and orange… I hadn't finished typing my description when I was provided with an answer. I read the text next to a photo of a bird that looked just like the one I saw outside the gate.

'The *hoopoe* is an African bird that belongs to the Family: *Upupidae*, which also includes the Eurasian Hoopoe (*Upupa epops*).'

'Look, he's come all the way from Morocco,' I tried to educate Bobby, but he was once again napping under the table.

Not the least discouraged by Bobby's lack of thirst for knowledge, I kept on reading. I found out that hoopoes were monogamous, at least during the breeding season, which was now, and that they made nests inside hollow tree trunks. There were thousands of trees outside the cottage, so I assumed that the female was probably hiding inside her new home.

I learned that, over the centuries, people have had somewhat divided opinions about hoopoes. They were considered sacred in many ancient Mediterranean cultures, including the Egyptian and Cretan civilisations. In medieval Europe, their cultural status changed, and they became harbingers of death and misery. The little bird had the misfortune to feature heavily in the *Munich Manual of Demonic Magic*, a fifteenth-century publication of which only parts have been translated from Latin into English. Apparently, the sacrifice of a hoopoe could summon demons and add efficacy to magical spells. I had so many questions for those sorcerers.

My first was: *How did you catch a hoopoe for your magic spells?*

It couldn't have been easy to catch a small, nimble bird in the middle of a forest. Even if they searched for the nests, climbing from one tree trunk to the other in those long wizard robes must have been a nightmare. They'd get caught on the brambles and branches all the time. A 'catch-a-hoopoe' expedition would take days of walking among the pine trees and oaks. All this energy would be exerted only to then chop the poor creature up and mix it with a toad's liver, spiders' legs, and some moonstone powder — a cure for warts.

I know I waste much of my day staring mindlessly at the tiny screen in my hand, but this was time-wasting on an unprecedented scale. Unfortunately, as I read on, I learned that the idea that animals do not possess supernatural powers has not yet gained traction in some parts of North Africa, where many exotic birds are traded live in herbalist shops since their body parts are deemed to have magical healing properties.

While I initially skipped over the name of the species — *Upupa epops* — since it looked positively unpronounceable, the origin of the strange name soon became self-evident. Later that week, I was sitting on the patio when I heard the call '*up-upa up-upa*' coming from the wheat field next to the house. It was a mixture of a cuckoo's call and a nesting pigeon but distinct from both. I knew instantly that it was the hoopoe marking his territory against competitors. That spring, I saw my little avian friend almost every day. He was frequently in the field, either looking for insects or sunbathing.

On the days that I didn't see him, I'd still hear him calling out, loud and clear. One April afternoon, I was on the patio cutting up seedling potatoes into halves. Between chatting to Bobby and listening to my resident hoopoe, I realised I was, in fact, very lonely. It was time I made good on the promise I had made to myself in Abu Dhabi — it was definitely time to create a circle of friends.

TWENTY-FIVE
HOW TO HOST AN OLIVE OIL TASTING PARTY

'Have you planted the potatoes?' Robert kept bugging me during our Skype calls about potatoes. 'I'd like to eat some new potatoes when I come home.'

'I have a ton of work every day,' I'd argue my case. 'I have a deadline from Cambridge, apartments to sort out, the builder, the weeds are sprouting, and the bottom of the pool consists of a layer of red sand from the Sahara.' The latter observation wasn't a metaphor. In February, a sandstorm, known locally as *calima*, had blown particles all the way from Africa to Andalusia and covered the east-facing walls of our white cottage with red dust.

I wasn't getting much empathy, so I continued my case of martyrdom: 'Also, I have to update the booking websites, edit new photos, and sync all the calendars.' These were all chores that were not complicated *per se*, but to Robert, who manages to break any electronic device as soon as he looks at it, it was rocket science.

'Why don't YOU update our website, and I will ponce around the field with the potatoes?' I might as well have asked him to split the atom in his free time.

Since the time when he tried to design a website for his school, I had banned Robert from making decisions that demanded any sense of the aesthetic and would never let him work on our *casa rural* website. I could only imagine the 'house of horrors' website that he would create for the holiday apartments. Once I made my case of how busy I was, there was not much else to do but buy the seed potatoes.

The next time Trish took me to Alcalá for my weekly shopping, I asked her to stop by the gardening shop. The small business is run by two brothers called Ruiz. One brother has a little shop in town where he sells small plants for balconies and terraces as well as vegetable seedlings for those who have *campo* houses and like to enjoy their own vegetables in the summer.

The other brother has a nursery right outside the town and sells trees of all varieties and bigger plants that are not suited for apartments. Both brothers look almost identical to each other, and if one day you decide to buy a tree at the nursery and then some seedlings in town, you are in for an uncanny experience.

Where did you come from? was my thought when it happened to me the first time. *I just saw you ten minutes ago in Santa Ana.*

I was now in the shop in town debating with the 'town' Ruiz about the number of seed potatoes that I wanted to buy. I agreed with him that it was a lot, but I also had strict instructions from Robert on how many potatoes to buy and which varieties.

'My husband is English,' I said in Spanish, thinking it would explain the quantity.

'But that's too much,' Ruiz was shaking his head in astonishment. 'You will be eating potatoes every day.' He used some hand gestures that suggested that we'd be sick and tired of eating them.

'The English love potatoes,' it was not the first and last time that, as a third party, I had to explain the way of the English to a confused Spaniard. 'They eat potatoes with every meal. Every day! They fry them, mash them, boil them, make chips, bake them...,' I ran out of Spanish cooking verbs that I knew.

Ruiz clearly did not want to argue with a client, so he just looked at me, questioning my mental state.

'They can't eat a meal without potatoes,' I made my case whilst simultaneously distancing myself from English culinary practices.

It was good that I stood my ground because later that day, I was interrogated by the other party — the potato eating Englishman in question — on whether I had followed his instructions vis-à-vis the volume of seed potatoes.

'Yes, and I've spent the whole afternoon with the hoe planting them. There are three rows.'

Robert seemed satisfied with the news that on his return, he'd be eating new baby potatoes that were now safely set in the ground.

'I'm going to hold an olive oil tasting party,' I announced my new idea.

'Have you collected the oil from the mill?'

Robert was already in Oman when I went to the mill to collect it.

'Yes, we have nine five-litre bottles. So, I need to sell some of it.'

'Who are you going to sell it to?' there was a slight tone of scepticism in his voice, but I wasn't discouraged.

'To the people from our Spanish class,' I said as if there were that many other people I knew. 'I saw Roy and Amy a few weeks ago in town. And Céline and Leon are back from their housesit. Keith and Delia are back from the UK. There is also a Dutch couple from Montefrio — they stayed with us in October. Do you remember?'

'The Zimbabweans?' It was a private nickname that we gave Liv and Julian, a Dutch couple who, after twenty years of running an agricultural business in Zimbabwe, had just moved to a rural property on the other side of Montefrio.

'Mmm...I told you that I saw her in the supermarket in Montefrio during Christmas. She invited us over for a barbecue, but my sister was with us with all the kids, so I told her that we would meet up in the spring.'

'Anyone else?'

'I put an advert on Facebook about an olive oil tasting session, and I told everyone to bring their friends and neighbours,' as I was reporting on these plans, I realised that I needed to start preparing for this party. Since I was by myself, I had to prepare the space for the party, prep the food, and then barbecue the meat on the day of the party.

'How much are you going to sell it for?'

'I had a look in Mercadona, and they sell their basic olive oil for four euros a litre, so I was thinking eight or ten euros a litre. I'm going to sell it in these glass bottles.'

I showed him an old-fashioned square glass bottle with a cork which I had decorated with the name of our house, the name of the mill where we had our olives pressed, and a cartoon image of olives on a branch. I posted a photo of the bottles together with the open invitation.

'I already have orders for eight bottles, so people seem to like the idea. Amy really loved how I decorated the bottles.'

The next day, while walking Bobby, I saw Rafa working in his vegetable patch and stopped for a chat. I told him that I was planning to sell our olive oil. When he heard *what* I was planning to charge *extranjeros* for the olive oil, he almost fell into his artichoke patch laughing. He already considered the price of our holiday accommodation to be highway robbery. From his perspective, anything north of thirty euros per night was extortion. But then, the only place he had ever stayed at was a small apartment near the beach in Almeria — the favoured summer destination for many Andalusians. So I wasn't bothered by his criticism and was definitely not planning to take business advice from him.

What Rafa could not understand was that I was not just dealing with the four walls of an apartment in an old Andalusian cottage but, instead, I offered our clients a bucolic dream — the idea of pastoral life where shepherds rest under olive trees, drinking wine, and eating goat cheese. What he saw was a tourist accommodation in the middle of nowhere with little to see and nothing to do. What I was selling were endless views of olive groves, grapevines shading a rustic patio, cascades of roses and geraniums, cherry orchards, asparagus fields, and quirky white villages with tiny town squares where old men spent their mornings playing cards and where swallows built their nests under the roof of a sandstone church. For him, a stone-paved street decorated with orange trees was just one of many; for a visitor from Northern Europe, it was an opportunity to trend in their friends' Instagram feed for a day or two.

Similarly, Rafa could not understand why anyone would buy our olive oil, especially at the price that I was suggesting. Like most families in rural Andalusia, he too had large bottles of top-quality extra virgin olive oil stashed away in his pantry. When the fresh olive arrived from the mill in December, he would gift the old bottles to any relatives in the cities and town who didn't own land, thereby making room for the new season's oil.

'I'm going to host an olive oil tasting party so that people can try the olive oil and buy it,' I explained to him.

In my mind's eye, I saw groups of delighted people seated under the bay leaf tree, dipping bread into our delicious olive oil, eating it, and telling me how wonderful it was. But Rafa had a more pertinent question about my idea.

'How many oils are they going to taste and compare?' he enquired.

'One?' I was embarrassed at my naivety. 'I only have one type, the one from our trees. I suppose I could get a small bottle from Mercadona and another one from Lidl to contrast it against.'

Since Mercadona and Lidl are both vast supermarket chains, it was as clear as day that I was pitting my purebred racehorse against a donkey and a mule. When Rafa heard my plan, he murmured something that sounded like *mierda* under his nose and gestured for me to wait while he went inside his cottage.

I wasn't sure if his observation was directed at the supermarket olive oil or my idea, but I decided to wait patiently as he seemed to have a better plan than mine. While awaiting his return, I stepped onto his patio to exchange greetings with Loli, his wife, and our other neighbour, Maria. Both women were sitting on small

Andalusian bulrush chairs, shelling a mountain of fresh *habas* or fava beans.

Shelling beans and cracking nuts are my least favourite domestic chores, so I did not offer to help. I was glad Robert wasn't there with me, or he would have quickly signed me up for a few hours of mindless shelling. Instead, I conducted an inane conversation about the things that were in my direct line of sight, which matched my linguistic expertise.

'It's a lot of work,' I pointed my chin at the mountain of fresh beans and another heap of discarded shells. I reminded myself of Old Gabi, who liked to come by whenever he saw me weeding and pontificate about how much work it is.

Both women nodded and repeated what I had just said. Echoing what one's conversational partner has just said is part of the Andalusian style of discourse.

'A lot of work, but little food,' I observed philosophically.

Loli agreed with me while Maria looked at me, enquiring.

'These are for winter. We're going to dry them for stews and soups,' Loli showed me the bucket of clean beans. 'You can eat baby beans without shelling them.'

She must have realised that I did not understand what she was saying because she grabbed a small baby bean from the pile, wiped it on her apron, snapped it in half and ate the first half. She gave me the other half, which I was obliged to consume in front of her. Luckily, baby fava beans taste just like snow peas or any other juvenile legume.

She then explained that I could *sauté* the fava beans when they were still small without having to shell them. She didn't use the word *sauté*, she used the Spanish word for *fry*, but I got the idea. With her usual Andalusian generosity, she grabbed a reused plastic bag, picked the smallest of the fava beans from her pile, and handed them to me. She reiterated how I should cook them in a frying pan with some *jamón*.

'I could serve it with grated cheese and pasta,' I suggested trying to show my neighbour that I wasn't just an idiot from abroad, but she didn't much care for my innovations to a classic Andalusian dish.

Instead, she gave me a strange look and smiled. It must have been her version of rolling her eyes at me.

While I was standing with my bag of baby beans in hand, Rafa came out with a small container filled with olive oil. I knew it wasn't their olive oil because theirs and ours come from the same mill. The olive oil from our groves is the colour of rusty wheat and is a bit cloudy. This sample was much darker but still very translucent.

'It's from my friend's mill in Frailes,' he explained and repeated the mill's name three times. By the time I had returned to my cottage, I had forgotten the name but was pleased to have two purebred horses in my race now. I was still going to buy the supermarket oils to compete against my quality examples.

I don't know why I decided to host an oil tasting party in the first place. I had never been to one. Neither were they common in rural Andalusia, where people consume olive oil daily. I think I stole the idea from an episode of *Hotel Impossible* where Anthony Melchiorri, the US version of Alex Polizzi, suggested to the owners of a rural retreat in California to organise olive tasting parties to attract future guests and help spread the word about their establishment.

I didn't remember the details of the actual olive tasting promotion that I saw on TV. What remained in my mind were the large tables covered in white cloths on the top of an olive hill. Each table had carefully arranged clay plates, chunks of rustic bread, olive dishes, and a selection of cheeses and fresh olives — the insignia of an Arcadian lifestyle. In the TV show, the guests gathered around the tables with their wine glasses and enjoyed their day out in the countryside while staring off into a horizon of never-ending olive groves. I felt I would be able to create a similarly pastoral backdrop for my party, but the exact details of what my guests were supposed to do during the tasting remained sketchy.

Will they just dip the bread in olive oil and eat it? I asked myself.

I couldn't understand how this activity would be different from a regular party in Andalusia, where copious quantities of olive oil are consumed with vigour and enthusiasm as a matter of course. In desperation, I resorted to my usual source of knowledge, the esteemed University of Google.

In seconds, I found a blog about how to host an olive oil tasting party, and just as quickly, I was ready to close the window on my laptop.

Olive tasting is not much different to wine tasting, it read.

I ground my teeth and let out a long sigh of annoyance. Few things in life are as obnoxious and pretentious as the phenomenon known as 'wine tasting'. The whole theatre of swirling the liquid, warming the glass with your hand, sniffing, sipping, and slurping makes my blood boil. If I hadn't already invited people over to this famous olive tasting party, I would have called it all off. Instead, I was forced to read on.

I skimmed over the frequently repeated words like *aroma, pungency,* and *whiff* and tried to get to the core of the olive tasting. It involved keeping the oil in your mouth while slurping air. The author suggested a few times that the taster *make a note of XXX aroma and YYY taste.*

Are we supposed to sit there with notebooks and write things down? I wondered.

I imagined a pompous gathering of great minds with their little notebooks, everyone taking one sip at a time and slurping away. The cacophony of disgusting mouth noises was overwhelming even for my imagination. I couldn't see how this would lead to a successful party, so I decided to wing it.

TWENTY-SIX

IN THE SHADE OF A NISPERO TREE

C éline and Leon, the Dutch-Belgian couple we had met at Blanca's Spanish classes over a year and a half earlier, were the first to arrive at my spring celebration-olive oil tasting party. In fact, they arrived an hour earlier than I expected. I had just got out of the shower when I heard Bobby barking downstairs and a car hooting outside. It had taken me two days to set up the party. One day was devoted to staging the rustic charm ambience and preparing all the plates, cutlery, glasses, napkins, and wines so that I would not have to run around like a headless chicken during the party.

The day before the party was spent preparing food for the unspecified but (I expected) large group of people. The bag of fava beans that Loli had gifted me earlier that week came in handy, but my experiment with the beans had not resulted in a culinary success, to say the least. Instead of following the trusted Andalusian recipe that Loli had entrusted in me, I decided to go Asian and cooked all the beans in a large Japanese wok that I had bought on a whim many years earlier and only used once before.

This culinary fusion resulted in an enormous pile of slop that had the colour and consistency of light-green baby vomit. All it needed was a middle-aged lunch lady with a net over her greasy hair and a ladle to dish the concoction out to the unsuspecting masses. I was not proud of whatever I had created, and my suspicion that the verdant swill was vile was confirmed when I tasted it. It was bitter and somehow raw even after being on the stove for a considerable amount of time.

I let it sit for the night in the fridge in the hope it would get better, but it never did. It was still unappetising in appearance and thoroughly disagreeable in taste the next day. Nevertheless, I decided to keep it on the menu in case a hungry vegetarian came to the party — they might not notice the small chunks of *jamón* between the overcooked beans. Not to be too brazen about my failure, I decided to hide the embarrassing dish behind the other entrées on the buffet table. Fortunately, I had prepared other food dishes which were tried and tested; a generous bowl of potato salad, chicken tandoori, and a variety of spicy chicken wings and chorizo sausages for the barbecue.

Even though I had started preparing two days earlier, I still had a lot of things to do on the morning of the party and was hoping to have an hour before everyone arrived to add the final touches, but it wasn't meant to be. Leon was so worried that there wouldn't be any parking outside our house that he had left his home well in advance to ensure that he secured a parking space close by. With the dog barking and the car hooting, there was no time to think of what to wear, so I donned the first summer dress that I could find in the wardrobe and ran downstairs to greet my early guests.

Being a Dutch housewife, Céline was highly domesticated and fluent in the art of social courtesies. As I stumbled outside onto the patio wearing an un-ironed dress and worn-out loafers, with my hair still wet from the shower, they stood waiting politely on the driveway.

In a stunning white gown with giant printed poppies and her make-up and hair all in perfect harmony with the outfit, Céline was holding a small bag that clearly contained a bottle of wine. She had a beautiful potted plant in the other hand. Leon must have tired of waiting for me because he was smoking one of his cigarillos. He was a small man with a swarthy, sun-burned complexion which, together with his well-trimmed goatee, gave him the appearance of a Spanish conquistador.

Flustered for having to rush downstairs, I came up with the terrible idea of giving these two domestic gods a tour of my household. I really should have known better. When I was a student in my early twenties, I lived for a year in a Dutch suburb in Nijmegen. Every day I would cycle to the university and back and admire manicured gardens, where no blade of grass was longer than the others. I would muse over their outdoor decorations that were ever-so-elaborately staged. A family of gnomes standing by their little cottages or working a minuscule windmill, their friends fishing in an artificial pond or enjoying a porcelain picnic. There were ceramic birds' nests with clay birds roosting in them. Or a group of merry geese wearing bonnets and aprons captured on their way to market. Everything was always immaculate. I'd never see any of the ceramic characters fall over and lie on the ground for weeks collecting dirt and growing moss as they would if they were left to their own devices in my garden. I imagined the interiors of the Dutch houses to be equally polished and presentable.

I had to imagine what such houses might look like inside since I had never actually been invited to a Dutch home for a meal. In late autumn, cycling through the suburbs of Nijmegen, I had just fleeting impressions of their brightly-lit living rooms and open-plan kitchens. As few Dutch believe in closing their curtains, I could catch a glimpse of domestic bliss and picture-perfect happiness as I cycled past.

Expensive bottles of wine would be placed carefully next to a pot of fresh Italian herbs. A saucepan of tomato sauce would be simmering gently while the couple would talk about their day while chopping onions and grating Parmigiano-Reggiano. A photographer from a lifestyle magazine could walk into those houses at any time and wouldn't need to stage anything. Their homes were always camera-ready.

Green with envy, I'd arrive back at my own student dwelling. I'd leave the bike in the garden shed, kick the piles of dead leaves out of my way as I entered the house, and quickly close the living room curtains so that no one could see me slob around, drink beer from a bottle, smoke cigarettes, and microwave a frozen meal from Lidl.

And now, in a total lapse of judgement, I had invited the same perfectionists whose scrutiny I feared the most to admire my bedroom. While Céline and Leon were from Belgium, they were *Dutch*-Belgians, and their attitude to cleanliness and tidiness was similarly Dutch.

'This is our bedroom,' I announced. 'I don't think you saw it last year.'

'No, the party was in the guest house next door,' Leon reminded me the last time they were here when we rescued Bobby.

'That's right.'

We reminisced for a minute about that day.

'I didn't know you have cats,' Céline pointed at Whitey and Twiggy sleeping on a sun lounger on the elevated terrace outside the bedroom.

'They stay upstairs because Bobby chases them, and then I have to get a ladder to get Twiggy down from whatever tree he escapes to.'

As we chatted, I looked around and spotted something in horror. The fact that the bed wasn't made was no surprise to me — I rarely make the bed. The dust and the messiness were at a regular level. What was appalling was that there, smack in the middle of the bed, was a pair of undergarments and a bra. I choked in embarrassment for a second, not knowing what to do. Obviously, I had taken them off when I went to shower, but then I had to get dressed quickly and run outside. I had forgotten to put my used underwear away in the laundry basket.

'Do you want to see the view from the terrace?' I suggested, and without waiting for an answer, I directed them out of the bedroom through the French windows and onto the sunny terrace.

'Your nispero tree is lovely!' I heard Céline say.

'What?' she occasionally mispronounces English words, so I wanted her to repeat what she had said.

'This is a nispero tree,' she came to the edge of the balustrade and reached out to a branch growing on the level of the terrace on which we were standing.

'Nispero? I've never heard of it.'

'It's a fruit tree. It has small orange fruit. You haven't seen them?'

I had no idea what she was talking about, but I trusted her. Céline knew most of the plants and flowers that grew in our area. She was an expert on plants and would often volunteer at the local florist's to make arrangements for parties and special events.

'Look, I'll show you,' she took out her smartphone and tried to connect to the internet, but I knew for a fact that she would not be able to get a signal.

'The phone signal here is terrible,' I explained. 'Let's go downstairs, and I can give you the Wi-Fi password.'

This redirection of their attention was a relief to me since it meant the grand tour of my empire of dirt could come to an end. We walked quickly past my dreaded bed, which was still adorned with my cringeworthy garments. I was sure that my domestic sloppiness would be the main topic of conversation in their car on the way back home to their village of Frailes. It was a good fifty-minute drive from my house, so I was confident that the compromising display would keep them entertained for the whole trip. But, being well-mannered, they did not say anything to my face.

As we made our way downstairs, I looked at my humble abode afresh and came to realise that I was, indeed, a lazy housewife. I could have told Céline that the house was in the state that it was because I was alone and couldn't manage to clean it properly all by myself. I could have said that I had too much work writing and couldn't find time to do house chores. I could have invented a reason. But the fact of the matter was that in the evenings when I was alone, I chose to settle down with a glass of wine and watch *Girls* instead of running around with a mop and a duster. While I was pondering the poor state of my femininity, Céline had managed to go online and find some images of the nispero fruit.

'It's evergreen, and it has orange fruit in the spring. Look.' I looked down at her phone and noticed her beautifully manicured nails.

'I don't understand why I haven't seen the fruit,' I said as I looked at my own fingernails. They were cut as short as possible yet still uneven, with the cuticles damaged by a lifelong habit of picking at them when I am stressed.

'Maybe you were busy renovating the house,' Céline was a kind soul and excused my ignorance.

'I'll look out for it this spring,' I promised.

There was not much more time to talk together. Soon, cars started to appear on the driveway and groups of people gathered on the patio. It seemed that everyone had brought their friends and neighbours, as my invitation enthusiastically suggested. I was about to start running around like a headless chicken when Céline and Amy asked whether they could help.

Amy was a military secretary in her first life and, like her husband Roy, oozed a certain martial discipline. Her hair, which was the colour of sunflowers, combined with her stubby nose and high cheekbones, reminded me of a Swedish milkmaid or a Russian farm girl. And indeed, she was very matter-of-fact and easy to talk to. I gave Céline and Amy the job of serving drinks and tapas. Seeing me scramble for more chairs and setting up additional tables, Roy offered to barbecue the meat. I was very grateful for the help because I had obviously overestimated my ability to host, serve, cook, and entertain all at the same time.

'Is Loki OK?' I motioned towards Roy's peregrine that was perched on a special bench on the window sill so that Bobby would not get to it. The initial precaution was not, in fact, necessary. Bobby must have smelled death on the raptor's sharp claws because he kept a very prudent distance from the bird and focused his attention on befriending people with slices of cured cheese and ham in their hands instead.

'As long as he has his hood on, he'll stay calm,' Roy answered with the confidence of an ex-military man, accentuated by the camo shorts that he liked to wear.

Since Roy was confident that his pet predator was comfortable in the shade of the tree and was merely listening in on the chatter, I explained what meat I was planning to barbecue. First to the grill were chicken wings in a spicy marinade and chicken kebabs marinated in yoghurt with tandoori spices that I had brought back from Oman. The rest of the meat that was to be grilled consisted of *panceta*, thick slices of bacon or pork belly, and a selection of chorizo sausages and *morcilla*, blood sausage filled with roasted onion.

My old Spanish classmates and I made a good team. Céline and Amy kept on refilling glasses and circulating tapas while I carried meat platters from the kitchen to the barbecue and back to the buffet table. While I was doing this, I finally figured out how to go about the olive oil tasting, ostensibly the main reason we were all gathered together.

Once everyone was comfortable with helping themselves to drinks and food, I could mingle and chat. I also started to collect orders for my olive oil, which was displayed on a separate table. There was plenty of bread for everyone to taste some olive oil before they made their purchase. It was lovely chatting with all these new people. Some were just visitors to the area, so I didn't spend a great deal of time talking to them. I wanted to make connections with people who lived in the area permanently. Trish introduced me to her friend, Lucas, who lived in the next village and was about to open a bed and breakfast business combined with a yoga retreat.

'You must know Keith and Delia,' I was ecstatic to get to know another neighbour. 'She does yoga too.'

'Yes, I know Deely,' it was a strange abbreviation for 'Delia', but as Lucas was Dutch, it must have made sense to him. As he spoke, I admired the collection of tribal-looking necklaces around his neck.

'My partner, Eduardo, organises the retreats. I do the bed and breakfast,' he explained as he lit another cigarette.

'Eduardo is in California right now taking a course in shamanic healing,' Trish informed me.

It was the first time I had seen Trish outside the context of her chauffeur work. She seemed to be having a good time with a brandy and coke in one hand and her tiny black dog, Ebony, on her arm.

'We want to combine the yoga retreats and shamanic healing,'

Lucas explained, but as I knew nothing about shamanic healing, I could not comment on this business idea.

'This chicken is lovely,' Trish mercifully changed the subject. 'Is it a curry spice?'

On hearing her, two English women, whose names I had forgotten, turned around.

'Ooh! I love a good curry,' said a short blond-haired one. 'You can't get the proper curry round here.'

'Next time I go to Iceland, I'll get you some,' said her friend, who also seemed to know Trish.

'Iceland?' Lucas was confused.

'It's an English supermarket in Fuengirola,' Trish explained to him.

'Isn't it a bit far to travel to Fuengirola just to visit a supermarket,' Lucas asked. It was a good point. Fuengirola is on the Costa del Sol, about two hours' drive away from where we were.

'We go there when we want to treat ourselves to some creature comforts from the UK,' the blonde's friend, a petite brunette with spiky hair, explained. It was noticeable that both women spent a lot of time on the coast — their upper bodies were covered in sun-liver spots accentuated by their matching strapless tops.

'It's no different in the UK ... shops selling foreign goods for those foreign nationals who can't buy what they like and enjoy from a mainstream supermarket...just saying,' the blonde went on, clearly defending a point that she had been criticised for before. 'Each to their own, I say...' she completed her argument with a flourish.

Being the host, I refrained from commenting on the rigour of her argumentation. I also was worried that Roy might overhear our conversation and join in. From our previous chats together, I knew how much he despised his fellow compatriots who spent their weekends driving around Andalusia looking for steak and kidney pies and other British delicacies.

'You don't need to go to Fuengirola,' Trish broke the uncomfortable silence. 'You can go to Dealz in Jaén.'

Dealz is another British discount shop. I knew about it because Trish would often recount her trips to her province's capital, a mere one-hour drive away.

'What can you get there?' the brunette inquired.

In response, Trish listed several British goodies: KitKats, Cadbury's chocolates, English bacon, Bovril gravy, and the ever-so-divisive Marmite. By now, we were joined by Liv, who was Dutch but, despite speaking perfect English, could not understand what the Brits were talking about. Lucas, equally, had a confused expression on his face.

'I think they sell all that stuff in Mercadona,' Lucas said.

I admired his bravery. Many Brits don't like to know the error of their ways, especially when it is pointed out by a European. This is particularly true for that class of Brit who is willing to spend half a day looking for a specific chocolate brand or type of canned custard. Liv, a newcomer to Spain, struggled to understand the English's obsession with their country's processed food.

'But there is bacon at Lidl and Mercadona or at any butcher's,' she pointed out. 'And you can find gravy in any supermarket, surely. Is this "Bovril" thing something special?'

'It comes in a jar,' the brunette took it upon herself to explain the product as if selling gravy *in a jar* was a uniquely British way of packaging it. 'Bill gets terrible leg cramps despite magnesium supplements and loads of water…this really helps, but the jars are quite small.'

Apart from the blonde and the brunette, no one in the little group seemed to know Bill. We looked at each other wild-eyed.

'Has he tried a slug of tonic water?' the blonde tried to be helpful. 'The quinine is what helps with cramps. I can't stand the stuff, but it does work for me.'

'Yes, he drinks loads of the sugar-free one. It's a sod when it starts.'

Now that we had Bill's cramps sorted out, I hoped they'd change the topic, but the British women were oblivious to the fact that all their references to English food classics were going over the heads of the Dutch and Belgians who were also listening to this riveting conversation.

'Do they have mint sauce in Dealz?' the blonde asked Trish.

'Didn't see it last time, but I have a small jar at home. You can have it.'

'Is it Colemans?'

'Yes, you can stop by next time you drive through the village.'

'It's not urgent. Just planning. I still have some left.'

I was trying to think of a situation in which mint sauce would be classified as 'urgent', but I was interrupted by Lucas, who had a better idea.

'You know you can make it yourself. There is a lot of mint in the field growing wild.'

I could see that the women were not interested in making their own mint sauce, but he went on to kindly explain the three simple steps to make it anyway. I knew we'd be friends.

It was time for me to go inside the house and prepare the olive tasting competition. I had prepared five sets of small glasses with four different olive oils to do the blind testing. The judges were to rank the oils from the best to the worst. As one of the oils was from Lidl, one from Mercadona, and two from local mills, everyone was excited to see the verdict. It was basic entertainment, as entertainment goes.

Liv, Amy, Delia, and two people who were strangers to me were the judges. In the final verdict, the oil that I got from Rafa was deemed the best, and ours came second. Delia — a self-confessed foody and a militant raw vegan, chose the Lidl oil as her favourite, but she was the only outlier. The others could clearly identify the quality oils from the supermarket ones.

Later that night, I Skyped with Robert.

'How was the party? Did anyone come?' I ignored the tease and gave him a brief account of the party.

'Of course, they came,' I was indignant at the mere suggestion that people would snub my party. 'I offered free food and booze.'

'Did you lose money on this event?' his Scottish genes started to tingle.

'No, I sold a lot of olive oil, so I'm even-steven.'

'Did you meet any nice people?'

'The people from the Spanish class were nice. They helped me with the barbecue and serving, and Céline even did the dishes.'

'Did you meet anyone new?'

'A nice Dutch couple who live near Keith and Delia, and the Zimbabweans were easy to talk with. The English stayed in their cliques, so I don't think I'll be seeing them again. Anyway, I have a lot of bookings for the rest of the month, and some of my Polish friends are coming to visit.'

'From Warsaw?' Robert asked since he knew some of my friends from the time he studied at Warsaw University.

'No, you don't know these people. They're from Gdynia, from my high school.'

TWENTY-SEVEN
BUONGIORNO!

I was standing on the steps to the guest accommodation when my old classmates came up the driveway. As Filip opened the door to the rental car and got out, he shouted out to me: *Buongiorno!* which is *Good morning!* — in Italian. The intonation and the delivery made me think of Super Mario. In fact, he even looked a bit like Mario but older, balder, and rounder. After not seeing each other for twenty years, the first encounter with an old classmate can leave a person speechless. For decades, they have been preserved in your memory as youthful and charming. To see them somewhat stouter and balding and generally worn out by life can be a shock to the system. Even more so when I realised that, in their eyes, I probably looked like Mario's resentful ex-wife. It took me a few minutes to absorb Filip's transformation into a middle-aged man, and as a result, I didn't correct him that we were in Spain, not Italy.

'It's *buenos tardes*,' I should have said. 'Do you know you are in Spain?'

It might have saved me days of the gentle frustration of listening to him and his wife constantly comparing Andalusia to its pretty sister, Tuscany.

'We'd like to visit an *enoteca*?' was one of their first requests after Filip, Aneta, and their five-year-old daughter, Maja, had settled in.

We sat on the patio under the budding grapevine and admired the olive groves. The golden hour made the green hills and trees shimmer with life as if they were modelling for one of Van Gogh's famous paintings. But something else was on their minds. They were both viewing my wine section with obvious disdain.

'A what?' I had no idea what he was talking about — I assumed he had mispronounced a name of a famous place.

'*Enoteca*,' he repeated louder as if I were hard of hearing.

'I have no idea where that is,' I admitted. 'I'll check Google maps.'

Now he was looking at me, wondering what kind of simpleton I was.

'It's a wine shop,' his eloquent, beautiful wife explained. She sported a dark, luxurious bob haircut and looked like an extra from a 1920s movie.

'A specific wine shop?' I couldn't apprehend what they wanted.

'No, it's not a brand. It's any wine shop where you have a large selection of wines from local vineyards.'

'Ahh! *Enoteca* is a wine shop in Italian,' I puzzled the pieces. 'There is wine in Mercadona,' I said. 'It's our local supermarket.'

I could see they were not happy. They wanted to go to an *enoteca* to replicate an experience that must have been imprinted on their brains since their epic holiday in Tuscany.

'I could find a *bodega*,' I said, using the Spanish word for a wine shop. 'There are also small shops with local produce that we could visit.'

It was an *enoteca* or nothing. The next day, they agreed to look for a wine that was more to their taste than my humble selection from Mercadona. At first, I was relieved as I thought it would save me from having to go to a bodega and translate descriptions of things I knew very little about. For the first forty-five minutes, they stood before the wine shelves in said supermarket fervently looking for Chianti and Pinot Grigio. I told them that these were not sought-after wines in rural Andalusia, but they insisted that there MUST BE Italian wines in the supermarket.

'What about Cabernet Sauvignon or Pinot Noir?' the sophisticated Aneta suggested, and they spent another half an hour looking for French wines.

'There are only Spanish wines here,' I tried to explain, but to no avail. By now, I was doubled over the supermarket trolley and ready to faint from physical and mental agony.

'Can I have an ice-cream sandwich?' their five-year-old daughter asked her mum.

'Let's have a *gelato*,' her mum agreed, and we left Filip reading the fine print on the labels on the wine bottles.

I directed Aneta and Maja to the frozen goods area, where there were three freezers full of Spanish ice cream products. Soon an argument was in full swing between Maja and Aneta because it turned out that the supermarket didn't sell the specific brand of sandwich ice cream that the child was used to eating. I left them to argue and went back to Filip, hoping that he had finally selected that very special bottle of wine that he was planning to drink. As I watched him inspect the shelves with the determination of detective Colombo, looking for clues, I wondered how things had changed since when we were all in high school together.

The three of us had been in the same class for several years. But back then, Filip and Aneta were not even good friends. It was Aneta and me who were close friends. Filip, on the other hand, had been obsessed with more refined, more elegant girls than the type that his future wife represented. He liked girls with long fingers, who played the clarinet, wore silk scarves, and went horse riding on the weekends. Such aspirational girls were of a better class of people than he was.

While he lived in a grey block of flats in an uninspiring post-communist suburb featuring a rusty old slide as the primary source of entertainment for the kids, the girls that he chased after were from affluent suburbs where modern villas had been built. They were daughters of local dignitaries and tycoons who summered on the Black Sea and wintered at Italian ski resorts. So, it came as a surprise to me when, years after we had left high school, I heard the news of Filip and Aneta's wedding. And while his obsession with the finer things in life continued, I was taken aback to see Aneta, once a down-to-earth and no-nonsense girl, participate in his aspirational foolishness.

I approached the wine shelves to see that Filip had cautiously placed two expensive bottles of red in the trolley.

'*Crianza* is good,' I tried to commend his selection, but in return, I received a lecture explaining to me that *crianza* is not a type of grape but merely an indication of how long the wine has been in the barrel or something like that. *Reserva* and *gran reserve* mean this, and *tempranillo* that, and *rioja* is something else. It felt like he kept on talking for a very long time, picking up random bottles and mansplaining to me what was written on them. I was about to lose my will to live when he concluded with an abbreviated lecture on the history of sherry from Jerez. I was hoping that he'd turned the corner and was now ready to explore Andalusia and stop thinking of Tuscany, but I was wrong.

At a local restaurant near the park in Alcalá, they asked the waiter for Peroni beer. This was, of course, not available. They then scoured the menu for Italian dishes. For starters, they asked for *bruschettas* with basil. Not knowing what that was, the waiter suggested *San Jacobos*, delicious breaded ham with melting cheese inside. They ate this small dish begrudgingly, regaling me about the lovely starters that they had consumed with gusto when they last visited Sienna. They wanted gnocchi and pasta for the main course but got fried *bacalao* (cod) and calamari instead. The precious child didn't touch any of the food that was placed on the table. She sat quietly chewing on a piece of dry bread and refused to try anything new. The peak of her culinary adventure was reached when, after a lot of encouragement, she dipped the edge of her bread in some olive oil and ate it. I was told that when she was in Italy, Maja polished off every plate of food that was presented before her. Her parents could not understand why she didn't want to eat anything here, in humble Andalusia.

For dessert, they demanded tiramisu, and on hearing that it was not served at this particular establishment, they declined the waiter's suggestions to try *crema catalana*, a Spanish version of crème brûlée or even the delicious *tarta de queso*, a cold cheesecake. Trying to show some cultural awareness, they asked the exhausted waiter for churros and chocolate, to which he, in turn, showed bafflement and stared at them for a long time as if they had asked him for a plate of dog turds.

'They don't serve churros after midday,' I explained to my guests.

'Why not?' Filip asked, almost demanding that the whole country change their eating habits to suit his whim.

'It's breakfast food, and it's served in a *churreria*, not a restaurant.'

The next couple of days were equally exasperating, and I felt just like the waiter in the restaurant in Alcalá — offering delicious local experiences but being continuously scorned and rejected. Nothing that Andalusia had to offer was good enough for these two Italophiles and their *bambina*. While our visits to restaurants and places of natural beauty were annoying because of their constant comparisons to Italy, the day trip to the Alhambra was simply disheartening.

For me, the Alhambra is a magical place where nature, architecture, and centuries of Moorish and Christian history are intertwined. With their cleverly designed labyrinths of ancient canals and aqueducts that feed streams and fountains and keep the flora alive, the gardens are my favourite. Centuries-old cypresses and oleanders line the pathways between castles, palaces, and fortifications from various periods of the Alhambra's history. Lush varieties of ivy, wisteria, jasmine, and hundreds of roses of all colours and species decorate the medieval fortifications. Secret courtyards are scented by orange trees and rosemary bushes. With the ghosts of great rulers, now long gone but not forgotten, strolling these timeless grounds, it's a place to reflect on one's life and one's mortality. But for my two guests, it just couldn't compare to Venice.

We were all silent in the car on the way home from the Alhambra. It was their third day in Andalusia, and I had failed to impress so far. I should have said something, but to be polite, I kept my peace and merely chewed over their hurtful comments in my mind. I wanted to suggest a visit to the castle in Alcalá la Real and the olive oil museum or a hiking trip to the spectacular gorge in Moclín, but I realised that I could only take a certain amount of rejection for that week. I had just reached boiling point.

As I sat in the back passenger seat watching a strange child playing a video game, her parents sat in front, taciturn and obviously regretting that they had not gone to Tuscany for the gazillionth time. I felt that I was back in high school, dejected and not knowing how to please anyone. Soon, I would be grateful for their presence, however.

TWENTY-EIGHT
A HOOPOE ON THE NISPERO TREE

W hen I painfully opened my eyes, it was pitch black and nothing that I felt or touched made any sense to me. I lifted myself up and felt the cold tiled floor beneath me. I was lying prone on the landing at the bottom of the staircase that led down from my bedroom to the living room.

Did I fall asleep here? I asked myself. *Did I pass out?*

I couldn't figure out what the time was or even what day it was. In complete darkness, I searched for the light switch. With the light on, I went to the adjacent bathroom to wash my hands because they felt sticky. As I placed them under the tap, I realised that the water looked dirty. My hands were covered in something gooey, but I couldn't understand what it was. I looked behind me to the landing and saw a pool of red that was now smeared everywhere. Bloody palm prints covered the white wall and the light switch.

What the hell? I thought to myself and looked in the mirror.

There is a scene in *Jane Eyre* when the madwoman, and Jane's *Other*, Bertha Mason, sees her own reflection in a mirror and gasps in horror. At that very moment, in my bathroom, I could relate to poor Bertha. The familiar face that I was so used to was gone, and in its place was that of a battered housewife. My right eye was swollen shut, and half of my face was covered in blood and still bleeding copiously from the eyebrow. Were I a Victorian madwoman, I would have screamed 'Vampyre! Goblin!' and ran back to the attic to hide from the monster in the mirror. Since I was an educated twenty-first-century woman, I immediately blamed myself for spoiling everyone's good time.

What have you done! I wanted to shout at myself.

I could look no longer at the macabre countenance that stared back at me.

What have you done!

The realisation came to me that whatever I had done to my face wouldn't fix itself. But always the optimist and not wanting to bother others, I decided to bandage myself up, get some frozen vegetables for the swelling, clean up the bloody mess, and hope that it would all go back to normal by the morning.

It's just a little bit of swelling and a cut, I convinced myself. *It's nothing.*

I put a wet towel over the cut on my face and searched the living room drawers for bandages or plasters. It wasn't easy with only one open eye. I also became aware of the fact that I wasn't using my right arm. Unconsciously, I kept it close to my chest and refused to move it. I walked around downstairs like a bird with a broken wing.

It will be fine by the morning, I kept reassuring myself.

Finally, I found the first aid kid that belonged to our old car. I had never imagined that I would ever need the items inside it, but here I was, using my mouth to rip open the packets with gauzes and bandages and thanking Robert's hoarding tendency for not throwing the kit away. I fastened the gauze with some plaster so it would stay on my head. Now that I had stopped dripping blood all over the place, I went to search for a bag of frozen vegetables to put on my face. I was about to go upstairs to lie down with this homemade cold compress when I saw the mess on the floor and the walls.

You need to clean this up in case Maja sees it, I told myself.

I imagined little Maja coming in first thing in the morning and being confronted with what looked like the set of a particularly gruesome episode of *Criminal Minds*. She'd be traumatised for life. And so, I put the vegetables aside and went to the pantry to get the mop and a bucket.

In hindsight, I should have immediately called for an ambulance or asked my guests to take me to the emergency clinic in Montefrio. But I was very confused, and instead of getting the urgent help that I required, I mopped the floors using my one good arm. In my defence, I had just accidentally fallen from the top of a tallish staircase all the way to the bottom and, in the proceedings, smashed my head on the tiled floor below.

More importantly, I'm a woman, and most women of my generation, who grew up in a patriarchal society, don't like to make a fuss. Someone stands on your foot in a crowded bar and breaks a few of your toes — *don't worry, I'll walk it off*, we say. You get terrible food poisoning from a dodgy restaurant — *I can do with a couple of days in bed. It's 'me' time*, we explain. Flu, pregnancy, a tumour, stroke, broken limbs — we wave them all away. Nothing is ever worth making a nuisance of yourself for others. Thus, I cleaned the floor and the walls, rinsed the bucket, and decided it was time to lie down.

It will be OK, I consoled myself. *By the sunrise, the swelling will be gone, and your arm will have rested.*

And thus, the longest night began. I expected a miraculous recovery by dawn, but the clock on my mobile phone seemed to have stopped. The frozen packet on my face made me shiver, and the cold penetrated my bones. I had never felt so cold in my life, but I was too tired to get up to get more blankets from the wardrobe. Nothing was changing. Nothing was getting better. By four a.m., I knew I needed a doctor. My arm hurt, and I could not move it.

*I think it's brok*en, I admitted to myself.

But again, following the same stubborn logic as before, I decided to wait until my guests were up and ask them to take me to the emergency room.

The time stretched itself thin that lonely morning mercilessly, and by sunrise, it felt like another lifetime had passed. I finally decided to get up and went to the bathroom to check the mirror, but the grotesque apparition that once was my face stared back at me. I took a shower and cleaned myself up, changed the dressing on my forehead, and noticed another big gash on my leg. I must have hit the edge of a sharp tiled step on my way down. I put a bandage on it too. Getting dressed with one working arm was a challenge and took some time, but finally, I was presentable.

I put on a pair of huge sunglasses to cover the gargantuan black eye and some of my eyebrow that was still bleeding. I wasn't fooling anyone with the sunglasses. The right-hand side of my face looked as if someone had attached half an overripe melon to it, but at least the makeshift disguise gave people time to ease into my horrendous physiognomy. I could see why the Elephant Man wore a potato sack over his head — the shock and horror on people's faces when they see a monster can be equally upsetting for both parties: the unsuspecting viewer and the owner of the detestable visage. I wished *I* had a potato sack, but instead, I donned a giant floppy hat as if I were preparing for a picnic at the beach and not a visit to *urgencias*.

I worried about Bobby and let him out of the house for a short walk before seeking help. As I made my way up the driveway after a very short but exhausting excursion with Bobby, I saw Aneta on the terrace. She was still in her sleeping attire, drinking coffee, and working quietly on her laptop. I was so glad to finally see a human face.

'I need your help,' I said quietly. 'I need to go to the emergency room to get some stitches.' I lifted my Jackie Onassis sunglasses and showed her my disfigured face.

'Oh my God! What happened?' I was bombarded with questions to which I didn't have any answers. 'I'll wake up Filip, and we'll go together. Give me five minutes.' She dropped everything and was halfway inside the apartment when I stopped her.

'I think it's best if we go alone. If a man is involved, the doctor may call the Guardia Civil to report a case and register a criminal file.'

Gender violence and domestic abuse are key features of many public awareness campaigns in Andalusia. Posters in public offices, local clinics, and town halls advise people to be brave and report such cases immediately. Having watched enough crime TV series, I knew exactly what kind of conclusion any public servant would come to; it was patent that I had been punched repeatedly in the face by a right-handed man, most likely my husband or a male relative. I didn't want to spoil Filip's holiday entirely by having him spend the day at the local Guardia Civil headquarters, which were located inside an impenetrable medieval barbican. And so, as a true battered woman would, I showed up at the *urgencias* with a female friend.

My family doctor, Francisca, immediately started to question me about the whereabouts of my husband and was not wholly convinced that he was in Oman. Then, she wanted to know how exactly I fell down the steps. I still could not remember what had happened. The last thing that I could recall was sleeping in my bed and hearing Bobby bark downstairs. I could now vaguely remember getting out of bed to go downstairs to shush him because I was worried that he would wake the child next door up. I also had a faint recollection of seeing our white cat run down the stairs in front of me. From these indeterminate thoughts, I pieced together the only plausible story: I had tripped over Whitey while going downstairs to quiet Bobby. If there ever was a cat-dog conspiracy to kill their owner, these two had almost succeeded.

Were they in cahoots? Why do they loathe me so much? I was wondering while Francesca was inspecting and cleaning my wounds.

Being a Spanish woman, she did not cease her chattering while she worked, which was starting to give me a massive headache. I was thankful to Blanca, my Spanish teacher, for drilling into us the vocabulary for different body parts, aches, and injuries, as now I could at least understand some of the things that my doctor was saying.

Francisca placed clean dressings on my wounds, inspected my arm, which I had not moved an inch since the fall, and determined that I needed to have an x-ray and see a specialist in Granada. I looked at poor Aneta, who never in a million years would have imagined spending her holiday visiting different hospitals in Andalusia. More importantly, I had no idea how to find the hospital that Francisca was talking about, and once there, where in the building I should go.

'I can't drive,' I told her.

'Of course, you can't drive. I mean your friend,' she pointed at Aneta, who was sitting quietly in a foreign emergency room and could not understand anything that was being discussed.

'She's not from here. She doesn't know where to go.'

'OK. Don't worry. You'll go in the ambulance.'

I explained to Aneta what Francesca and I had been talking about. I asked her to take Bobby for a walk later in the afternoon and told her that I'd be in touch from the hospital. Ten minutes later, I was fastened securely in the back of the ambulance. I waved my friend goodbye, and off I went for the first time in my life in an ambulance. The trip from Montefrio's *Centro Salud*, or health centre, to the hospital in Granada took almost an hour. Even though there were no windows to look out of and no way to chat to the driver, who occasionally shouted something at me to check if I was still awake, I found great solace in the back of this dark, air-conditioned vehicle.

Seeing that there were people who knew what they were doing and who were ready to help lifted a great weight off my shoulders. I would experience the same feelings of immense gratefulness three years later, in the back of the very same ambulance, but then I would be lying flat on a stretcher with a pretty nurse by my side, injecting me with first-class morphine. Little did I know how my subsequent encounter with Montefrio's paramedics was going to turn out. This time, it was just a dress rehearsal.

Once we arrived at San Cecilio Hospital, a vast medical complex on the outskirts of Granada, I was handed over from one team of nurses to the other. The paramedic had a paper that he had received from my family doctor, which he handed over to the head nurse. At no stage did I have to show my national health card. There was no red tape to overcome, just swift efficiency. No one asked for my ID number or how I spell my name, which was for the best because my head hurt so badly, and I was not in the mood to be spelling my super-long Polish surname in the Spanish alphabet.

Unlike many other public services in Andalusia, the hospital ran like a well-oiled machine; highly experienced nurses passed me from one set of hands to the other. When I say hands, I can't stress enough how many hands touched my face, stroked my hair, and gently held my hand during the treatments that I received. Spanish people are known for their close-contact culture, and on a typical day, it may not be to everyone's liking. But when one is in hospital after experiencing a trauma, there are few things as comforting as the human touch.

The first set of nurses checked my vitals and flashed lights into my eyes, the second stitched up my eyebrow and bandaged the leg, then a female doctor analysed my x-rays and announced that my forearm was indeed fractured and sent me to the plaster room to be fitted with a splint. No one believed my story that I had tripped over the cat in the middle of the night. I could see the sadness in the nurses' eyes as they felt sorry for the abused foreign wife who had invented a pathetic excuse for her violent husband. They nodded their heads in compassion and told me condescending stories of other women who they knew who had also tripped over their cats.

'It happens all the time *guapa*,' they assured me. 'It's not your fault.'

Once they were done fixing me up, I was wheeled into the waiting room with my one working hand full of instructions and prescriptions. I was asked to wait for the patient's minibus to take me back home.

I waited for an hour or so before the transport was ready. In the meantime, I sent Aneta and Filip a message and told them I was coming home. I hadn't told Robert or my family anything about my accident because I was emotionally and physically drained and wasn't ready to have to calm people down. Once the bus was full, mostly with senior citizens from various remote villages in the province who were visiting the hospital for their regular check-ups, we took off on what soon became a magical mystery tour.

After leaving the hospital premises, we did not continue onto the

Granada-Cordoba highway, which leads directly to Montefrio, but we went off in the direction of Sevilla. This made me really worried. I did not want to spend the night in Sevilla. I asked the driver if he was going to drop me off in Montefrio, and he assured me that he was. Montefrio was the final stop on his route, he told me. But from what I could see out of the window, he was driving further and further away from Montefrio. We were now heading south, towards Loja and Malaga.

There could be another Montefrio outside Malaga, I thought to myself in dread. *It's not a very original name, after all.*

'You said MONTEfrio, right?' I asked again, emphasising *mountain*. 'Not RIOfrio?'

Riofrio is another village that is close to Loja. I had learned about its existence two years earlier when our new fridge-freezer was delivered to Riofrio and not Montefrio. Whoever took our delivery address in Carrefour in Granada must not have heard of Montefrio and thus decided that we were probably mispronouncing Riofrio, where they sent the order.

'We're going to MONTEfrio,' the driver seemed confident. 'I'm from Montefrio, don't worry.'

The route we took was the longest way anyone could rationally go from Granada to Montefrio — we stopped in every single tiny hamlet on the way to drop off patients from villages up in the mountains and down in the valleys. Once I knew that I would eventually end up at home that day, I calmed down and stared out of the window at the endless olive groves and mountains. I wasn't looking forward to seeing people in my house — I was upset and wanted to be alone.

Where was the new, fresh life that we had envisaged? It had all turned to ashes in my mouth. We were supposed to live deep, close to nature, and enjoy life together — instead, we were eight thousand kilometres apart. Robert was stuck in a tiny apartment in Sur, Oman, not being able to go outside because of the oppressive humidity. I was alone, making parties for strangers and living in squalor in a half-finished house.

We need a better plan, I thought. *I don't want to be here by myself anymore.*

Three hours after we had left the hospital, we arrived outside my gate.

'Is there anyone in the house to help you?' the driver was concerned about leaving me alone in the middle of nowhere.

'I have friends. They can help me,' I lied and thanked him for taking me directly to my house. Filip and Aneta were due to leave in two days, and I wasn't planning to bother anyone further with my predicament.

I could barely walk up the driveway. I moved like a zombie after a rough night of hunting humans around a rural town. The adrenaline was now long gone, and all I wanted to see was my bed. I felt heavy, tired, and despondent. I could hear my guests playing in the pool.

At least they had a good day. I was relieved.

I walked to the pool and was greeted with cheers. I couldn't just go to bed after keeping them waiting at the house all day, even though they could swim and enjoy the pool. I briefly described my time at the hospital and asked them whether everything was OK.

'We had a lovely time in Montefrio,' Filip said. 'We went to the top of the castle and then had some ice cream on the square.' It seemed that, in my absence, they had decided to stop wishing they were in Italy and started to appreciate Spain.

'I think there is a problem in the house,' he said. 'I've been hearing this alarm go on and off all day. We checked everywhere, but we can't find it.'

'The fire alarm?' I asked, my heart sinking.

'No, we checked the fire alarms. They are fine. It's something else. Like a car alarm.'

'We don't have a car alarm,' I said. 'Maybe there is something else in the car that is making a noise. Let me see.'

Our 4X4 was parked outside the garage. As we walked toward the car, Filip stopped and raised his finger.

'This one. Do you hear it?'

I knew the sound very well.

'It's a hoopoe,' I told him.

He looked at me, not having the faintest idea of what I was saying.

'Look!' I pointed up at the long branches of the nispero tree. 'There is a hoopoe on the nispero tree.'

But before Filip could turn to look, my little harbinger of death and misery had flown away. I heard his last *'upupa upupa'* from the hill opposite as he disappeared for the night to spend time with his wife and chicks, safe in the oak forest.

EPILOGUE

FORKING PATHS

'Oh, gosh! It must have been a terrible fall. Tish told me all about it,' I heard a petite older woman say to me as I entered Tish's patio. 'By the way, I'm Sarah.'

As I appraised my new acquaintance, the word *bohemian* immediately sprang to mind. Should Cambridge Pictionary ever need a photo to illustrate this adjective, they wouldn't need to look any further. Her clothes were a patchwork of fabrics and colours, all different yet complementing each other. The eye shadow and lipstick matched the clothes, and the somewhat spiky white hair gave her moxie. I felt that if a gipsy band came from around the corner with violins, guitars, and an accordion, she would fit right in with their singing and dancing. I took an immediate affinity to this *nispero*.

I wanted to hear more, and *Oh! Gosh!* did I? Sarah could talk for hours without a break.

'It was terrible,' I decided to fill her in as it was an obvious topic of conversation in Venta, the tiny village where Sarah and Trish lived. I explained how I tripped over my cat in the middle of the night — I decided it was a more interesting version than I tripped on a worn-out slipper, which had also become a suspect in causing my accident.

289

'But you know what's worse, everyone in my family is convinced that I was drunk out of my mind.'

'Weren't you?' Trish looked at me curiously as she set coffees on the garden table.

'No, I was angry because my guests had annoyed me. I had only one glass of wine with them before I turned in.'

Hearing my own protests, it became evident to me that while I had spent the last few weeks recovering in the seclusion of my cottage, my family, friends, and neighbours were developing their own colourful versions of my accident. The insinuation that I was a raging alcoholic did not bother me very much. What bothered me the most was the implication that I could not walk up and down steps when tipsy because — in my humble opinion — *I have perfect balance when intoxicated and years of adventures to prove it.* As I ruminated on this idea, I became conscious of the fact that I was, in fact, acting like a drunkard who insisted that they could walk in a straight line. It was time to stop protesting and accept my new social persona.

'Well,' Sarah was contemplating the still fresh scar on my eyebrow while stirring her coffee. 'You must have hit your head really hard because your eye is still quite blue. How long has it been?'

'Four weeks, more or less. I can move my arm now a little bit. The doctor at the *Centro Salud* removed my cast a few days ago, but I'm wearing this to protect my arm since it still hurts when I move it.'

I pointed at the rollerblading wristguard that I wore to drive the car and do jobs around the house. My forearm was still very sensitive, and the thick plastic guard gave me some confidence whilst limiting any movement in my wrist. I came up with the idea to wear it the day the doctor removed my cast because I felt that, after not having been in use for over three weeks, my arm needed some support. That's when I remembered our old rollerblading gear that Robert stashed in the wardrobe and refused to throw away in case we wanted to go rollerblading again. Once again, his inability to throw things away had saved the day, and as I fitted the old wristguard on my weak forearm, I started to reconsider my philosophy of throwing things away if not used for more than four years. The wristguard worked better than anything else I had seen at the pharmacy.

'How have you been managing by yourself with one arm? Are you left-handed?'

It was the sixty-four-thousand-dollar question. I was not left-handed, so losing the ability to move my right arm for the most part of May was very limiting. Being obstinate and unwilling to change plans, I kept all the bookings that I had for that month.

'Trish has been helping me a lot,' I explained. 'She does all the ironing and cleaning, and I do the final check of the rooms before the guests arrive and put the final touch to the rooms.'

'You do more than that,' Trish interjected. 'She moved a tonne of wood with one arm,' she told Sarah.

It sounded ridiculous, but I did move a trailer of firewood when my cast was still fresh. What happened was that a few days after my accident, I got a message from our old builder, Dani, who had delivered wood to us previously. He told me that he had finished pruning his olives and wanted to start getting rid of the wood. His trailer was loaded with fresh wood and ready to deliver. I didn't want to delay him in his work, so I agreed for him to drop off the firewood the next day. To my despair, Dani, who was very familiar with our house as he and Robert worked on it together, had dropped off the load in the middle of the driveway before I managed to go outside to ask him to leave it in a more convenient corner. As soon as I came close, he saw my freshly battered face. I saw horror and pity in his eyes. His reaction was why I refused his kind offer to move the wood out of the way. I insisted that my friends would help me with it instead.

It was a lie. I did not intend to ask anyone to come to the house to move a tonne of olive wood to clear the driveway. As soon as he had left, I went to the garage to get a working glove for my left hand and started to throw the wood off from the driveway to a place where it did not block the guests from coming and going. Half an hour into my labour, in an extraordinary act of pathetic fallacy, it started to rain. I put on Robert's raincoat since the sleeves were big enough to fit my arm with its plaster cast and went back to my work, which had slowly turned into self-punishment. Each log was a lash, and each stick was a means of self-flagellation.

Why are you doing this? The logical part of the brain asked.

Shut up! The emotional part responded curtly. *I do whatever I want to do! It has to be done! One can't go through life asking people for favours!* I was shouting in my head.

You hit your head really hard, insisted the frontal lobe. *Go to bed and call your friends to come and help you.*

No! I can do it myself! The limbic system was not going to change its mind. I was going to move the tonne of wood and feel sorry for myself.

Perhaps it was for the best. Since my accident, I did not have time to feel sorry for myself. Standing in my driveway in the rain and doing mindless physical work was very cathartic. Once the wood was moved, I cleaned up my face, put some dry firewood into an olive picking basket, and made the fire. Even though it was May, the nights were still bitterly cold. As I was reflecting on these events, I noticed that Sarah was looking at me curiously. I realised I hadn't explained myself.

'Well, it had to be done,' I said. 'Since Robert has been in Oman, I have learned to fend for myself. I don't like to ask other people for help.'

I can't explain why I was so candid with this complete stranger, but there was something in her mannerisms and the way she chose her words that was very honest and trustworthy.

'When Peter died, I did everything myself. I had to organise the *tanatorio* where he was cremated and do all the paperwork.'

I assumed Peter was her late husband.

'Sarah can be very stubborn,' Trish interjected, remembering the events. 'She only told the neighbours and me of what had happened weeks after he passed away. If I had known, I would have helped.'

'I didn't want to talk to anyone. The months after he passed away, I had a horrible migraine all the time. Sometimes I could not get up from my chair. I just sat there for hours looking at a crack on the floor tile. If it weren't for Fifi, I would not have left the house at all.' I assumed Fifi was her dog.

'I could not think straight,' she continued. 'I could not do anything around the house. I went to a doctor after a few months, and he told me that it was from grief. It was like a black fog inside my head.'

'When was it?' I prompted, hoping to hear more.

'Three years ago, but it was not sudden. Peter had dementia for several years before he passed away. It was horrible. Sometimes, he could not remember who I was. One day we were having tea in the garden, and he told me that his wife Sarah would love to meet me; that I should come over for drinks.'

She smiled wistfully at the heart-breaking memory. I wanted to hear more about her husband's death. I liked how forthright she was as she spoke about one of the biggest losses of her life. In a world where most of our time is devoted to sharing happy moments, we forget to share tragedies. I had met some widows in the past. Most don't talk about their loss. They tear up at the mention of their dead spouse's name and close down the conversation. As if losing someone dear was something to be ashamed of, a new age taboo. I, on the other hand, liked to be prepared. I wanted to know everything about the death of one's spouse so that I would know what to expect one day when the inevitable happens.

As it turned out, I did not have to prompt Sarah at all. She was an eloquent and eager speaker; her stories span from her 1960s hippie life in Ibiza to running a respectful bed and breakfast business in Cornwall. She'd lived in a tent with an infant child, in various caravans, in an attic as a seamstress, by the docks in London where Peter started to hone his oil-painting skills, and in various self-reformed cottages in Spain. She'd met some of the top artists in Europe and socialised with their families. She lived her life to the full; a lifetime of experiences and projects and things to do. I did not hear all of these stories that one afternoon, of course — she is not a self-indulgent bore. I heard them over the next few years during our frequent get-togethers. As a writer, I have been tempted to reappropriate these wonderful tales, but they are not my stories to tell. Besides, Sarah is a much better storyteller than I am.

As I sat on Trish's patio, I didn't have that insight. I was simply captivated by Sarah's words. We moved away from the topic of her husband's death and were now discussing our dogs — a topic normally dreary to anyone who is not the owner of the dog in question. Yet, my charming new acquaintance regaled us with stories, each with its own twists and turns. I looked to the village road that ran outside Tish's patio and couldn't put my finger on why HER stories were so engrossing and bewitching. Perhaps the Japanese have a word to describe a personality which is immediately engaging but honest, without trying to be the centre of attention.

'Trish said that you have done a lot of house renovations on your cottage.'

'Yes, we have,' I explained some of the changes that we had to make to our old stone house to modernise it. Sarah was all ears about the house renovation stories.

'You'd love to see our house in Alicante,' she said when I finished. 'We built it from scratch in the middle of nowhere. There wasn't even electricity. I had to go every night to a nearby *barranco* to put petrol in the generator so that we could run the lights and have running water. If you can come round one day, I'll show you the photos.'

'That would be great! I'd love to see it!' I said over-enthusiastically, ignoring the two facts that I still had no driving licence and I was driving a manual car with a semi-healed broken right arm.

Trish, who knew about my driving licence shenanigans since she was the one who had been taking me to *Centro Salud* for check-ups and to Mercadona for my weekly shopping, explained that Sarah lived very close to her house, but down the valley *over there* — she gestured in the general direction toward the olive hills.

'Sarah's house is a little bit more secluded than ours,' Trish explained.

Anyone would be more secluded than Trish's house, I thought to myself as a delivery truck whooshed by her patio, literally three or so metres away from the coffee table. In the sixteen or seventeen hundreds, her house would have been in a perfect location for a traveller's inn. In fact, the name of her village and many other villages in the area started with the word *venta*, which in olden times indicated a roadside establishment catering to travellers. I imagined merchants on horses with caravans of donkeys carrying fabrics and other luxury goods from North Africa to Toledo; couriers on fast stallions taking messages from the king's deputies in Granada to the royal palace in

Madrid; farmers with oxen pulling the wooden wagons full of goods all the way from Jaén to Sevilla.

A *venta* was once a lively, almost a cosmopolitan place, where people of all walks of life and from all parts of the Iberian Peninsula met, drank cold beer, ate a bean stew with rabbit and *jamón* and embellished stories of their travels. I imagined they shared stories of heroism, tales of fighting with road bandits or *bandoleros*, legends of great wealth and riches to be found in the New World, anecdotes of foreigners who they had met, and their strange customs and habits. As it remained, in the twenty-first century, Venta was a somewhat forsaken village. The location of the cottages right on the main road deemed the houses unsellable. What was once a great asset was now a curse.

'So when is Robert coming home?' Sarah asked as if she had known him for ages.

'At the end of June. I'm thinking of buying an automatic car because these hills are killing me. Then, we will be busy with guests the whole summer.'

'Is he going to go back to Oman after the summer?'

I didn't know the answer. We were at a forking path.

'I don't think I can stay here alone for another year. It's OK in the spring and the summer, but the winter was very long,' I said. 'I think we may have to admit defeat and return to the Middle East together to make some money, or we try to put down roots here.'

I really did want to settle down in our new home, but I still had no idea how we could achieve it.

ABOUT THE AUTHOR

Sabina is a non-fiction writer. She has lived and taught English in Poland, Sweden, the Netherlands, the UAE, and Spain. Her memoir series depicts her and her husband's adventures of starting a new life in rural Andalusia.

She currently lives in the middle of olive groves outside the picturesque village of Montefrio and runs a language school in the town of Alcalá la Real.

For the occasional glimpse of Cortijo Berruguilla and the nature around Montefrio, follow us on Instagram or Facebook:

Facebook @cortijoberruguilla

To get updates about new books, subscribe to her website or social media:

www.sabinaostrowska.com

Facebook @sabinawriter

For the occasional glimpse of Cortijo Berruguilla and nature around Montefrio, follow Sabina on Instagram or Facebook:
Instagram @cortijob
Facebook @cortijoberruguilla

Chat with Sabina and other memoir authors
and readers in the Facebook group,
WE LOVE MEMOIRS:
https://www.facebook.com/groups/welovememoirs/

A REQUEST

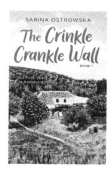 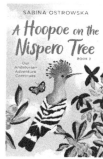 

If you enjoyed *A Hoopoe on the Nispero Tree*, please do leave a review.

To get updates about the next books in this series and to read other free stories, subscribe to my website or follow me on social media:

www.sabinaostrowska.com

Facebook @sabinawriter

Instagram @cortijob

ACKNOWLEDGMENTS

A writer's journey can be lonely. One sets off alone in search of new worlds, unsure whether there is anything to be seen beyond the horizon. While the writing itself is done solo, everything else demands the help of other people.

As a self-published writer, I rely on the advice and companionship of fellow self-published writers. Without the help of writers' groups, it would be impossible to navigate the vast ocean of information, apps, and tricks of the trade that one needs to learn in order to publish and market your own writing. One in particular is We Love Memoirs Authors' Group.

Another group of people whose assistance is essential towards the end of your journey are beta readers. I wish to thank all my beta readers for volunteering their time and expertise and for their candid feedback which has greatly improved the final version of *A Hoopoe on the Nispero Tree*. These include fellow memoir authors: Simon Michael Prior, Jacqueline Lambert, Tammy Horvath, and Lisa Rose Wright, and memoir readers: Jude Mossad, Susan Jackson, Lynne Hewitt, Judith Benson, Sue Raymond, Eileen Kuriger Huestis. And finally, my dear friend, Julie Ross for her feedback on the penultimate draft.

And most of all, I wish to say thank-you to all the readers who took the time to post their opinions of *The Crinkle Crankle Wall*, shared my first book with their friends, and reached out to tell me that they enjoyed it. It gave me the encouragement to continue writing and to finish the second book.

Cortijo Berruguilla, June 2022

Made in the USA
Monee, IL
22 October 2022

16397354R00174